HOLLYWOOD INCOHERENT

HOLLYWOOD INCOHERENT

Narration in Seventies Cinema

TODD BERLINER

University of Texas Press | Austin

Requests for permission to reproduce material from this work should be sent to:
    Permissions
    University of Texas Press
    P.O. Box 7819
    Austin, TX 78713-7819
    www.utexas.edu/utpress/about/bpermission.html

∞ The paper used in this book meets the minimum requirements of ANSI/NISO
Z39.48-1992 (R1997) (Permanence of Paper).

LIBRARY OF CONGRESS CATALOGING-IN-PUBLICATION DATA

Berliner, Todd, 1964–
    Hollywood incoherent : narration in seventies cinema / Todd Berliner. — 1st ed.
        p.   cm.
    Includes bibliographical references and index.

    ISBN 978-0-292-73752-5 (paper)

    1. Dialogue in motion pictures.   2. Incongruity in motion pictures.   3. Motion
picture plays—History and criticism.   4. Narration (Rhetoric)   5. Motion pictures
—United States—History—20th century. I. Title.
    PN1995.9.D49B47   2010
    791.43'6—dc22

                                                                    2010019946

For Dana

CONTENTS

ACKNOWLEDGMENTS

A lot of minds improved this book, but two of them made such valuable contributions that I must single them out. They belong to Stephen Booth and Dana Sachs. Stephen Booth helped me develop the project at its beginning, and his impact on the book is everywhere. Dana Sachs read the entire manuscript with as much care as I used to write it, sometimes more. Many of the ideas within it result from conversations we had, and, if those ideas make sense, they do because she made me write them so that they would. She also gave me the love and moral support I needed to complete the book, as did Jesse Berliner-Sachs and Samuel Berliner-Sachs, who helped keep me spiritually fit by placing toys between me and my computer.

I want to acknowledge the valuable help of several colleagues and friends. Tim Palmer, Stephen Prince, Carl Plantinga, and Scott Higgins commented scrupulously on complete drafts. Andrew Escobedo read several chapters when I shouldn't have let them out of the house looking the way they did. Dale Cohen helped me obtain and analyze the data in my empirical studies. Ray Carney offered instructive comments on Chapter Seven. Ira Sachs gave me insightful criticism of Chapters One and Six. David Bordwell, William Nestrick, Marilyn Fabe, Ann Martin, Frank Tomasulo, Lynne Sachs, Vern Cleary, and Barbara Namerow each helped me with portions of the manuscript. Jennifer Raspet provided research assistance. Leo Hageman and Felix Trolldenier helped me reproduce the still frames. The University of North Carolina Wilmington provided several research grants and a year-long research reassignment. At the University of Texas Press, Jim Burr, Lynne

Chapman, Sally Furgeson, and Kaila Wyllys gave me all of their support, and I am grateful to them.

I owe special thanks to Philip Furia, who coached me, encouraged me, and championed me from the time I was an assistant professor through the publication of this book.

My colleagues—friends—in UNCW's Film Studies Department continue to surround me with a supportive working and thinking environment. I could hardly imagine a more delightful place to work than the department we've created together.

Portions of this book appeared in "Hollywood Movie Dialogue and the 'Real Realism' of John Cassavetes," *Film Quarterly* 52, no. 3 (Spring 1999): 2–16, reprinted with the permission of the University of California Press; "The Genre Film as Booby Trap: 1970s Genre Bending and *The French Connection*," *Cinema Journal* 40, no. 3 (Spring 2001): 25–46; and "The Pleasures of Disappointment: Sequels and *The Godfather, Part II*," *Journal of Film and Video*, 53, nos. 2–3 (Summer/Fall 2001): 107–123. I am grateful for permission to reprint revisions of that work here.

I have saved my most long-standing debt of thanks for last. I have a huge and supportive family, most of whose members love movies and learning as much as I do, but who didn't choose professions that allowed them to squander their lives in movie theaters and libraries as I have. Their passion nurtured mine, and their love for me has always nurtured me.

HOLLYWOOD INCOHERENT

PART I

An Introduction to Narrative Incongruity

Great works of art are daredevils. They flirt with disasters and, at the same time, they let you know they are married forever to particular, reliable order and purpose.

—STEPHEN BOOTH, *Precious Nonsense*

CHAPTER 1 POETICS OF SEVENTIES CINEMA

The film *Nashville* (1975) opens with a jolt. The Paramount Pictures logo, black-and-white and faded, initiates a quiet display of credits that gives way unexpectedly to a peppy advertisement for the film in the form of a late-night TV commercial for a country music compilation album. The commercial sounds so cacophonous and moves at such a blistering pace that spectators could not possibly make out half of the information it presents. A hawker's shrill voice-over clashes with brief song clips; album covers quickly scroll behind drawings of the principal actors, as the camera whips from one drawing to another; and the bogus commercial asks spectators simultaneously to read one set of text crawling up the left side of the screen and another set crawling down the right (Figure 1.1).

The segment is, in some revealing ways, an emblem for seventies storytelling. It displays the wry self-consciousness indicative of the era's filmmaking, but even more indicative is its combination of incongruous styles and narrative devices. The commercial fits neither with the subdued style of the credits that precede it nor with the narrative mode of the rest of the film, which never again addresses the audience directly or adopts the form of an out-and-out parody. Moreover, the commercial occupies a precarious position within the film, functioning paradoxically as credits for the twenty-four lead actors, an introduction to their characters, an advertisement for the movie, an advertisement for the movie's soundtrack album, and an advertisement for the movie as though the movie were itself a country music album. The remainder of *Nashville* is less disorienting than its disjointed

FIGURE 1.1. A bogus TV commercial at the beginning of *Nashville* appears unexpectedly and employs a style and narrative form incongruous with the rest of the film.

opening credit segment, but only barely; the film persists in straining the cognitive capacities of its audience. Although distributed by a major Hollywood studio, *Nashville* resists the clarity, formal harmony, and narrative linearity that had distinguished studio filmmaking for more than fifty years.

Under the studio system, the American film industry perfected a coherent narrative design that made Hollywood movies accessible to almost any filmgoer. Then, in the 1970s, a group of talented filmmakers set out to dismantle it. Film commentators have variously regarded the work of these filmmakers as a triumph of the artist, a failed political critique, or a display of self-indulgence, but most recognize that, during this period, the industry made some of the best movies ever to come out of Hollywood.[1]

The 1970s marks Hollywood's most significant formal transformation since the conversion to sound film and is the defining period separating the storytelling modes of the studio era and contemporary Hollywood. Certainly, traditional narrative forms persisted during the period: Consider the popularity of *Airport* (1970), *Love Story* (1970), *What's Up, Doc?* (1972), *The Sting* (1973), *The Way We Were* (1973), *Benji* (1974), *Jaws* (1975), *Rocky* (1976), and *Star Wars* (1977), each of which earned well in excess of $15 million in domestic rentals in its first run. At the same time, however, the mainstream American film industry released a group of films that challenged the narrative orthodoxies of its own tradition: *M*A*S*H* (1970), *Patton* (1970), *Little Big Man* (1970), *A Clockwork Orange* (1971), *The French Connection* (1971), *The Godfather* (1972), *Cabaret* (1972), *Deliverance* (1972), *The Getaway* (1972), *The Exorcist* (1973), *American*

Graffiti (1973), *The Godfather, Part II* (1974), *Dog Day Afternoon* (1975), *One Flew Over the Cuckoo's Nest* (1975), *Shampoo* (1975), *Tommy* (1975), *All the President's Men* (1976), *Carrie* (1976), *Network* (1976), *Annie Hall* (1977), and others.[2] Such films are, in various ways, unusual for American cinema, yet each one also earned in excess of $15 million in domestic rentals in its first run, and many film fans and film commentators today consider them some of Hollywood's greatest achievements. Although $15 million may not sound like much today when profits for the most popular films are calculated in hundreds of millions of dollars, before the seventies the large majority of almost any year's top ten highest earners returned less than $10 million in domestic rentals. Even today, in dollars adjusted according to ticket prices, the seventies produced more of Hollywood's highest-grossing films than any other decade. And in terms of the quality and creativity of the output, the years 1970 to 1977 could rival any eight years in Hollywood's history.

What matters most about films of the seventies—what makes people remember them and return to them—is not so much their themes, politics, or cultural relevance, as previous studies of the period have contended, but their unusual manner of storytelling and the gripping, unconventional experiences they offer spectators. No previous studies have examined in depth the narrative design that defines this watershed period in film history. This book identifies the period's defining narrative strategies and explains their aesthetic contribution. It further sets out to demonstrate that the artistic achievements of the 1970s permanently expanded Hollywood cinema's narrative possibilities.

NARRATIVE PERVERSITY

Seventies cinema spotlighted the very disunities that previous generations of Hollywood filmmakers had labored hard to conceal. The period's startling disunity led movie critic Leslie Halliwell to write an essay on the "arrogance" of seventies filmmakers. Writing in 1977, the then-forty-eight-year-old Halliwell said about these young directors:

> Steeped in the history of Hollywood's golden age, they have no idea what made it work so well, and as soon as they become successful they begin to despise their audiences and are concerned only to over-spend enormous budgets while putting across some garbled self-satisfying message which is usually anti-establishment, anti-law-and-order and anti-entertainment. (930)

The unsettling change in narrative design troubled many filmgoers. Americans of Halliwell's generation, those born before 1940 or so, had stopped attending movies in a routine way, replaced by college-age and younger audiences, many of whom sought out the very films that Halliwell derides. Looking back on the era in 2000, film historian David Cook (born sixteen years after Halliwell) comes to an opposite conclusion: "The results were often extreme, even explosive . . . but the industry has never produced better [films], not even during the studio system's golden age" (396).

A peculiar narrative design became prevalent in American cinema during the years 1970 to 1977. A majority of the most acclaimed films of that eight-year period—films that have tended to win industry and critical awards and appear on critic and fan lists[3]—resisted some of the cardinal principles of "classical" Hollywood filmmaking, which, according to Bordwell, Staiger, and Thompson, include among other things "decorum, proportion, formal harmony, respect for tradition, mimesis, self-effacing craftsmanship, and cool control of the perceiver's response—canons which critics in any medium usually call 'classical'" (4). Several American movies from both right before that time (for example, *Bonnie and Clyde* [1967], *Faces* [1968], and *The Wild Bunch* [1969]) and right after (*Deer Hunter* [1978], *Manhattan* [1979], and *Raging Bull* [1980]) adopt narrative strategies prevalent during the period 1970 to 1977. The earlier group, however, presages a movement that hadn't yet taken hold in mainstream American cinema and the later movies are more isolated examples of a kind of film that starts to peter out about the time of *Rocky* (1976) and *Star Wars* (1977).

Influenced, in part, by Asian and European art cinema of the 1950s and 1960s—with its looser narrative structure, elliptical flashbacks, radical changes in mood, and emphasis on character ambiguity—seventies filmmakers, working within the classical Hollywood model, tested that model's flexibility by adapting the radical techniques of more truly subversive filmmakers to Hollywood's classical form. Indeed, a large number of the most successful directors of the period—among them, Martin Scorsese, Robert Altman, Arthur Penn, Dennis Hopper, Sidney Lumet, Clint Eastwood, Sidney Pollack, William Friedkin, and Peter Bogdanovich—have named as influences the works of De Sica, Rossellini, Bertolucci, Antonioni, Visconti, Bergman, Godard, Resnais, Rivette, Rohmer, Truffaut, Renoir, Buñuel, Ray, Kurosawa, and Ozu. These foreign filmmakers enjoyed a popularity among American audiences that surpassed even that of the Film Arts Guild, the art-house cinema movement, and the ethnic theaters of the 1920s and

1930s. "During the late 1950s and 1960s," Douglas Gomery observes, "the international art cinema reached an apogee" (*Shared Pleasures*, 189).[4]

Many seventies filmmakers adopted narrational strategies popularized by these art-house filmmakers. David Bordwell has identified several features characteristic of the historical mode of narration known as "art cinema," and we see them exhibited in seventies films to an uncommon degree for Hollywood cinema.[5] *Deliverance, The Conversation* (1974), *The Godfather, Part II*, and *Nashville* foreground the kind of narrative ambiguity regularly found in European and Asian art films, such as *Rashomon* (1950), *Hiroshima mon amour* (1959), and *L'avventura* (1960). Their plotting is not as redundant, clear, or tightly constructed as is customary in Hollywood cinema, and story exposition is delayed and distributed more broadly across the plot; we consider these qualities more closely when we examine the narrative strategies of *The Godfather, Part II* in Chapter Three. The characters of *Five Easy Pieces* (1970), *Wanda* (1970), and *Scarecrow* (1973) slide passively from situation to situation in an episodic series of events, like the protagonists of *Alfie* (1966), Ray's Apu trilogy, and Truffaut's Antoine Doinel series. They lack clear-cut traits, motives, and goals, and character psychology often fluctuates from one scene to the next. Such films focus on what Bordwell calls the "vagaries of real life," loosening the cause-and-effect relationship between story events and dramatizing not just climactic but also trivial moments (*Narration*, 206). Like *Carnal Knowledge* (1971), *The Last Detail* (1973), *Lenny* (1974), *The Conversation*, and *Mikey and Nicky* (1976), these and other seventies films also cue the spectator to perform what Bordwell calls an "inquiry into character," which he regards as one of the defining features of art-cinema narration and which "becomes not only the prime thematic material but a central source of expectation, curiosity, suspense, and surprise" (209).

Like art films, many seventies films flaunt their processes of narration. *A Clockwork Orange, Nashville, Taxi Driver* (1976), and *Annie Hall*, because they contain the kinds of narrative and stylistic idiosyncrasies found in much foreign art cinema (e.g., *8 1/2* [1963] and *Persona* [1966]), create curiosity about their modes of narration and stimulate an interest in their stylistic devices that diverts attention from the films' stories (see Bordwell, *Narration*, 213). Such films, as we will see in Chapter Six, develop a more self-conscious narration by intermittently foregrounding the role of the filmmaker as the architect of the film's style and plot patterning. Films such as *Annie Hall* and *The Godfather, Part II* disorder their chronological events, and *The Offense* (1972) depicts scene fragments that only gradually reveal an event, so as to, as Bordwell says of *The Conformist* (1970), "tantalize the viewer with reminders of his of her limited knowledge" (210). Furthermore, like *The Umbrellas of Cherbourg* (1964) and *Day for Night* (1973), Hollywood films of the 1970s "quote" previous cinema through a process of pastiche that not only makes the filmmaking more self-conscious but also reveals the filmmakers' own fascination with film history. We see this fascination exhibited in Arthur Penn's *Little Big Man*, Robert Altman's *The Long Goodbye* (1973), Herbert Ross's *The Last of Sheila* (1973), and Martin Scorsese's *New York, New York* (1977), which, as we see in Chapter Four, quote the Western, the private detective film, the whodunit, and the Hollywood musical, respectively, as well as in Brian De Palma's various quotations of Hitchcock in *Sisters* (1973), *Obsession* (1976), and *Carrie*.

One can easily overstate, however, the similarities between seventies cinema and the foreign art cinema that influenced it. The impact of art cinema on Hollywood in the 1970s is somewhat more complex than many scholars of the period have noted.[6] Mainstream seventies films do not violate Hollywood classicism in the radical way that, say, Resnais's *Last Year in Marienbad* (1961) undermines classical cinema's insistence upon narrative clarity and logic or Ozu's *Early Spring* (1956) defies the Hollywood continuity system. Seventies Hollywood offers no equivalent of Kon Ichikawa's *Odd Obsession* (1959), with its self-conscious and minimally motivated freeze-frames, ambiguous character behavior, and perplexing, obscure plot. Seventies films by and large follow the protocols of Hollywood narration. They only intermittently make narration manifestly self-conscious, and, when they do, generally either genre or story events motivate the flagrant display of technique. As compared to art cinema, they also tend to make character motivations overt and comprehensible. And, although more cognitively demanding than traditional Hollywood cinema, most seventies plots do not tax viewers' memory, attention, perceptiveness, and analytical ability to the extent that foreign art films do. According to Bordwell, Hollywood selectively assimilated art-film practices and bent them to its purposes. "In Hollywood cinema," he observes, "there are no subversive films, only subversive moments" (Bordwell, Staiger, and Thompson, 81).

Still, along the route of classical narration, seventies films inject incongruous devices that violate narrative unity but that never gain enough prominence to undermine the films' classical foundations. Hollywood films of the seventies, in more tempered ways than *Marienbad*, *Early Spring*, and *Odd Obsession*, challenge the harmony of the classical Hollywood model even more so than *films noirs* or the works of Hitchcock, Welles, or Preminger, films that, some scholars suggest, represent idiosyncratic deviations from the Hollywood paradigm. While stabilized by Hollywood's codified formal system of narrational devices, seventies cinema resists Hollywood's insistence upon efficiency, linearity, and conceptual harmony. Consequently, unlike foreign art cinema, which advertises its own idiosyncrasy and complexity, Hollywood cinema of the 1970s tends to nestle idiosyncratic and complicating devices within a familiar and stable structure. And whereas art films flaunt their violations of classical norms, seventies films commit surreptitious, intermittent, and often trivial infractions of their classical plot patterning. With the stability afforded by classical narration, they can risk a measure of narrational incoherence and still remain anchored to classical cinema's structure and purpose.

Classical filmmaking provides a harmonious form into which seventies filmmakers integrate a faint cacophony of incongruous ideas and narrational devices. The incongruities in seventies cinema keep viewers mentally alert as they attempt to integrate into their experience of a movie thoughts and emotions antipathetic to the movie's overt formal appearance and narrational purpose, even as such viewers, unlike many of their art-cinema counterparts, retain trust in the underlying coherence of the work before them. The quotation from literary critic Stephen Booth that begins this book attests to the aesthetic value of works of art that seem at the same time structurally stable and on the verge of collapse. William Friedkin made the same sort of point, albeit more crudely, when he said about his directorial work in the 1970s, "That's the thrill of filmmaking to me, the thrill of failure, potential failure. This may not work. Yeah, but if it does work it's going to be terrific" (*A Decade*). According to this line of reasoning, the Hollywood paradigm stimulates the most intense aesthetic excitement when pushed almost to its breaking point.

In a word, seventies narratives are *perverse*. They not only deviate from classical narrative norms more than Hollywood films from other eras, but their narrative and stylistic devices also threaten to derail an otherwise straightforward narration.

The word "perverse" normally implies a moral judgment, even in film scholarship (see, for instance, Smith, "Gangsters," 217 and Staiger, 2). Following Booth, I use the term here in its literal sense to mean *turned around*.

Perversity denotes a disposition to act contrary to what is reasonable or expected. For Booth, perversity adds to an artwork "a usually gratuitous and potentially distracting and counterproductive extra system of coherence that rivals . . . the narrative, polemic, or other ideationally essential organization of the work" (*Precious Nonsense*, 37–38). Such systems range from common literary devices, such as rhyme and metaphor, to narrative and stylistic devices one encounters in cinema and other arts, such as stylistic patterning, narrative diversions, and other deviations from an artwork's substantive essence.

In the context of this study, *narrative perversity* means a counterproductive turn away from a narrative's linear course. Causal linearity—the principle of linking story events by cause-and-effect—is the governing principle of Hollywood storytelling. In a classical narrative, events are linked not arbitrarily (x *and* y) or chronologically (x *then* y) but causally (x *therefore* y), one story event bringing about another. Causality generates "linear" narratives because it organizes story events into lines of action (x *therefore* y *therefore* z). Perverse elements in a narrative threaten to undermine, interfere with, or distract spectators from a story's causal logic.

Narrative perversities manifest as story detours and dead ends, ideological incongruities, logical and characterological inconsistencies, distracting stylistic ornamentation and discordances, irresolutions, ambiguities, and other impediments to straightforwardness in a film's narration, and they jeopardize an artwork's narrative and conceptual coherence. Narrative perversity adds something incongruous to an artwork—something out of harmony with the work as a whole. Alex's wit and love of Beethoven in *A Clockwork Orange* run counter to the narration's portrayal of him as a sadistic thug. The stylishness of the cinematography in *Taxi Driver* seems, in some ways, unsuited to the film's otherwise gritty narration. The grandfatherly charm of John Huston's portrayal of Noah Cross in *Chinatown* (1974) undercuts his depiction as a depraved, incestuous child molester. The bizarre image of Elliot Gould dancing down the street after shooting his friend at the end of *The Long Goodbye* not only violates our image of Philip Marlowe from previous movies but also our sense of him here as a blundering and unsure private eye. In fact, the presence of the uptight, mumbling Gould himself adds a pointed incongruity to the private detective film. The injustice of our hero's imprisonment in *One Flew Over the Cuckoo's Nest* is undermined by the fact that he is not wrongly imprisoned, as in *I Am a Fugitive from a Chain Gang* (1932), or imprisoned for something minor, as in *Cool Hand Luke* (1967), but for five assaults and the statutory rape of a fifteen-year-old girl. Although the movie treats his crimes trivially, and spectators likely forget them soon after they learn of them, their inclusion in the narration gratuitously hampers what seems the film's essential goal of enlisting sympathy for a nonconformist facing an unjust system.

Although all narrative films employ a degree of perversity (without turns, there *is* no narrative), the relatively prevalent, pointed, and superfluous narrative perversities in seventies cinema do more than delay satisfaction and narrative resolution: They preclude the definitive and satisfying resolutions characteristic of more normative Hollywood movies. Counterproductive to narrative unity, linearity, and resolution, narrative perversities are exceptionally productive in creating the rich aesthetic experiences that have made seventies films among Hollywood's most treasured creations.

THE FILM INDUSTRY IN THE 1970S

Several industrial factors broadened the range of Hollywood's narrative and stylistic options in the 1970s and help explain why mainstream film narration took such a strange turn. Normally, I wait for the particulars of particular films to invite discussion of industrial changes, such as the industry's increasing reliance on series films and sequels (Chapter Three), changes in genre filmmaking (Chapter Four), the "blockbuster syndrome" and the rise of mainstream exploitation cinema (Chapter Five), the elimination of regulatory restrictions on the depiction of lurid material (Chapters Five and Six), the influence of "auteurism" on seventies filmmaking and the relaxation of limits on idiosyncratic expressions of a director's style (Chapter Six), and governmental and industrial incentives for independent film production (Chapter Seven). Presenting historical material in this way makes it less likely that readers will think they have a comprehensive grasp on the research concerning historical and industrial factors that influenced filmmaking trends in the seventies, research that is often speculative. However, some general factors have been fairly well established, mostly by David Cook in his extensive historical study of the period, and we can begin now to consider some of the large-scale industrial changes that helped create the conditions for seventies narrative innovations.

The most persuasive explanation for the artistic changes in studio filmmaking can be summed up in a word: insecurity. At the beginning of the decade, the film industry suffered an unprecedented financial crisis, and industry executives did not know how to respond. The "Recession of 1969" plagued the film industry, resulting in $600 million in losses for the major film studios between 1969 and 1971 (see Cook, 3).

The financial crisis had several causes. First among them, the major studios no longer controlled the industry through a system of vertical integration, which had been deemed monopolistic by the U.S. Supreme Court in the 1948 case, *United States v. Paramount Pictures*. The case led to a series of "consent decrees" between the studios and the Justice department that forced studios to divest their holdings of theater chains and ended practices that inhibited independent production, such as "block booking," the practice, prevalent in the studio era, of forcing exhibitors to take blocks of studio pictures.

Second, the film industry saw a twenty-five-year decline in film attendance. Weekly attendance in the United States dropped from 90 million attendees in 1946 to an all-time low of 15.8 million in 1971, the decline particularly steep between 1956 and 1971 when weekly attendance fell 62 percent in just fifteen years (see Steinberg, 371). Meanwhile, ticket prices between 1956 and 1972 rose 160 percent, while the cost of living rose only 53.9 percent (Belton, 258). Audience demographics also changed dramatically. The baby boomers (those born after 1945) would, according to Douglas Gomery, "constitute the core movie audience of the 1970s," keeping theatrical exhibition alive and altering moviegoing behavior ("Motion Picture Exhibition," 398). As a group, baby boomers enjoyed more unusual film entertainment than their parents—darker, bolder, and more challenging, stylized, and eccentric. Clearly, the sensibilities of the typical moviegoer had changed when *Charge of the Light Brigade* (1968), which had a negative cost of $12 million, returned a domestic rental of $1 million, and *M*A*S*H* (1970), which had a negative cost of $3 million, returned a domestic rental of $36.7 million.

Finally, slow to respond to changing demographics in the late 1960s, the studios financed a large number of expensive, artistically conservative flops, such as *The Bible* (1966), *Doctor Dolittle* (1967), *Star!* (1968), *Sweet Charity* (1969), and *Battle of Britain* (1969). Meanwhile, foreign films and offbeat American films, geared toward the youth market, returned surprising profits, including *Blow Up* (1966, $6.9 million in domestic rentals), *Bonnie and Clyde* (1967, $24.1 million), *I Am Curious (Yellow)* (1967, $19 million), *The Graduate* (1967, $49 million), and *Easy Rider* (1969, $19.2 million). Tino Balio notes that the number of U.S. theaters that regularly played art films rose from approximately one hundred to seven hundred between the 1950s and the 1960s (63). The increase in art-film exhibition during this period, Gomery notes, "represented a rare trend upward in movie attendance" (*Shared Pleasures*, 188).

The crisis conditions created financial and artistic opportunities. The film studios, low on cash but holding lucrative real estate (indicating temporarily undervalued shares), proved attractive for corporate takeovers by major conglomerates looking to diversify their holdings (see Cook, 301). Except for 20th Century Fox, Columbia, and Disney, conglomerates had purchased all of the major studios one by one by the decade's end. The structural change in studio filmmaking altered the executive culture at the studios, which were no longer run by movie moguls, who had owned substantial shares in the studios they headed, but, as Thomas Schatz notes, by salaried employees, "one percenters" more readily replaced than their predecessors from the studio era ("Boss Men," 28). Compared to the veteran moguls, the executives, lawyers, agents, and bankers who now ran the industry had little knowledge of film production. Frustrated by rising debt and their own inability to gauge audience tastes, they began to rely on filmmakers to make executive decisions. Brought up on cinema and television, young directors seemed to know better the appetites of the baby boomers who now constituted the core audience.

The studios sometimes recruited these new, youthful directors from film schools, where they studied film as an art form. Francis Ford Coppola studied at UCLA, George Lucas and John Milius at USC, and Martin Scorsese graduated from and taught at NYU. The new generation of American filmmakers sometimes emulated the artists of the French New Wave and other foreign filmmakers from the fifties and sixties, who had developed cinematic techniques and sensibilities strange to American film. The studios hired these new directors for relatively small salaries, compared to more established directors, and budgeted their films at B-movie rates. "These filmmakers," Cook says, "brought fresh, cost-effective talent to an industry embroiled in financial crisis and structural change, and, for a few brief years, the studio chiefs gave them unprecedented creative freedom" (6). According to Ned Tanen, head of production at Universal Pictures, the executives at Universal

> said to the [young directors] who could not have gotten an appointment on the lot two weeks earlier, "It's your movie, don't come back to us with your problems, we don't even want to know about them." . . . [T]he studio left

> them alone because they thought they'd screw it up if they interfered, and the
> movies didn't cost anything. They realized that here was a fountain of talent.
> That's how, in the late '60s and early '70s, it became a director's medium.
> (Cited in Biskind, *Easy Riders*, 125–126)

The unusual change in studio culture accounts for why several directors, including Scorsese, consider the seventies "the last golden period of cinema in America" (Hirschberg, 92).

Together, the changes in the industry—the consent decrees, demographic changes, an industry recession, corporate buyouts, and a reliance on a new breed of directors influenced by television, film school training, and modern European and Asian filmmaking trends—created the conditions for a rare atmosphere of innovation and a new kind of mature cinema that enjoyed a brief popularity through the mid-1970s.

It would be difficult not to tell this story as one of the rise and fall of the artist in Hollywood because, by the end of the decade, the industry, now back on a firm financial and structural foundation, no longer relied on directors as a barometer of the tastes of the average filmgoer. Indeed, by the late seventies, the moviegoing demographic had again changed. A 1977 survey indicated that "57 percent of all movie tickets were purchased by those under twenty-five, a group whose tastes were inherently more conservative than those of the late 1960s counterculture" (Cook, 23). According to Richard Maltby, "by 1979 every other [movie] ticket was bought by someone aged between 12 and 20" ("Nobody," 24). The studios responded by putting the majority of their finances behind blockbuster films in genres that appealed to young audiences—science fiction, comedies, and action—so that films such as *Star Wars* (1977), *Close Encounters of the Third Kind* (1977), *Animal House* (1978), *Superman* (1978), *Star Trek* (1979), *The Empire Strikes Back* (1980), and *Raiders of the Lost Ark* (1981) increasingly dominated film production and the box office. Their success showed studio executives that blockbusters could generate more profit than anyone had previously suspected, and executives began to focus their energies and studio finances almost exclusively on the production of expensive movies that would draw huge rental returns, ensured in part by saturation marketing techniques. Marketing costs, for the first time, began sometimes to exceed negative costs, and marketing and distribution executives increasingly controlled studio policy. Films marketed to juveniles also enabled a lucrative ancillary market in product tie-ins, including soundtrack albums, games, toys, clothing, books, food, and candy, which also helped advertise the films; the merchandise sold the films and vice versa. By the end of the seventies, *Star Wars* had made more money in merchandise than at the box office (Maltby, "Nobody," 24). Ancillary merchandizing deals, for the most part, applied to children's movies and sci-fi and action genres. Few people would want action figures, games, and candy associated with *Chinatown* or *Dog Day Afternoon*.

By the late seventies, the cost of production had risen drastically relative to inflation, and studio executives felt pressure to make movies with wide audience appeal. By the end of 1979, the average negative cost of a movie was $7.5 million, nearly twice the figure for 1977 (Cook, 349). To recuperate costs, the industry relied increasingly on the successes of a few extraordinarily popular films. The number of feature productions dropped, and each year most major studios laid their money on five or six potential blockbusters. "Increasingly," James Monaco wrote in 1979, "we are all going to see the same ten movies" (393). Presale agreements with television and cable networks (and, after 1985, home video licensing fees) provided much of the production capital for Hollywood films and biased the industry toward genres that would attract TV viewers and away from the more slow-paced and complex films that populated theaters in the earlier seventies.

In such an environment, a smaller-budgeted movie, geared to make a modest profit with a niche audience, seemed hardly worth pursuing. Hollywood still produced a handful of artistically "mature" movies, and some of the filmmakers who had become popular in the early seventies had the clout to continue making them. In 1979, Francis Ford Coppola made *Apocalypse Now*, Woody Allen made *Manhattan*, and Martin Scorsese was in production on *Raging Bull*. But, as Monaco notes, "By the mid-seventies, with costs escalating rapidly and the studios now solidly under the control of accountants and businessmen [films geared toward small audiences] were ruled out. Simply put, it's harder to make a profitable small picture than a profitable large one" (20). Once industry executives felt more secure in their ability to predict successful projects, they no longer gambled on relatively low-budget films with limited markets and limited potential for blockbuster success. Such films became increasingly harder to sell, as "event films" displaced the more innovative movies that only critics and the dying breed of routine filmgoers would attend. By the end of the decade, Hollywood had survived and solved its financial crisis, and its brief artistic renaissance ended.

POETICS VS. CULTURAL STUDIES

Despite the attention scholarship has already paid to seventies cinema, previous film scholars, using by and large the same methods (usually a variation of cultural studies and ideological analysis), have largely come to the same conclusions: In general terms, films of the seventies replicate or react to the ideological conflicts and social upheavals of the era. This study's revisionist account of seventies cinema adopts a text-based approach—one that focuses on the films as experiences for spectators—and thereby offers a new way of understanding the cinema of the period.

Previous studies—most notably David Cook's *Lost Illusions: American Cinema in the Shadow of Watergate and Vietnam, 1970–1979* and Robin Wood's *Hollywood from Vietnam to Reagan*—have speculated as to *why* Hollywood produced so many artistically innovative films in the 1970s, but none of them has adequately explained the films' innovations. The concentration on cultural history causes scholars to see the "Hollywood Renaissance" of the 1970s in mostly ideological terms and to emphasize the films' politics and cultural contexts. Such studies examine the impact on American cinema of the antiwar movement, the drug culture, the Watergate scandal, and other cultural events of the period and see the blockbuster successes of the middle and latter part of the decade as the reflection of an encroaching Reagan-era conservativism. One film scholar says that "the aesthetic trends of the [1970s] corresponded rather directly to conflicting ideological currents" (Lev, 185); another, that the "blockbuster spectacles" of the late seventies "return to the cultural myths of the pre-Vietnam, pre-Watergate era" and reflect "the conservative politics that underpinned society during the Reagan-Bush era" (Man, 3); and a third, that "the blockbuster syndrome returned Hollywood to its bedrock profile of reactionary ideology and capitalist greed with a newly sophisticated emphasis on commodity packaging" (Cook, xvi). Equating artistic value with progressive social values, several cultural studies of the period end up disparaging some memorable movies—such as *Rocky* (1976), *Star Wars* (1977), *Heaven Can Wait* (1978), and *Kramer vs. Kramer* (1979)—and inevitably extolling some dull ones, such as *Joe* (1970) and *Go Tell the Spartans* (1978), that reflect ideas the critics consider important.[7] The "blockbuster spectacles" of the mid- to late seventies indicate changes in narrative strategies, more than ideological changes, occurring in Hollywood cinema. In fact, two blockbusters of that period—*Jaws* (1975) and *Alien* (1979)—far from reflecting "reactionary ideology and capitalist greed," contain liberal critiques of capitalism and government almost as forceful as those in the so-called "social criticism" films of the earlier part of the decade, such as *McCabe & Mrs. Miller* (1971) and *Chinatown* (1974). Cultural and ideological analysis may demonstrate the ways in which seventies films respond to the ideologies of the time, but it threatens to foul up aesthetic analysis.

Indeed, analyzing ideology and culture does not much account for the attraction of one film over another. I have seen no compelling evidence that a film's ideology and social relevance influence its popularity or acclaim over decades.[8] All movies can be said to reflect their social climate (even by ignoring it). *The Graduate, Little Big Man, M*A*S*H, A Clockwork Orange,* and *One Flew Over the Cuckoo's Nest* tackle the same left-wing social issues—the generation gap, the Vietnam War, violence, racism, abuse of authority—as *The Trip* (1967), *Catch 22* (1970), *The Strawberry Statement* (1970), *Johnny Got His Gun* (1971), and *The Trial of Billy Jack* (1974), yet the films in the second group have not drawn many viewers since their initial release or earned much praise from critics, scholars, or film fans. The films in the first group are valued *and* (not because) they tend to lean politically to the left. Liberal films, moreover, do not appear to attract the culture's interest more than conservative ones. Filmgoers and film commentators express aesthetic admiration for many films with conservative ideologies, including *Sunrise* (1927), *Triumph of the Will* (1935), *White Heat* (1949), and *Die Hard* (1988). By the same token, if Francis Ford Coppola could take a book by Mario Puzo commonly regarded as pulp (even by Puzo) and, with minimal thematic changes, turn it into what most commentators and filmgoers consider one of the best movies of the decade, then ideology and social relevance cannot be fundamental to artistic value.

In short, ideological and cultural analysis does not explain why some films draw more affection, attraction, and admiration than others that offer essentially the same ideological content. Narrative and stylistic analysis, by contrast, can help explain the ways in which individual movies function as works of art. The two scholarly books devoted to the narrative and stylistic strategies of contemporary American film, Kristin Thompson's *Storytelling in the New Hollywood* and David Bordwell's *The Way Hollywood Tells It*, deal only in passing with the narrative innovations of the seventies. Bordwell notes the ways in which directors from the mid-1960s to the early 1970s explored "oblique and ambiguous storytelling," albeit in a more tempered way than the foreign directors who inspired them (72). He focuses primarily, however, on narrative devices popularized during the 1990s: "paradoxical time schemes, hypothetical futures, digressive and dawdling action lines, stories told backward and in loops, and plots stuffed with protagonists" (73). Thompson, too, focuses on more recent American cinema (her most distantly released case study is 1979's *Alien*). She does say in her introduction that the "youthquake/auteurist films of the period from 1969–1977 or so were not harbingers of a profound shift in Hollywood storytelling but a brief detour that has had a lingering impact on industry practice" (4). And she's right: Such films *were* a brief detour and *have* had a lingering impact. However, the route of the detour and the quality of their impact have yet to be explained.

Both Thompson's and Bordwell's studies adopt a neoformalist approach. In an earlier work, *Breaking the Glass Armor*, Thompson defines neoformalism as "an approach to aesthetic analysis" that studies "how artworks are constructed and how they operate in cueing audience response" (6). Neoformalism, she says, is not itself a method (which, following Boris Eikhenbaum, she defines as an "instrument" for answering questions), but rather an "approach" or "principle" that "allows us to judge which of the many (indeed infinite) questions we could ask about a work are the most useful and interesting ones" (7). Hence, neoformalist critics use a variety of methods, depending on the particular questions posed by particular artworks. Adapted to film analysis from the works of Russian formalist literary theorists, neoformalism regards art as "set apart from the everyday world" since, in the everyday world, "we use our perception for practical ends" (8). Although artworks cause us to employ the same perceptual capabilities that we use to interact with the everyday environment, with art we employ them for what Thompson calls a "playful," rather than practical, interaction.

Although this type of analysis runs contrary to some trends in contemporary film theory, it addresses key aspects of the cinema that many contemporary approaches neglect. Political, historical, and ideological analysis, although potentially useful in understanding how movies function within culture, cannot answer myriad fundamental questions about cinema that neoformalist film analysis addresses directly, the most fundamental being, "How does a film construct an aesthetic experience?" Neoformalism does not regard audiences as passive recipients of artworks and other cultural forces, such as marketing and ideology, but rather acknowledges that audiences engage actively and selectively with works of art. Film scholars sometimes write about viewers as though they could not distinguish between the works of art they like and the ones the culture tells them to like. If viewers were indeed so undiscriminating, then one would expect most Hollywood movies to make money in theatrical release (most do not) because the same cultural forces promoting profitable films also promote unprofitable ones. Neoformalism studies the ways in which artworks stimulate spectators to perform mental operations. Film spectators, according to this approach, form mental models—they draw inferences and make predictions—that they continually revise based on information provided by the film as it unfolds, a type of cognitive activity that E. H. Gombrich calls "the interplay between expectation and observation" (*Art*, 60). Active and creative, the viewer constructs a story based on stimuli from the film, anticipating events and rethinking hypotheses and inferences as the plot progresses.[9] Neoformalist film analysis sets out to explain the interaction between the film, which provides the stimuli, and the spectator, who converts the stimuli into an aesthetic experience.[10]

More broadly, we can (following Aristotle, Igor Stravinsky, the Russian Formalists, and others)[11] define the study of the form and construction of artworks as "poetics," which seeks to describe and explain the design of artworks and their effects on perceivers. This research project is in part an instance of what Alexander Veselovsky called "historical poetics," which traces the course of development of artistic forms or, as Bordwell defines the term, explains "how artworks assume certain forms within a period or across periods" (Bordwell, *Poetics*, 13). Mainly, however, this study sets out to explain the peculiar attraction of so many peculiar films coming out of Hollywood during the seventies. In the pages that follow, then, we seek answers to the following key questions: First, what principles govern the narrative strategies characteristic of Hollywood films of the 1970s? Second, why have these principles come about at this moment in Hollywood history? Third, what effects do some exemplary films of the period have on people watching them? And fourth, why might people value such effects?[12] Wherever we are, we will always be working on at least one of these four questions.

NORMATIVE VS. NON-NORMATIVE SPECTATORS

This study, then, endeavors in part to explain the interaction between, on the one hand, a film's narrative and stylistic devices and, on the other, the common mental activities of its spectators. Inevitably, the question arises whether—given the apparent variety of responses to films and the presumption that, as Janet Staiger says, "each spectator is a complex and contradictory construction of such self-identities as gender, sexual preference, class, race, and ethnicity" (13)—scholarship can say anything at all about the shared experience of a movie.[13] It can. At the very least, it can offer informed speculation. When discussing films, we rarely acknowledge that much of what we experience at a movie is practically indistinguishable from what the person sitting next to us experiences: We generally perceive the same figures, objects, and settings; we often laugh, gasp, and scream in the same places; and we typically understand more or less the same story. I am referring here to elementary aspects of cinematic experience; however, film scholarship has time and again demonstrated how films guide spectators toward complex mental processes.[14] Indeed, although in *Perverse Spectators* Staiger denies the validity of "normative descriptions" of spectator responses, her use of the term "perverse" admits some form of a normative response: Perverse responses must turn away from *something*. If one can describe a perverse response to a film, then one can describe a normative one.[15]

The film industry itself banks on the assumption that millions, if not hundreds of millions, of viewers from a variety of backgrounds will have a particular, predictable experience of a new film, just as theme park owners bank on the assumption that a number of park patrons will have a particular, predictable experience of a new roller coaster. No one would bankroll such an expensive enterprise as a Hollywood movie without some assurance that the movie could at least guide the responses of its spectators. Although the industry accounts for variation in spectator responses, targeting individual films to subsets of the world population, it also assumes a likely amount of cognitive sameness, particularly within a demographic. A filmmaker, moreover, could hardly design a movie if spectators' experiences were so varied that they responded in largely indeterminable ways. From scriptwriting to post-production, filmmakers must assume that large numbers of spectators will perform a foreseeable repertoire of similar mental activities—including highly complex activities, such as story reconstruction, hypothesis testing, inferential reasoning, and emotional engagement—in response to cinematic stimuli.[16] That assumption makes industry filmmaking, and every other commercial artistic enterprise, possible.

A colleague once accused me of excluding non-dominant, non-normative experiences in my scholarship. I instinctively sought to defend myself against the accusation, until I realized that she was right. I do sometimes exclude non-dominant and non-normative experiences, just as scholars such as Staiger sometimes exclude the dominant, normative experiences that I want to illuminate in this book. Any degree of specialization is exclusive. My specialization here offers a way to understand the means by which a movie stimulates shared experiences for spectators.

If filmmakers can *create* an experience for people, then scholars can study it. Although, as William Paul says, "determining exactly what an audience might be thinking is always a tricky thing" (73), art theoretician-critics (including neoformalist, cognitive, and reader-response critics) have devised methods for understanding the ways in which works of art *cue* spectators to perform mental activities.[17] According to Thompson:

> The analyst's task becomes to point out the cues and . . . discuss what responses would reasonably result, given a knowledge of backgrounds on the part of the viewer. The neoformalist critic thus analyzes not a set of static form structures . . . but rather, a dynamic interaction between those structures and a hypothetical viewer's response to them. (*Breaking*, 30)

Her reference to a "hypothetical viewer" will likely raise some eyebrows: For some people, it might seem impossible to reconstruct viewers' experiences in any confident way. Although a reconstruction might remain speculative, scholarly speculation is not the same as guesswork, and the risk of flaws in an analysis of spectator experience does not undermine the endeavor. "In accounting for the effects of history on spectators," Thompson says, "critics need not go to the opposite extreme of dealing only with the reactions of actual people. . . . The notion of norms and deviations allows critics to make assumptions about how viewers would be likely to understand a given device" (26). Understanding an art form's historical norms (such as Hollywood's customary narrative strategies) allows the scholar to determine individual artworks' obedience to and deviations from standard practices.

Other types of research also aid analysis. Accounts of film receptions— movie reviews, box office statistics, contemporaneous essays, trade reports, marketing information, anecdotal reports of audience reactions, and empirical studies—help guide, advance, complicate, and confirm analyses. Cultural history, industrial history, auteur criticism, genre research, and research on modes of film production and exhibition enable us to understand spectators' expectations of a film, the conditions under which they view it, and the conventions that help guide their responses. Psychology research helps us understand the workings of the mind and the ways in which people typically respond to a controlled stimulus, such as a movie. Together with this book's central activity—the analysis of narrative and stylistic devices—such methods can help us reconstruct some of the moment-to-moment experiences that attend an individual film. "In the spirit of reverse engineering," Bordwell says in his study of modern American cinema, "I want to tease apart the finished films and see what strategies of plot and visual style govern their design" (*The Way*, 17). Film scholars have done little of this type of historically informed "reverse engineering" on even the most thoroughly studied Hollywood films of the 1970s. Consequently, the methods used in this study reveal fundamental aspects of seventies cinema that scholarship has left previously undiscovered.

CHAPTERS, FILMS, AND FILMMAKERS

In the following chapters, I examine seventies cinema's characteristic narrational strategies. Throughout the book, I use the term "seventies cinema" to signify not all films of the decade but rather a popular and prominent subset of films of the period 1970–1977 that helped expand Hollywood's narrative options and that seem to define the era for many filmgoers and commentators; the term is an abbreviation. The same principle applies to my use of the term "seventies filmmakers," which generally refers to a group of mostly writer-directors who helped shape the period's narrational strategies, most notably Woody Allen, Robert Altman, John Cassavetes, Francis Ford Coppola, William Friedkin, Stanley Kubrick, and Martin Scorsese. Many other directors and screenwriters of the era, however, often worked in the same vein, namely Hal Ashby, Peter Bogdanovich, John Boorman, Paddy Chayefsky, Brian De Palma, Bob Fosse, Arthur Hiller, Milos Forman, Sidney Lumet, Terrence Malick, Paul Mazursky, John Milius, Mike Nichols, Alan Pakula, Sam Peckinpah, Arthur Penn, Roman Polanski, Bob Rafelson, Michael Ritchie, Nicolas Roeg, Paul Schrader, Robert Towne, and others.

Continuing the introduction to narrative incongruity begun in this chapter, Chapter Two explains and illustrates the principles that distinguish the narrative strategies that develop and become prevalent in seventies cinema. Chapter Two also addresses why people might value incongruity in a narrative, particularly when watching films made within a tradition devoted so fully to organic unity. Finally, the chapter offers some empirical evidence that cinema from the 1970s deviates from Hollywood narrative norms (including classical standards of coherence and resolution) more than films from other periods and that a majority of the most highly regarded films of the decade, according to a variety of independent ratings, exhibit narrative incongruity to an uncommon degree.

Whereas Part I of this book describes the characteristic principles of Hollywood narratives in the 1970s, it does not explain seventies cinema "narration": the process of "selecting, arranging, and rendering story material in order to achieve specific time-bound effects on a perceiver" (Bordwell, *Narration*, xi). Each of the three chapters in Part II examines a key mode of perverse narration in 1970s cinema, modes that I abbreviate as 1) narrative frustration, 2) genre deviation, and 3) conceptual incongruity. To see, in a vivid and detailed way, how each mode operates, each chapter examines a key case study that illustrates the narrative mode in an exemplary way. Rather than systematically analyze a random sampling of films, it seems to me most useful for understanding narration of this period to engage in close, illustrative, revisionist analyses of films that readers likely know, that film fans have demonstrable affection for, and that film scholars have already shown interest in.

The three films under primary consideration in Part II of the book—*The Godfather, Part II*, *The French Connection*, and *The Exorcist*, each a model of seventies narrative design—achieved popular success and also received a great deal of critical attention at the time of their release and in subsequent years. In the context of the popular trend of sequels in the 1970s, Chapter Three studies the sequel to *The Godfather* in order to illustrate the peculiar tendency of seventies cinema to frustrate straightforward narration and to refrain from fulfilling narrative promises in conventionally satisfying ways. More conventional sequels of the seventies, such as *Magnum Force* (1973) and *Jaws 2* (1978), attempt to outdo the pleasures of the original films, but *The Godfather, Part II* systematically eschews the sentiment, suspense, excitement, clarity, and narrative momentum that helped make the first movie so widely appealing. Chapter Four studies the tendency of seventies narration to exploit and modify conventional genre devices in order to create unsettling and unresolved narrative incongruities. The chapter examines *Chinatown*, *Dog Day Afternoon*, *Taxi Driver*, and other films, but it focuses primarily on *The French Connection*, which uses the familiar conventions of the police detective film to mislead spectators into expecting conventional outcomes. Chapter Five studies the ways in which seventies narration intensifies conceptual incongruities already present in some traditional Hollywood scenarios. *The Exorcist*, the chapter's principal case study, creates conceptual incongruities that violate the film's "high concept" and impede linear narration. The chapter also traces the genealogy and evolution of conceptual incongruity in Hollywood cinema, from its ancestry in films of the studio era, particularly in studio-era crime films and horror films, to its narrative descendants in recent Hollywood cinema.

What are the limits of seventies narrative design? Part III offers two answers, one for classical Hollywood films and one for films uninhibited by Hollywood's strict norms of narration. The answers come by way of examining the work of two directors, Martin Scorsese and John Cassavetes, whose films embody the narrative strategies this book sets out to explain. Neither director would have found funding, distribution, or a market for his idiosyncratic work had not industry instability in the 1970s and a popular taste for challenging and unconventional film entertainment created a brief period of support for narrative and stylistic transformation in American cinema. Chapter Six studies the ways in which the films of Martin Scorsese, particularly *Taxi Driver*, test the parameters of the classical Hollywood model. *Taxi Driver* flirts precipitously with narrative and stylistic incoherence, at the same time that formal patterning holds together the film's incongruent pieces and inspires confidence in its underlying structure and harmony. Whereas Scorsese rides along the edge of Hollywood classicism, John Cassavetes leaps right over into radical cinema. Chapter Seven examines Cassavetes's uncompromising films, especially *A Woman Under the Influence* (1974), which show us the extreme, and some of the commercial hazards, of the narrative design that characterizes American films of this period. In Cassavetes films, we see what narrative perversity looks like when severed from classical Hollywood's stabilizing structures.

Together, these chapters demonstrate the centrality of this period to the history of Hollywood narration and the lasting impact of seventies modes of narration on contemporary Hollywood film. During the 1970s, more intensely and prevalently than ever before, narrative perversity became a leading strategy for Hollywood filmmakers. Now part of Hollywood history, the strategy that shocked many critics and audiences in the 1970s has become an established and accepted narrative tradition.

CHAPTER 2 NARRATIVE INCONGRUITY IN SEVENTIES CINEMA

In this chapter, we examine the qualities that broadly characterize Hollywood narratives of the 1970s and the principles that govern the period's narrative design. We furthermore examine the aesthetic value that incongruous narrative devices add to an otherwise unified film. Finally, we consider empirical evidence that films from the period 1970–1977 show a distinct tendency toward narrative incongruity and that a majority of the period's most admired and celebrated films exhibit such a tendency. Later chapters examine the era's processes of narration, but I intend to demonstrate by this chapter's general introduction to the period's characteristic narrative patterning that seventies cinema exhibits traits that distinguish it from Hollywood cinema from other periods.

Films of the 1970s often aim for moments of narrative incoherence. I use the word "incoherence" here, and everywhere in this book, not in its common metaphoric sense of irrationality or meaninglessness but rather in the literal sense to mean a lack of connectedness or integration among different elements. The incoherencies in seventies cinema are like those of a drawer full of knickknacks. "Coherence," by contrast, refers to a congruity of elements, the separate parts united to form a harmonious whole. A wind-up wristwatch is coherent, all of its integrated pieces working toward a common end. All artworks display a tension between incoherence and coherence since "organic unity"—the integration of a work's different parts—can only be achieved by bringing together materials that seem decisively separate. While some works of art (atonal music, avant-garde cinema, paintings by Picasso) stress the disunity of their form, classical Hollywood narration stresses unity through a set of codified formal principles, including narrative clarity, communicativeness, and linearity; unambiguous presentation; goal-oriented protagonists and character consistency; an emphasis on definitive story resolution; and an aversion to narratively superfluous story information or stylistic devices.[1] Without overtly violating the order and stability of the classical model, seventies cinema exhibits relatively more superfluous, pointed, and irresolute narrative incongruities than those in Hollywood films from other periods.

My argument might at first sound similar to the one Robin Wood makes in his 1981 essay, "The Incoherent Text: Narrative in the '70s." Indeed, like Wood, I want to examine layers of incoherence in seventies films that (unlike, say, avant-garde films) do not advertise their incoherencies.[2] But for Wood, seventies films are not incoherent *as* films (that is, as aesthetic experiences) but rather as allegories of political ideas. Wood only shows concern for contradictions in what seventies films are "trying to say" (50).[3] So he examines the films' ideological incongruities, which, for him, point to a failed political critique of mainstream ideology. "We can already look back to Hollywood in the '70s," he concludes, "as the period when the dominant ideology *almost* disintegrated" (69). Wood's essay touches on, but ultimately dismisses, what is most interesting and provocative about seventies narrative, namely its tendency to flirt with incongruities of all sorts.

The seventies teems with Hollywood films that display one or another form of *conceptual incongruity*, which we can define as a discordance of concepts, ideas, or principles. Conceptual incongruities include:

> 1. *Moral* or *ideological incongruities*, which denote a discrepancy between different ethical beliefs or belief systems. For example, war is noble vs. war is senseless and vain (*Patton*, 1970);
>
> 2. *Factual contradictions*, when story information contradicts other story information. For example, Michael Corleone tries to have Frankie Pentangeli murdered vs. Hyman Roth tries to have Pentangeli murdered (*The Godfather, Part II*, 1974);
>
> 3. *Logical inconsistencies*, which denote inconsistencies in a story's underlying system of principles or in the inferences one derives from them. For example, getting shot with a "splurge gun" (it shoots whipped cream) means death to the victim, until the finale, when the gunshots are all in fun (*Bugsy Malone*, 1976); and

4. *Characterological inconsistencies*, when characters behave in ways inconsistent with their previous characterizations. For example, the senatorial candidate has unbending integrity vs. the candidate does what he must to get elected (*The Candidate*, 1972).

We will encounter instances of all four types of conceptual incongruity throughout this study.

Conceptual incongruities are not the same as ambiguities. Ambiguity denotes an uncertainty or inexactness of meaning and indicates that an artwork elicits more than one interpretation. Conceptual incongruity, by contrast, denotes a lack of connectedness among the ideas generated by a film. Although conceptual incongruity is *one* way to generate ambiguity (other ways include imprecise storytelling or narrative or visual obscurity), incongruity does not inevitably result in an ambiguous spectator interpretation. A film may present incongruous concepts, yet spectators may never feel uncertain about the film's meaning, and the film may not elicit different interpretations from different viewers. In seventies cinema, ideological incongruities, factual contradictions, and logical and characterological inconsistencies often prompt spectators to understand and evaluate story information on the basis of incongruous but equally valid concepts.

David Thomson, in his 1993 essay, "The Decade When Movies Mattered," acknowledges these same sorts of conceptual incongruities when he says about films of the 1970s:

> Many of them had unfamiliar shapes, new narrative structures or strategies. They began late. They switched course. They didn't say this guy is reliably good and that one write-off bad. They didn't stick to the rules. And they did not end well, or happily, or comfortably. Sometimes they broke off in your hands or your mind. People you had come to like took it in the head, or turned traitor. The world of the films was as complex and as frightening as anything you'd come into the theatre to escape from. And you were left there when the lights came up, having to work it all out. (74)

Thomson here responds to various ways in which seventies films require viewers to supply some of the definition and logic that American cinema customarily provides *for* its viewers. His description of seventies cinema conveys, in the most vivid language I've encountered on the subject, the aesthetic vitality of the era's narrative incongruities.

Film scholarship has offered several compelling accounts of the aesthetic value of *unity* in cinema, most notably V. F. Perkins's *Film as Film* (also Noël Carroll's *Interpreting the Moving Image*, Stefan Sharff's *The Elements of Cinema*, and Warren Buckland's *Directed by Steven Spielberg*). However, we have seen no book-length studies devoted to the aesthetic contributions of cinematic *dis*unity. Perkins's "synthetic" theory of "balance, coherence and complexity" values, above all else, integration, clarity, proportion, and harmony, which he regards as prerequisite to cinema's aesthetic value (189):

> At the level of detail we can value most the moments when narrative, concept and emotion are most completely fused. Extended and shaped throughout the whole picture, such moments compose a unity between record, statement and experience. At this level too, sustained harmony and balance ensure that the view contained in the pattern of events may be enriched by the pattern of our involvement. When such unity is achieved, observation, thought and feeling are integrated. (133)

When Perkins finds fault in a movie—such as John Frankenheimer's *The Train* ("we can observe a disproportion between the effect produced and the means employed to produce it" [87]) and Franklin Schaffner's *The Best Man* ("[t]he weakness of Schaffner's approach is suggested by the extent to which the use of decor can be separated from the other elements in the film's treatment" [92])—the fault rests invariably in some illogic, imbalance, or disproportion.

Perkins's approach, however, is blind to the aesthetic value of precisely the illogic, imbalance, and disproportion one finds in so many great artworks.[4] Coherence is, as Perkins says, "a prerequisite of meaning" (116); however, meaning is only one of an artwork's components. An incongruity between, say, a film's meaning and its effect on spectators can generate an aesthetic excitement that more coherent works of art cannot offer. For instance, as we see in Chapter Five, much of the complexity of Hollywood crime films comes from aesthetically productive incongruities between the films' overt condemnation of crime and the narrations' successful effort to enlist viewers' sympathetic engagement with criminals. This type of complexity is of an order completely different from Perkins's conception of complexity, which relies on the harmonious integration of an artwork's meanings, devices, and emotional impact.

THE VALUE OF NARRATIVE INCONGRUITY

The most compelling account of narrative incongruity's aesthetic value comes from humor scholarship, which offers us a comprehensive body of research on the mental processes involved when encountering incongruity. Furthermore, humor research helps us understand the ways in which narrative incongruities generate not just mirth or laughter but other sorts of aesthetic pleasure as well.

Most scholars of humor and laughter—psychologists, anthropologists, linguists, social scientists, and theorists of aesthetics—ascribe to some version of the Incongruity Theory, which dates back to Aristotle's *Rhetoric* and was developed by Immanuel Kant, James Beattie, Arthur Schopenhauer, and others. According to the theory, humor results from the recognition of a violation of the patterns of an orderly world, and laughter, as humor researcher John Morreall describes it, is a "reaction to something that is unexpected, illogical, or inappropriate in some other way" (*Taking*, 15). For Morreall, something is incongruous "relative to someone's conceptual scheme" (60–61).

Incongruity Theory has over the years been elaborated upon and refined, most notably as Incongruity-Resolution Theory (advanced separately by psychologists James M. Jones, Thomas Shultz, and Jerry Suls) and Appropriate Incongruity Theory (by anthropologist Elliot Oring). Incongruity-Resolution Theory suggests that humor arises when the perceiver meets with an incongruity and is then motivated to resolve it. Consider the Woody Allen joke, cited by Suls, in which a group of prisoners escape, "twelve of them chained together at the ankle, getting by the guards posing as an immense charm bracelet" (*Woody*). Listeners resolve the incongruous punch line about prisoners posing as a charm bracelet because, as Suls says, prisoners on a chain gang "do in an odd way resemble a charm bracelet" (42). Oring's Appropriate Incongruity Theory makes essentially the same point, but he emphasizes the perception of an "appropriate relationship" between concepts or categories that perceivers normally consider incongruous (e.g., prisoners and charm bracelets). "Whereas nonsense can be characterized as pure or unresolvable incongruity," Shultz says, "humour can be characterized as resolvable or meaningful incongruity" ("Cognitive-Developmental," 13).

I introduce Incongruity-Resolution Theory here not to advocate for it. (It is the leading approach in humor and laughter studies, but many researchers find the theory inadequate in explaining all humor[5]). I am not trying to develop a comprehensive account of humor but rather to demonstrate that one established aspect of humor appreciation—the inducement to resolve incongruous information—helps us understand how minds respond to incongruity in cinema and other narrative forms. Moreover, research into the theory offers compelling empirical evidence (and probably the only scientific evidence) for the aesthetic pleasure of resolving incongruities.

Indeed, a wealth of empirical research supports the theory, legions of ethnographic and controlled psychological studies, many of them conducted by Shultz and his colleagues in the 1970s.[6] For instance, Shultz and Horibe found that children between ages eight and twelve considered verbal jokes to be funniest when the jokes had both an incongruity and a resolution (e.g., "Why did the cookie cry? Because its mother had been a wafer so long") and less funny when the jokes had an incongruity and no resolution ("Why did the cookie cry? Because its mother was a wafer") or a resolution and no incongruity ("Why did the cookie cry? Because he was left in the oven too long"). Shultz also identified incongruity and resolution features in the large majority of Chinese jokes, riddles from nonliterate cultures, and Japanese riddles and folktales.

Our laughter at jokes and other humor expresses our enjoyment in resolving or finding appropriate relations between incongruous story information. In *The Art of Laughter*, Neil Schaeffer says that laughter gives free expression to creative mental processes—imaginative associations, improbable linkages, illogical resolutions—that serious situations and "our practical investment in the process of reason" inhibit and treat as dysfunctional (24). I propose that the pleasure expressed when laughing at incongruities in a humorous context is a more flagrant version of the pleasure offered by narrative incongruities contained in a variety of more serious aesthetic contexts, such as those found so prevalently in seventies cinema. Incongruity sometimes leads to laughter (research suggests that it depends mostly upon contextual cues)[7]; however, laughter is just one manifestation of the pleasures of resolving incongruity, and mirth merely a subset of those pleasures. "We enjoy incongruity in other ways than by being amused," Morreall observes ("Funny Ha-Ha," 204).

Recall that the standard tropes of both humorous and nonhumorous literature—rhyme, metaphor, metonymy, paradox, puns, irony—have at their root an appropriate or resolved incongruity. Film narratives regularly prompt spectators to connect elements that seem resolutely incompatible. For example, whodunits generally reveal the least likely character (the butler, a dead victim, all of the suspects together) as the criminal, not only to surprise us but also to allow us to see an intriguing correctness and inevitability to events that had previously seemed improbable or unimaginable. Screwball comedies often bring together seemingly mismatched characters—a rich heiress and a working man (*It Happened One Night* [1934], *Holiday* [1938]); a stuffy intellectual and a sexy vamp (*Ball of Fire* [1941]); a stuffy intellectual working man and a ditsy rich heiress (*Bringing Up Baby* [1938])—enabling us to perceive oddly appropriate connections between incongruous elements within a narrative.

Whether in humor or in serious situations, narrative incongruity induces us to mentally resolve a discrepancy between what context tells us must be true and what logic, pattern, or probability tell us should not be true. Resolving incongruity may result in mirth or the mere delight of making connections between elements in conflict. In either case, the endeavor to repair incongruous elements in a narrative exercises our cognitive agility and our creative problem-solving capacities.[8] Narrative incongruities prompt us to perform dexterous feats of imaginative reasoning.

It may seem strange to think of a joke's laughable incongruities as equivalent to the incongruities in a gritty narrative feature such as *Badlands* (1973) or *Chinatown*. However, the incongruities in jokes are structurally identical (although the ludicrous context makes jokes feel different) to those in any number of narratives that spectators take more seriously. The comic genre provides a context and a pretext for incongruous narrative information. However, whether we consider incongruities within a brief gag or across an extended and serious narrative, the perceiver's process of resolving incongruity is the same and has the same potential to inspire creative mental associations freed from the governance of pattern, probability, and strict story logic. Like incongruities in jokes, narrative incongruities in seventies films have the potential to excite in us a playful process of free association. They prompt spectators to *find the fit* between narrative elements that do not readily coordinate. Relying on our imagination, narrative incongruities liberate us from the limitations of probability, story logic, and conventional Hollywood plot patterning. In short, narrative incongruities offer us the creative pleasure of making sense of something that probability, story logic, and our experiences with film formulas might inhibit us from understanding.

Although narrative incongruities trouble a film's organic unity, they add richness and variety to a film that would otherwise come off as merely linear and logical. By defying probability and familiar plot patterning, they make films less predictable and straightforward. Spectators attempting to resolve narrative incongruities must make surprising (and sometimes logically suspect) connections among narrative elements that do not connect in any firm or foreseeable way. A mind making such precarious connections is a mind in a state of excitement, a mind gracefully working out the order of a disorderly narrative and using its imagination to correct a story that refuses to settle down and behave.

NARRATIVE INCONGRUITY IN SEVENTIES CINEMA

Since incongruity is, I propose, the defining characteristic of seventies narrative design, we should understand from the beginning of our study its manifestation in movies of this period. We should moreover understand the qualities that distinguish the relatively superfluous, pointed, and irresolute incongruities in seventies cinema from incongruities typically found in more traditional Hollywood cinema. We begin this examination by looking at instances of two types of conceptual incongruity in two prominent seventies films: characterological inconsistency and ideological incongruity in *Nashville* (1975) and *Dog Day Afternoon* (1975).

As *Nashville*'s narration toggles among characters interacting in a variety of scenarios, the film regularly violates what had seemed firmly established characterizations. At the end of the film, for instance—during the ruckus after a gunman shoots country singer Barbara Jean (Ronee Blakley) at Nashville's Parthenon—when Haven Hamilton (Henry Gibson) ignores his own bullet wound in order to help maintain calm at the rally, he reacts with an intrepidness incongruous with the narration's previous portrayal of him as petty and self-serving. The film's depiction of Hamilton at that moment would have seemed more consistent with its previous depiction of the character had he cowered and fled. The moment does not designate an unexpected reformation in Hamilton (as might an equivalent moment at the end of a studio-era melodrama) or cause spectators to develop sudden affection for the character: His courageous behavior contains the same stiff arrogance that has made him so abrasive all along. Rather, the moment opposes the film's previously scornful attitude toward Hamilton by portraying him briefly, and finally, as fearless.

Nashville complicates, in similar ways, its portrayal of several of its twenty-four principle characters, including, for instance, Tom Frank (Keith

Carradine), the rudest member of a rock trio performing in Nashville. Capitalizing on the image of male rock artists as womanizers, *Nashville* establishes Tom as a Casanova, careless of women's feelings, using them for sex and temporary companionship. In an unexpectedly affecting scene at a nightclub, Tom dedicates his song "I'm Easy" to Linnea Reese, an unsatisfied wife played by Lily Tomlin, whom he later beds. At the nightclub, interspersed between shots of an earnest-looking Tom and a visibly affected Linnea, the film depicts the reactions of three other women, all of whom Tom has previously seduced. The moment would seem slimier if Tom's ballad were not so beautiful, as seductive to the movie's spectators as it is to Linnea, and if his performance did not appear genuinely tender toward her. Despite that the song's refrain ("I'm easy") accords with his carefree ways and sexual promiscuity, its romantic style, earnest lyrics ("It's not my way to love you just when no one's looking"), and Tom's apparently heartfelt performance create a positive impression of a character who had, until that time, seemed a comfortable stereotype of callousness and vanity.

Nashville's characterological inconsistencies seem carefully measured to provoke curiosity and surprise by exploiting incongruities between two cognitive biases: the "primacy effect" (the tendency for initial stimuli, such as our first impression of a character, to have a salient influence on our thinking) and the "recency effect" (the disproportionate salience of recent stimuli). The incongruity between the two biases prompts *Nashville*'s spectators periodically to reassess their understanding of the film's characters. *Nashville* prompts spectators to *find the fit* between what they already know about a character and what they observe at the moment.

Nashville, like *Husbands* (1970), *Five Easy Pieces* (1970), *Klute* (1971), *Scarecrow* (1973), *Lenny* (1974), *California Split* (1974), and *Mikey and Nicky* (1976), generates characterological complexity through plausible incongruities in the portrayals of its lead characters. The characters themselves do not necessarily develop, but our experience of them does, as the narration periodically adds information about characters that opposes salient prior information. Such films do not cause us to radically reevaluate characters, as is the case in, say, *Mission Impossible* (1996) when the character of Jim Phelps, who for most of the film seems the prototype of spy film integrity, turns out to be a villain. Rather, little by little, the films reveal conflicting nuances of characterization, not wiping out previous impressions but complicating them through plausible incongruities. Fictions, like sporting events and board games, allow us to think about things within a system of options that is closed to the kinds of impertinent information that makes ordinary experience so much more mentally taxing. *Nashville* strategically admits the mental inconveniences that many people go to the movies to escape.

We can see in studio-era films antecedents of the inconsistent characters found in so much seventies cinema. Although studio-era screenwriting manuals admonished writers to maintain character consistency (see, for example, Vale, 102–105), many studio-era films, such as *Citizen Kane* (1941), *The Maltese Falcon* (1941), and *On the Waterfront* (1954), created ambiguity by inserting prominent incongruities into a protagonist's characterization. Charles Foster Kane, for instance, is the prototypical ambiguous protagonist, coming across sometimes as noble and likable and at other times as vain, petty, and narcissistic.

In Sam Spade, *The Maltese Falcon* has probably the most ambiguous protagonist of any private detective film from the studio era, with the possible exception of Mike Hammer from *Kiss Me Deadly* (1955). The film portrays Spade as a talented, at times heroic, detective, but he also behaves cold-heartedly and his motives appear dubious: He never seems sufficiently upset about the murder of his partner, Miles Archer; he is having an affair with Archer's wife, whom he can't stand; he exploits his relationship with Brigid O'Shaughnessy for sex and money; and, when he thinks he has acquired the notorious black bird, he maniacally grabs the arm of his ever-supportive secretary and greedily barks, "We've got it!" oblivious to her troubled face and whimpered response, "You're hurting me."

Similarly, *On the Waterfront*'s Terry Malloy seems a mass of contradictions—angry and virile yet passive and indolent, cold yet caring, a bum and a champion—depending on the situation. Compare, for instance, the focused intensity of Marlon Brando's portrayal of Malloy in the taxicab scene toward the end of the movie with his passivity in an early scene in the poolroom. In the taxi, Brando plays the character as insistent and forceful,[9] whereas, in the earlier scene, the character seems essentially reactive and passive. When Lee J. Cobb pushes on Brando's shoulder, for instance, Brando rolls with the shove, moving in the least resistant manner possible, a mannerism characteristic of Malloy in the early parts of the movie.

Citizen Kane, *The Maltese Falcon*, *On the Waterfront*, and other studio-era films with inconsistent lead characters indicate that the seventies did not invent characterological inconsistency in Hollywood. But seventies filmmakers modified the practice in ways that, like foreign art films, highlighted the impression of unpredictability and narrative diversion. To illustrate this point, let's consider the differences between the treatment of characterological inconsistency in the two Hollywood eras.

In studio-era films, a character's inconsistencies would likely become a crucial link in the narrative's cause-and-effect chain. According to Seymour Chatman, events linked by causality are hinges in a narrative structure and "cannot be deleted without destroying the narrative logic."[10] Characterological inconsistencies generally functioned as narrative hinges. *Citizen Kane*, for instance, makes the ambiguity of the title character the primary focus of narration. Structured around flashbacks inspired by the memories of characters who knew Kane, the narration stresses the investigation of Kane's psychology, variations in characters' impressions of him, and the difficulty of reconciling such impressions. Similarly, the ambiguity of the portrayal of Sam Spade in *The Maltese Falcon* helps to establish one of the film's central cruxes: Is Spade really so ruthless and mercenary or is he merely pretending in an effort to obtain answers and seek justice? The final scene, in which he foregoes money and love for the sake of principle ("Don't be too sure I'm as crooked as I'm supposed to be," he says to Brigid O'Shaughnessy before he turns her over to the police), answers the question audiences have probably been asking since they witnessed Spade's cold-hearted reaction to the death of his partner. *On the Waterfront*'s inconsistent depiction of Terry Malloy indicates the character's own struggle and forecasts the transformation he undergoes by the end of the film, when he turns from passively accepting the corrupt institution that employs him to bravely championing the law and human dignity.

Whereas, in the studio era, characterological inconsistencies tended to fit securely into cause-and-effect narration, in seventies cinema they often remained unanchored to causality. Consequently, the inconsistencies—like those in *Nights of Cabiria* (1957), *Hiroshima mon amour* (1959), *Odd Obsession* (1959), *Jules et Jim* (1962), and other foreign art films—often come across as random, unpredictable, and narratively incidental.[11] The inconsistencies don't always attach themselves to character goals or desires, instead functioning merely as indications of complex psychologies.

Consider the portrayal of Sonny Wortzik (Al Pacino), the endearing protagonist of *Dog Day Afternoon*. Sonny's characterization grows increasingly more incongruous as the narration periodically reveals nuanced character information inconsistent with salient prior impressions. Spectators are no doubt surprised to learn, halfway through the film, that Sonny is bisexual, but when they hear Sonny's gay lover, Leon (Chris Sarandon), say that Sonny put a gun to Leon's head and beat up Leon's friends, it is more than surprising: It violates firmly established details of Sonny's characterization, such as his sweetness, clumsiness, and aversion to violence. When Leon tells the police that Sonny said, "Go to sleep, Leon, so it won't hurt when I pull the trigger," we have little reason to doubt Leon, yet the words sound like nothing that has issued from Sonny's mouth. Nonetheless, the character's inconsistencies never become the primary focus of narration and hardly further the cause-and-effect progress of the story. For instance, the inconsistency between Sonny's sweetness and his violent threats against Leon doesn't create an enigma that the film's narration sets out to resolve. It remains an incidental incongruity, largely superfluous to the causal progress of the narrative, which never reconciles the depiction of Sonny with his boyfriend's description of him. In fact, the incongruity seems counterproductive to story logic, interfering with the narration's more blatant and essential effort to enlist our sympathy for the character.

We should not regard *Dog Day Afternoon* as art cinema, however. Unlike European art films, the movie is not highly self-conscious, the role of the author/filmmaker is not foregrounded, the break with Hollywood tradition is not radical or sustained, and the film never highlights its deviations from classical narrative norms—norms the movie obeys most of the time (see Bordwell, *Poetics*, 156). More precisely, we should say that the film has adopted a convention appropriate to both classical and art-cinema narration (an ambiguous protagonist) and modified it to achieve effects that momentarily lean toward those of art cinema and away from classical Hollywood (a sense of randomness and narrative drift; a focus on psychological complexity per se, rather than on character goals and actions). Because *Dog Day Afternoon* remains moored to the classical model, which stabilizes narration, it can briefly incorporate art-cinema techniques that—though they make the film less tidy, smooth, and linear—add nuance, richness, and unpredictability to classical narration.

Let's turn to ideological incongruities in seventies cinema, which further demonstrate a tendency among some of the era's films to risk narrative incoherence. *Dog Day Afternoon* periodically highlights, as one of its key themes, the news media's exploitation of Sonny's bank robbery attempt and the prurient fascination of outside spectators, who excitedly watch events behind barricades set up by the police. Sonny reviles the TV news station for its grotesque curiosity. "The audience is interested in you, Sonny," a TV reporter says, to which Sonny replies, "Yeah, we're hot entertainment, right?" The crowd of onlookers appear impudent and voyeuristic, especially, for instance, when they boo police or cheer Sonny and scramble for money he tosses. The movie, however, also places its own audience in a position that has uncomfortable similarities to that of the news media and the crowd. The media and the rubberneckers depicted in the film are doing almost precisely what the movie's spectators are doing: voyeuristically watching an entertaining media event, rooting for criminals and denigrating police.

We should return to *Nashville* because, even more pointedly than *Dog Day Afternoon*, Altman's film contains so many ideological incongruities that the ethos of the film is unintelligible. The performance of the film's final song, "It Don't Worry Me," emblematizes *Nashville*'s ideological incongruities. A determined performer named Albuquerque (Barbara Harris) finally gets her break when she sings the song immediately after Barbara Jean's shooting. On stage at the Parthenon, Albuquerque begins singing tentatively, but she performs finally with a big and charismatic voice that encourages not only gospel singers to join with her but also the entire rally audience.

My description makes the scene appear unified, but the presence of numerous ideological incongruities impedes efforts to define the film's moral position on the depicted events. For instance, written and performed in the style of a protest song, "It Don't Worry Me" is precisely the opposite. Although it advocates a free spirit that corresponds with shots of the singing crowd— shots reminiscent of *Woodstock* (1970)—the song's complacent message does not accord with the image of a countercultural mass and also denies the horror and senselessness of Barbara Jean's assassination. Interspersed shots of the American flag just before the shooting, presumably from the viewpoint of the gunman, make the assassination feel vaguely seditious, but the crowd's response looks like neither a patriotic reaction to the shooting nor a gesture of ideological sympathy with the gunman. It remains unclear, moreover, exactly what the singing crowd might be protesting since Barbara Jean, the gunman, and the candidate featured at the rally do not represent any distinct idea or institution. Finally, whereas various, infrequent shots of stunned characters register the shock of the shooting, the revelation of Albuquerque's heretofore hidden singing talent seems paradoxically to applaud the triumph of her moment on stage. Her song sounds so catchy and hymn-like and the moment seems so uplifting that it might take the time to get to the movie theater parking lot before one fully considers the shooting that instigated the song and the appalling message of its refrain: "You may say that I ain't free, but it don't worry me."[12]

At *Nashville*'s climax, numerous incongruous ideas seem *almost* to rally together. Critics have called the scene "bitterly ironic" (Wood, 29); "a sad acknowledgement of social problems and personal pain" (Klein, 7); a "satire and deconstruction of myths" (Man, 164); and "a creative, energetic view of society gone awry" (Lev, 65). Critics have also said that the scene reveals a "potential source of strength" among the crowd (Klein, 7); condemns the crowd's "inherent passivity" and "alienation from power" (Kolker, 356–357); and depicts the American people either as "a flock of sheep" or as exhibiting a "stubborn strength" (McCormick, 25). However, none of these ideas can be maintained without contradiction from opposing ideas provoked by the film's narration, and the incongruities prevent the film from reaching any stable ideological closure.[13]

Hollywood movies outside the 1970s also display conceptual incongruities. *His Girl Friday* (1940), for instance, prompts spectators to ally with Rosalind Russell's efforts to outwit Cary Grant, even though doing so would cause her to give up her rightful career as a newspaper reporter and end up with dreary Ralph Bellamy, rather than with Grant, who we know is perfect for her. *Gladiator*'s (2000) protagonist defies the Roman's prurient desire for bloody combat—the very bloody combat that presumably everyone in the audience went to the movie to see. However, two qualities distinguish the kinds of conceptual incongruities that tend to appear in seventies cinema: 1) seventies films pointedly intensify incongruous elements in the narrative, and 2) whereas Hollywood movies from other periods generally smooth over their conceptual incongruities with harmonious resolutions, many seventies films leave their incongruous elements relatively unresolved. Chapter Five traces the genealogy and evolution of conceptual incongruity in Hollywood cinema, but we begin the discussion here by examining the ways in which seventies cinema manifests *pointed incongruity* and *narrative irresolution*.

POINTED INCONGRUITY

Scarface (1932), *White Heat* (1949), *Kiss Tomorrow Goodbye* (1950), and other studio-era crime pictures can be said to challenge the harmony of the Hollywood model in some of the same ways that seventies films do. In *Kiss Tomorrow Goodbye*, when escaping prisoner Ralph Cotter (James Cagney) recklessly kills a pursuing officer, the movie appears both to celebrate his escape and condemn the murder he commits along the way. However, because the film does not highlight the officer's death, the clash between celebration and condemnation does not gain any grip on the audience's attention. The movie, for instance, does not show the murder's impact on the officer's family or provide a close-up of his dying face. Since the film has not made Cotter's pursuer human to us (he is defined principally by his function as an obstacle to the escape of our gangster protagonist), the narration does not emphasize the conflict between *Kiss Tomorrow Goodbye*'s celebration and condemnation of Cotter's criminality.

A typical crime film of the 1970s would more likely intensify the incongruity between the appealing goals of a criminal protagonist and the upsetting effects of the protagonist's actions. *The Godfather*, for example, offers the gangland revenge that such movies have taught spectators to expect, but the narration also emphasizes revenge's unsettling consequences. Consider the scene in which the new Mafia don, Michael Corleone (Al Pacino), has one of his captains, Sal Tessio (Abe Vigoda), killed for betraying the Corleone family. In the movie's moral universe, Tessio deserves death for having helped another don try to kill Michael, but the narration goes out of its way to highlight Tessio's sympathetic response to the discovery of his betrayal. He behaves so sweetly as he is led to his death—"Tell Michael it was only business; I always liked him"—and, just before a forlorn rendition of one of the movie's musical themes enters the soundtrack, a medium close-up shows Vigoda's long, dejected face and puppy-dog eyes (Figure 2.1). The film's incongruous attitudes of sympathy and vengefulness toward Tessio is pure seventies filmmaking.

Chinatown (1974) creates similarly pointed incongruities in its attitude toward its protagonist. When private detective Jake Gittes (Jack Nicholson)

FIGURE 2.1. *The Godfather*: Abe Vigoda's dejected face elicits sympathy for his character at the moment of vengeance against him.

confronts his client Evelyn Mulwray (Faye Dunaway) about her relationship to a girl he has been trying to locate, he repeatedly slaps Mulwray, yelling "I said I want the truth!" But she had been telling him the truth since before he began hitting her: "She's my sister *and* my daughter!" As he tries to grasp what she is saying about her incestuous relationship with her father, Gittes looks dumbfounded and Mulwray fragile and broken. Although slapping an obstinate rival is a commonplace of the private detective genre—"When you're slapped, you'll take it and like it," Humphrey Bogart says to Peter Lorre in *The Maltese Falcon*—the equivalent moment in *Chinatown* makes the detective, having lost his cool demeanor, look like a jerk. Here, as in many seventies films, *Chinatown* takes a conventional Hollywood narrative device (a determined detective obtaining crucial information by slapping a rival) and modifies it to create a pointed incongruity (the detective succeeds both in obtaining the information and in looking foolish and obnoxious).

The Godfather and *Chinatown* seem to cheer on their protagonists even as the films portray them as contemptible. We could say the same about the protagonists of *Patton* (1970), *Husbands* (1970), *The French Connection* (1971), *A Clockwork Orange* (1971), *Straw Dogs* (1971), *The Getaway* (1972), *Death Wish* (1974), *The Godfather, Part II* (1974), *Shampoo* (1975), *Carrie* (1976), *Network* (1976), and *Taxi Driver* (1976). The male protagonist of 1973's *Badlands* is a charming, homicidal sociopath, the female protagonist an indifferent observer. In *The Missouri Breaks* (1976), the outlaw played by Jack Nicholson murders the bloodthirsty "regulator" played by Marlon Brando while the character is sleeping. Nicholson's line to the startled manhunter, delivered with chilling composure, is, "You know what woke you up? That you just had your throat cut." Sam Peckinpah's *Cross of Iron* (1977) portrays Nazis sympathetically. The Nazi protagonists, moreover, are not the righteous pacifists of *Das Boot* (1981) but vicious soldiers, placed in a narrative that aligns spectators with the Germans as they attempt to kill America's Russian allies.

Even seventies movies marketed to children often display pointed conceptual incongruities, uncommon for children's films, which, as a rule, tend toward moral simplicity and conformity. *Willy Wonka and the Chocolate Factory* (1971) mostly portrays its title character (Gene Wilder) as a weary, but essentially moral, role model; his test of Charley, for instance, is designed to ensure Charley's character. Yet, throughout the movie, he barely acknowledges the danger the kids inflict upon themselves in his chocolate factory. "Stop, don't, come back," he whispers sardonically as Mike Teevee sets about atomizing himself, and he speaks wryly of the fact that Veruca Salt and her father have only a 50 percent chance of having themselves incinerated in one of his furnaces: "Well, I think that furnace is only lit every other day, so they have a good sporting chance, haven't they?"

Coach Buttermaker (Walter Matthau), the alcoholic protagonist of *The Bad News Bears* (1976), is equally mean to the children in his care, and, even after his transformation at the end of film, still immoderately guzzles beer and never expresses regret for screaming at the kids abusively. Coach Turner, the story's "bad" coach (played by Vic Morrow, who made a career of playing one sort of heavy or another), hits his son in the midst of a game— to the consternation of his wife, the crowd of spectators, and the movie's audience—when the boy refuses to do what his father tells him. However, the moment would be more ideologically coherent if the father were not attempting to discipline his son, who had intentionally fast-pitched a ball at the head of one of the Bears: "He could have killed that kid," Coach Turner says with surprising logic, sympathy, and moral clarity, a line that pointedly violates the narration's characterization of him as an overly competitive brute. Far from simplifying the moral incongruities inherent in the story, such moments intensify them.

The more intense the incongruity, the more mental activity is required to resolve it. Intensifying incongruity so pointedly exposes a film to conceptual failure—if *The Bad News Bears* spectators found themselves sympathizing more with Coach Turner than with Coach Buttermaker, the entire concept of the film would suddenly collapse—but it can also increase a film's potential to stimulate aesthetic pleasure. Humor research supplies a large body of empirical evidence for a positive correlation between the degree of pleasure and the degree of incongruity. Jones, for instance, found that one group of adult subjects' rating of the funniness of cartoons was a positive linear function of another group's rating of the cartoons' degree of incongruity. Nerhardt and other cognitive researchers found that subjects smiled or laughed more in proportion to the degree of discrepancy between the weight of an object and subjects' expectation of its weight.[14] Deckers and Salais found that humor increased in a negatively accelerated fashion with the degree of incongruity. Several researchers (e.g., Deckers and Buttram, Hoppe, McGhee, Wilson) have found what's known as an "inverted-U" relationship between incongruity and humor, such that humor indicators increased for a period relative to the degree of incongruity and then began to decline. The inverted-U results indicate that humor increases with the level of incongruity but that at a certain point—perhaps the point at which perceivers had too much difficulty resolving incongruity—the pleasure of incongruity decreases. Such research suggests that the greater the strain on our ability to resolve incongruous information, so long as the strain does not overburden our efforts at resolution, the greater we enjoy it.

I do not want to suggest that seventies movies alone contain pointed conceptual incongruities that tax spectators' efforts at resolution. We can find examples from the studio era and post-seventies cinema: *You Only Live Once* (1937), *Citizen Kane* (1941), *The Naked Spur* (1953), *The Searchers* (1956), *Anatomy of a Murder* (1959), *Lawrence of Arabia* (1962), *Do the Right Thing* (1989), *Unforgiven* (1992), *Starship Troopers* (1997), *V for Vendetta* (2006), and others. However, such movies permeated American theaters only in the first eight years of the 1970s.

NARRATIVE IRRESOLUTION

As the foregoing remarks indicate, seventies cinema not only creates pointed narrative incongruities, it also strains spectators' ability to resolve them. Hollywood cinema, as film commentators and screenwriting manuals frequently observe, generally insists upon definitive story resolution. Film scholars Richard Neupert (73–74) and Murray Smith (*Engaging Characters*, 213) have separately argued that Hollywood cinema also tends to insist upon moral resolution. During the 1970s, Hollywood filmmakers resisted both.

Resolution is a relative term. All movies, including classical Hollywood movies, have some measure of irresolution: Minor story lines are sometimes left unsettled (e.g., Mollie Malloy's story in *His Girl Friday*), or some characters might be left out of the film's concluding moments or are never given what justice says they deserve (e.g., Mr. Potter in *It's a Wonderful Life* [1946]). By the same token, even the most unresolved movie endings have a measure of closure, provided, for example, by a long shot, still frame, closing credits, or simply the film's termination. However, when placed on a continuum of resolution, most Hollywood films fall along the high end, European and Asian art films of the fifties and sixties (e.g., *The 400 Blows* [1959], *The Sword of Doom* [1966]) tend to fall along the other end, and a lot of seventies films fall in the middle.

Moral Irresolution

A comparison of the two versions of *Get Carter* (1971 and 2000) illustrates the 1970s penchant for *moral* irresolution. Written and directed by Englishman Mike Hodges and filmed entirely in the United Kingdom, the 1971 *Get Carter* was financed and distributed by MGM, capitalizing on America's newfound taste for European-style cinema by channeling it through Hollywood's production and distribution system. In its narrative strategies too, *Get Carter* demonstrates a "middle way" charted by seventies filmmakers between classical Hollywood filmmaking, which affords a stable paradigm and time-tested narrative devices, and foreign art cinema, which provides a looser, more playful, and less unified and resolute set of narrative strategies. In particular, *Get Carter* typifies the tendency of seventies films to develop and sustain moral incongruities without fully resolving them. In both the 1971 and 2000 versions, a mob hit man seeks to avenge his brother's death, but the Carter portrayed by Michael Caine in the original film sadistically kills anyone associated with the murder, including characters who simply knew of it and didn't tell him.

Many of the scenes of murder in the original film create an incongruity between, on the one hand, the narration's investment in Carter's revenge, and, on the other, Carter's excessive cruelty toward characters who do not seem to deserve it. For instance, in one scene, Carter pumps one of the meeker characters, Albert Swift (Glynn Edwards), for information and then proceeds to stab him to death for no good reason. Just before Swift, who doesn't fight back during any part of his ordeal, is killed, the camera focuses not on Carter, whose face remains out of the frame, but on the victim's kneeling body, tortured face, and pleading hands (Figure 2.2). Imploring, Swift says about Carter's brother, "Christ, I didn't kill him." Carter proceeds to stab him twice in the gut, punctuating each stab with his words, "I *know* you didn't kill him. I *know*." This is the first murder we see Carter perform—it takes place eighty minutes into the movie, after he has long ago enlisted audience sympathy—and, like later ones, the murder is morally irresolute: both admirably uncompromising and overly vicious.

Revenge movies regularly elicit positive attitudes toward cruelty: Violence and cruelty "deliver the goods." Although *Get Carter* gives spectators the violence and cruelty that the vigilante situation inspires, the extremity of Carter's cruelty and the haplessness of some of his victims prompt reactions counterproductive to the film's ethos of vengeance. For instance, Carter murders his brother's girlfriend, Margaret (Dorothy White), by forcing her to strip, shoving a handkerchief in her mouth, and injecting her with something lethal while kneeling on top of her arms. Viewers probably don't know for certain that Carter is killing her until after she dies. In an astonishingly

FIGURE 2.2. The excessively cruel protagonist of *Get Carter* kills a character who pleads for his life.

unsettling moment, the camera centers on her eyes as they transform from terrified to lifeless. That's not delivering the goods; that's perverse. Such scenes—which led Pauline Kael to write that the film launched "a new genre of virtuoso viciousness" (*5001 Nights*, 282)[15]—at the same time portray Carter as a sympathetic protagonist, overcoming obstacles in order to achieve his objectives, and portray those obstacles as human victims of a cruel monster. Although classical in structure, the film has modified classical narrative strategies to create pointed and relatively unresolved moral incongruities.

Caine's charismatic performance of the vicious, immaculately dressed cockney gangster accounts for much of the character's blend of charm and repugnance. The performance is measured, but in most scenes we sense a seething violence buried beneath the character's restrained demeanor, a violence suggested through clenched jaws—to indicate anger, Caine likes to thrust his bottom row of teeth forward and pull his upper lip above his top teeth—and the actor's tight movements, such as the way he moves his entire torso when swinging his head. The performance combines a prim fussiness (in the first-class dining car of a train, Carter fastidiously cleans his spoon with his napkin before eating) with bursts of startling brutality, his actions simultaneously cool and appalling.

One might assume that spectators delight in Carter precisely because of his excessive cruelty, in which case their moral attitude toward him would be coherent and the scenes of murder morally resolved. However, it is probably more accurate to say that spectators delight in Carter mostly for other reasons—Caine's charismatic performance, Carter's charming disregard for anyone's opinion of him, the character's uncompromising loyalty toward his brother, and his determination to achieve his goal—and that the narration periodically injects elements that challenge one's willingness to support him. Murray Smith has shown that spectators rarely respond sympathetically to characters "on the basis of their embodiment of socially or morally undesirable traits" ("Gangsters," 222). According to Smith, cinema might ally us with immoral characters but not with their immorality. He argues that even in such cases as Alex in *A Clockwork Orange* (1971) or Hannibal Lecter in *Silence of the Lambs* (1991)—cases that would seem to illustrate spectators' allegiance to evil behavior—such allegiances develop "in spite of rather than because of" the characters' immorality:

> Do we find Lecter sympathetic and attractive *because* of his taste for human liver? . . . Rather, I would argue that we find him (relatively) sympathetic because he possesses a number of attractive and appealing traits. . . . The film keeps his immoral traits and actions in the background and stresses his positive attributes. (227)

Similarly, in *Get Carter*, we *condone* Carter, despite his viciousness, because he exhibits several appealing qualities. *Get Carter* elicits sympathy for Carter's avenging mission and then upsets straightforward allegiance to the character with scenes of revenge in which he acts monstrously and his victims appear defenseless and pitiable.

In the 2000 remake, Sylvester Stallone portrays an equally tough and determined Carter, but Stallone's Carter has a more conventional morality, and the film regularly harmonizes common notions of decency with the character's vengeful goals and actions. A more typical Hollywood production than the original film, the remake supplants moments of moral ambiguity with story events that more fully resolve the film's moral incongruities. For instance, at one point the narration emphasizes Carter's triumphant decision *not* to kill one of the villains responsible for his brother's death—"I'm going to do for you what nobody ever did for me: Give you a second chance"—after the villain comes across, all of a sudden, as pathetic. The seventies Carter shows no such charity, not even toward his most pitiable victims, nor does the earlier film emphasize Carter's own pathetic background as justification for his criminality (Caine's Carter would never remark on what nobody ever did for him). Unlike the relatively irresolute *Get Carter* from the 1970s, the remake periodically aligns Carter's acts of revenge with conventional ethical behavior.

Story Irresolution

Let's turn away from moral irresolution to look at the era's penchant for a relatively high degree of *story* irresolution for mainstream cinema. Astonishingly few Hollywood movies from the studio era end on moments of narrative instability; examples might include *I Walked with a Zombie* (1943), *The Wrong Man* (1956), or even *Gone with the Wind* (1939), the last line of which, "After all, tomorrow is another day," signals commencement as much as closure. By contrast, during the 1970s doing so became a regular practice, and open endings were far *more* open than those of studio-era films. Consider the final moments of *Five Easy Pieces* (1970), *McCabe & Mrs. Miller* (1971), *The Candidate* (1972), *The Apprenticeship of Duddy Kravitz* (1974), *The Parallax View* (1974), *Nashville* (1975), *The Killing of a Chinese Bookie* (1976), and other films of the decade that force spectators to resolve what the films' narration neglects to resolve for them. William Paul says about the open-ended conclusion of *Carrie* (1976), "Although there were certainly some precursors for this (especially in *Psycho* and *The Birds*), *Carrie*'s ending was the most direct assault yet on closure's dominance in Hollywood films" (410).

Still other seventies films conclude with story resolution that leaves behind a *feeling* of irresolution. At the end of *A Clockwork Orange* (1971), our protagonist declares himself "cured" after enduring the grueling horrors of the "Lodovico Technique," but the moment provides narrative stability only when the character returns to his state as a sadistic brute. The film's ending feels more irresolute than the original ending of Anthony Burgess's novel, which contains a final chapter absent in the American edition on which Kubrick based his screenplay; in the British edition, Alex renounces violence.

All the President's Men (1976) has one of the more abrupt endings in a mainstream Hollywood movie. Although the movie achieves full closure (indeed, most viewers knew the story's ending before they stepped in the theater), the narration creates a feeling of irresolution by practically skipping over the climax—we never, in fact, see Bob Woodward and Carl Bernstein fully get "the story" of Watergate—and moving right to the epilogue: the guilty verdicts, displayed over a teletype, of members of the Nixon White House and the news of Nixon's resignation. The scene that stands in for the climax—and it only feels like a climax in retrospect; watching it, it feels like a continuation of the plot—is a series of shots of Woodward and Bernstein typing while a television depicts Nixon taking the oath of office. The TV screen and Nixon's voice dominate the image and soundtrack. Part of the reason the scene does not feel like a climax is that it portrays Nixon beginning his second term. Had the scene depicted Nixon on the way down (say, his 1973 "I am not a crook" press conference, in which he denied involvement in Watergate), the climax would have felt more conclusive: a visual illustration that Woodward and Bernstein's reporting would eventually lead to the president's demise. The filmmakers could have taken that poetic liberty, and few would have complained, but instead they included footage of Nixon that is gratuitously counterproductive to the scene's dramatic function as the climax of Woodward and Bernstein's goals.

In some of the decade's most critically celebrated films—such as *The Godfather* (1972), *Mean Streets* (1973), and *Manhattan* (1979)—the stories develop in such a way that, no matter what endings the films were to offer, they could never provide full and fulfilling resolution. At the end of *Manhattan*, for instance, forty-two-year-old Isaac (Woody Allen) dashes through the streets of New York to try to prevent seventeen-year-old Tracy (Mariel Hemingway), with whom he has broken up, from heading out for London, a six-month trip that he has all along encouraged her to make. If he succeeds in stopping her, we're likely to feel that their romance is nonetheless doomed and that he has prevented her from moving beyond the relationship and growing up. If he doesn't succeed, then he'll be left alone, regretful about encouraging her to leave in the first place. Either way, the story feels unfinished. Seventies movies, not just at their ends but in scene after scene often leave unresolved those aspects of the narrative that we are accustomed to having Hollywood movies resolve for us. As we see in the next section, irresolution is one of the defining characteristics of the period's narrative design.

EVIDENCE FOR A CHARACTERISTIC SEVENTIES NARRATIVE DESIGN

Here, I offer some empirical evidence in support of my hypothesis that, as a group, Hollywood films from the period 1970 to 1977 deviate from classical narrative norms more than films from other periods. I have said that seventies cinema contains relatively superfluous, pointed, and prevalent narrative incongruities and that the films resist the coherence and resolution characteristic of more normative Hollywood movies. I furthermore hypothesized that a majority of the most admired and celebrated films of the period exhibit narrative incoherencies to an uncommon degree.

We can extrapolate from my hypotheses two testable predictions, one pertaining to the *relative prevalence* of narrative incoherence and irresolution in 1970s cinema and the other to the movies' *aesthetic value*:

> 1. Films from the period 1970 to 1977 will tend to be less coherent and resolute than films from other periods in Hollywood cinema.
>
> 2. In critical, industry, and film fan ratings of films from the period 1970–1977, a majority of the most highly rated films will exhibit relatively overt narrative incoherencies.

Relative Prevalence Prediction

For a systematic evaluation, I compared the highest domestic box office-grossing films of the first two years of the 1970s to the highest domestic box office-grossing films of the first two years of the 1960s and 1980s, respectively. A group of film experts (with earned terminal degrees, working in film studies at academic institutions throughout the United States), unfamiliar with my hypotheses about seventies cinema, provided me with an unbiased determination of narrative coherence: Each expert coded the movies according to whether each film was "less coherent" than or "as coherent" as most Hollywood films in its genre. The experts, I found, coded the seventies films as "less coherent" almost three times as often as they did films from the sixties and eighties (35 percent for seventies films, as opposed to 12.5 percent for sixties and eighties films).[16]

Would a broader sample of films, from a wider period in Hollywood history, achieve comparable results? In order to empirically test one component of my prevalence hypothesis—that films of the 1970s are less resolute than those of other periods in Hollywood—I enlisted a separate sample of sixteen film experts to rate the degree of resolution of the top ten-grossing American films for each year between 1954 and 1992 (390 movies total).[17] The results of the study show a greater-than-average degree of irresolution in films released during the period 1970–1977. Graph 2.1 depicts the average standardized rating for each year in the study.[18] Higher numbers indicate less resolution, with zero indicating the average rating for all movies in the thirty-nine-year period. Hence, all but one year (1976)[19] during this book's chief period of study (1970–1977) contained top ten movies with endings on the whole more unresolved than average.[20]

The evidence from my studies is not definitive. One or two studies cannot settle any complex question, and, like all studies, this one makes

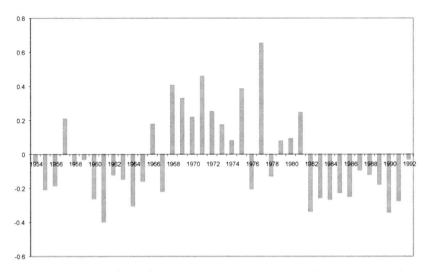

GRAPH 2.1. Degree of Irresolution of Top Ten-Grossing Films between 1954 and 1992 Average Standardized Rating by Year

compromises. First, the sample of 60 films (first study) and 390 films (second study), though large, may not be large enough: The top ten grossers of each year may not accurately represent the periods' narrative trends, and my studies do not include all years of Hollywood film production. Second, my expert coders rated the films based on their memories, rather than on direct observation of the films. And third, film expert ratings may not reflect the experiences of average viewers. I employed film experts, however, because I anticipated that they would be familiar with the large majority of the films in the surveys (they were) and have a better grasp than average viewers of the films' structural features. In summary, my studies provide credible, albeit qualified, empirical evidence that films from the period 1970–1977 deviate from Hollywood narrative norms and also support my prevalence hypothesis that Hollywood cinema of the 1970s tends to be less coherent and less resolute than Hollywood cinema from other periods.

Aesthetic Value Prediction

Let's move on to the prediction that a majority of the most highly rated films released between 1970 and 1977 exhibit relatively overt narrative incoherencies. We should remember that the large majority of Hollywood films from *any* era are highly coherent. Even during the first two years of the 1970s, the experts still only rated 35 percent of the top ten-grossing films as less coherent than other films in their genres. Therefore, it would be significant to find that a majority of the highest rated films of the period display relatively overt incoherence. And indeed, the available data of film fan, industry, and critical ratings support the prediction.

As one measure of aesthetic value, we may consider the twenty-five highest-rated American films from the period 1970–1977 according to the participating users of the popular Internet Movie Database (IMDB), as close to a representative sample of film fans as one could find anywhere. Of IMDB's highest-rated films of the period, the film experts coded 55 percent as "less coherent" than most Hollywood films in their respective genres.[21]

Combined film critic and industry ratings show an even greater preference for narratively incoherent films than do IMDB's film fans. If we compile the "Best Picture" lists for the period 1970–1977 from the New York Film Critics Circle, the Los Angeles Film Critics Association, a survey for *American Film Now* (AFN) of twenty leading international film critics,[22] as well as the Academy of Motion Picture Arts and Sciences (AMPAS)[23] and the American Film Institute (AFI),[24] then we come up with a list of twenty-five acclaimed films from the period. Of those films, 64 percent are, according to the experts, "less coherent" than the typical Hollywood film, offering even stronger support for the aesthetic value prediction.[25]

Many film scholars do not trust the aesthetic opinions of AMPAS and AFI's blue ribbon panel, but, if we limit the sample solely to nationally and internationally renowned critics, then the evidence supports the aesthetic value prediction even more overwhelmingly. Of the nineteen films listed by the New York Film Critics Circle, Los Angeles Film Critics Association, and the AFN survey, the experts coded 74 percent as "less coherent" than most Hollywood films in their genres.

In summary, we find that the period 1970–1977 appears to have a higher proportion of "less coherent" films than other periods in Hollywood and— using the most systematic aesthetic ratings available of industry, critical, and film fan opinion—that a majority of the most highly regarded films of the seventies exhibit relatively overt narrative incoherence. Such evidence helps substantiate my hypotheses that, compared to other Hollywood films, films of the seventies exhibit a distinct tendency toward incoherence and irresolution and that the most admired and celebrated films of the period contain more incoherent narratives than most Hollywood cinema.

FIVE PRINCIPLES OF SEVENTIES NARRATION

We understand enough now to formulate some general principles that govern the narrative strategies characteristic of Hollywood films of the 1970s. The following five principles, to which we shall return throughout the book, can serve both as a detailed definition of narrative perversity in seventies cinema and as a series of hypotheses for this study to investigate, illustrate, and prove.

1. *Seventies films show a perverse tendency to integrate, in incidental ways, narrative and stylistic devices counterproductive to the films' overt and essential narrative purposes.* The films insist on including incongruous ideas and formal devices that seem out of harmony with the work as a whole and threaten its narrative, generic, or conceptual logic. Rather than furthering causal narration, such incongruities gratuitously hinder causality. Moreover, many seventies films include narratively superfluous stylistic ornamentation that draws viewer attention away from plot patterning and creates distracting stylistic systems that rival classical narration and compete with it for prominence.

2. *Hollywood filmmakers of the 1970s often situate their filmmaking practices between those of classical Hollywood and European and Asian art cinema.* Seventies filmmakers exploit unrealized potentials within Hollywood cinema, often modifying classical devices in ways that result in narrative practices more typical of art cinema than classical Hollywood (e.g., sudden tonal changes, gaps in story information, delayed exposition, illogical events, loosening of cause and effect, narrative detours, distracting stylistic ornamentation, character ambiguity).[26] At the same time, seventies filmmakers avoid the experimentalism and mercurialness of art cinema by securing their films to the classical Hollywood narrative structure, which serves as both an anchor and a jumping-off point for a variety of unconventional practices and aesthetic effects. This "middle way" adopted by many seventies filmmakers affords their films significant aesthetic advantages, tying their work to a stable tradition yet still allowing them to draw inspiration and new narrational strategies from non-classical filmmaking practices.

3. *Seventies films prompt spectator responses more uncertain and discomforting than those of more typical Hollywood cinema.* The films often cue spectator responses that fluctuate in unpredictable, incongruous, or uncomfortable ways: They enlist viewer sympathy for contemptible figures;

they resist establishing a coherent moral order; they present multifarious, and often inconsistent, perspectives on the same events and prompt spectators to evaluate stories and characters in antithetical ways; they present story information that is obscure, incomplete, or incongruous; and they sometimes display striking indifference to spectator curiosity and informational needs.

4. *Seventies narratives place an uncommon emphasis on irresolution, particularly at the moment of climax or in epilogues, when more conventional Hollywood movies busy themselves tying up loose ends.* Seventies cinema often resists the resolutions necessitated by the Hollywood paradigm, intensifying narrative and conceptual incongruities already present, but unexplored, in some traditional Hollywood scenarios. Preferring to sustain, rather than smooth over, such incongruities, the filmmakers often refuse to fully resolve incongruous ideas provoked by the films' narration.

5. *Seventies cinema hinders narrative linearity and momentum and scuttles its potential to generate suspense and excitement.* Rambling and digressive, seventies narratives tend to resist straightforwardness. The films fixate on narrative detours and add gratuitous impediments to narrative efficiency and causality. Consequently, during moments that offer opportunities for suspense and excitement, seventies cinema tends instead to provoke uncertainty and frustration.

The remainder of this book offers evidence to support the validity of the foregoing principles and fleshes them out with textual analyses.

This chapter has described general narrative tendencies in seventies cinema, but such descriptions do not explain the processes by which seventies films engineer their narratives to create specific aesthetic experiences. In short, we do not yet understand *narration* in seventies cinema: the period's characteristic processes for selecting, arranging, and rendering story material and the effects of such processes on spectators' mental activities. Part II of this book studies seventies cinema's key modes of perverse narration.

PART II

Modes of Narration in Seventies Films

To understand the ways in which seventies narratives stimulate specific aesthetic experiences, we must analyze the modes of narration of individual films. Three key modes of perverse narration permeate Hollywood cinema of the 1970s. Illustrated with an exemplary case study, each of the next three chapters addresses one of the three modes: 1) *narrative frustration*—seventies films frustrate straightforward narration and avoid fulfilling narrative promises in conventionally satisfying ways; 2) *genre deviation*—they exploit and modify conventional genre devices in order to create subtle, unsettling, and unresolved narrative incongruities; and 3) *conceptual incongruity*—they generate ideas and emotions counterproductive to the films' essential concepts and overt narrative purposes. In Part II, we set out to understand these three modes through analyses of exemplary films and in light of seventies cinema generally.

CHAPTER 3 NARRATIVE FRUSTRATION
From *The Godfather* to
The Godfather, Part II

We begin our analysis of seventies modes of narration with *The Godfather, Part II* because critics'
initial complaints about the film's incoherence, and its subsequent status as
arguably the most critically admired Hollywood movie of the decade, help
introduce a premise central to this book: that many Hollywood films from
the seventies have enjoyed lasting acclaim not despite but *because* of their
disruptions in logic, the disharmony of their narratives, and their propensity
to avoid fulfilling narrative promises in satisfying ways. Seventies filmmakers
seem intent upon disappointing audiences and frustrating spectator expectations, and this tendency shows itself most baldly in the narrative strategies
of *The Godfather, Part II.*

Part II's perverse narrative mode seems all the more surprising since, had
the film adopted a more traditional approach to sequelization, it might have
better cashed in on the anticipation and excitement generated by the first
Godfather, which, by the time of the sequel's release in 1974, was already
one of the most beloved films of all time. When *The Godfather* debuted in
1972, it shattered all of the major box office records. It made $8 million in
rentals in its opening week in national release. It brought in at least a million
dollars a day for twenty-six days and at least $2 million a week for twenty-
three consecutive weeks. In fewer than six months, it surpassed *Gone with
the Wind* (1939) to become the most profitable movie to that time, earning
$86,275,000 in domestic rentals by the end of its first year in release. The
film won Oscars for Best Picture, Best Screenplay (Francis Ford Coppola

and Mario Puzo), and Best Actor (Marlon Brando). Most critics lauded it, although some complained that it glamorized the Mafia.

The astounding success of *The Godfather* surprised everyone involved with the picture, including the executives at Paramount Pictures, who immediately began badgering director Francis Ford Coppola for a sequel. The reason is not hard to figure out: If the *Godfather* sequel had only a fraction of the financial success of the original movie, it would mean enormous profits for Paramount.

More than ever, Hollywood executives coveted successful formulas at a time when investing in American cinema seemed something akin to gambling. The industry faced unprecedented market unpredictability as the negative costs of filmmaking increased 11 percent or more each year, marketing costs often exceeded negative costs, and the industry was weathering a twenty-five-year decline in audience attendance. Most Americans had stopped going to the movies in a routine way and theater attendance dropped to record lows. In 1946, 90 million Americans attended the movies each week. That figure dropped to 47 million per week in 1956, and by 1967 attendance fell to a mere 17.8 million, finally hitting a historic low of 15.8 million in 1971, the year before *The Godfather*'s release (see Steinberg, 371). Commentators blamed television, the high cost of movie tickets, and the poor quality of the films. Whatever the cause, between 1969 and 1971 Hollywood studios recorded their worst financial losses in history. Scrambling for audiences, studio executives in the early seventies banked on the successes of earlier hits by producing strings of horror movies and disaster movies and whatever else they hoped would satisfy the public. *The Godfather* spawned a litter of Mafia movies (including *The Don Is Dead* [1973], *Lucky Luciano* [1974], *The Black Godfather* [1974], and *Lepke* [1975]), just as *Bonnie and Clyde* (1967) and *Easy Rider* (1969) had engendered movies about sympathetic outlaws and what had come to be called "youth culture" (*Little Fauss and Big Halsy* [1970], *Getting Straight* [1970], *Dirty Mary Crazy Larry* [1974], *The Sugarland Express* [1974], and many others).

Sequels to popular movies had an almost guaranteed audience, typically earning two-thirds of the profits of the original films (Chown, 103). In the 1970s, Hollywood began to rely increasingly on sequels and series films to hedge against the risks of ever more costly and financially unpredictable filmmaking; consequently, the 1970s saw the greatest incidence of film sequels in Hollywood's history to that time. Unlike studio-era films, most seventies megahits gave rise to sequels, and many of them—including *Airport* (1970), *Billy Jack* (1971), *Dirty Harry* (1971), *Shaft* (1971), *Jaws* (1975), *Rocky* (1976), and *Star Wars* (1977)—became series. David Cook notes that "sequels, series and reissues accounted for 17.6 percent of all Hollywood releases from 1974 to 1978," as opposed to 4.4 percent for the period 1964 to 1968 (30). By 1974, he writes, "sequels and series, the very fodder of B-film production during the studio era, loomed as a major strategy for risk reduction among the majors" (4).[1]

The large majority of seventies sequels have had limited success since their initial release, whereas *The Godfather, Part II* has had several profitable video releases and theatrical re-releases and has regularly played on network and cable TV. Many film critics, moreover, now regard it as the finest movie of the 1970s, superior even to the first *Godfather*. What makes *The Godfather, Part II* so much more admired than the numerous other film sequels released around the same time, probably more admired than any other sequel in film history?

This chapter sets out to demonstrate that the film's renown results in large part from a perverse narrative mode characteristic of Hollywood cinema of the 1970s: a striking refusal to give spectators what they seem to want most. Unlike the first *Godfather*, the sequel often leaves narrative promises unfulfilled and squanders opportunities for suspense and excitement. The film emphasizes spectator disappointment over satisfaction and narrative convolution and inconsistency at the expense of clarity, coherence, and forward momentum. Indeed, *The Godfather, Part II* epitomizes the ways in which seventies cinema—even a movie financed specifically to cash in on the success of the most profitable blockbuster of all time—frustrates straightforward narration and frustrates spectator expectations. I hope to show, however, that the film's aesthetic of frustration and disappointment stimulates an emotionally and intellectually rich experience unavailable to spectators of either the original *Godfather* movie or more conventional Hollywood sequels.

In order to understand *The Godfather, Part II*'s novel approach to sequelization, we must first understand the typical ways in which filmmakers respond to the burdens of sequel making, particularly the disappointment with which spectators normally greet sequels. Like most sequels, *The Godfather, Part II* disappoints its audience, but it does so in a peculiarly extravagant way.

SEQUELS, NOSTALGIA, AND LOSS

Film commentators normally regard sequels as exploitative products that capitalize on the popularity of earlier blockbusters and are invariably inferior to the original films. Most critical treatments of sequels, as a genre, regard them as a sign of Hollywood profiteering and creative bankruptcy. Film scholarship has hardly addressed the phenomenon of film sequelization, and the few existing scholarly treatments focus almost exclusively on the horror film series that began inundating theaters in the late seventies and haven't tapered off since.[2] One full-length book has been devoted to literary and film sequels: *Part Two: Reflections on the Sequel*, a chronologically organized collection of essays, mostly by period specialists, begins by examining epic sequels of the Greek Bronze Age and ends by looking at movie sequels of the 1980s and 90s. It will come as no surprise that the theme common to the essays is that sequels let their audiences down. The essayists normally regard audience disappointment as an unavoidable consequence of publishers' and movie studios' attempts to profit quickly on the successes of earlier hits by churning out invariably inferior products.[3] Paul Budra and Betty Schellenberg also note "the inevitably changed [historical] conditions which make it impossible to achieve a precise repetition of the experience" of the original work (5). In their treatments of the sequel, however, the essayists deal only in passing with perhaps the most pertinent historical fact when considering spectators' common disappointment with sequels: one's prior experience of the original work. Even if a sequel were every bit as good as the original and experienced by an otherwise identical culture in equivalent historical circumstances, it would nonetheless tend to disappoint audiences because nothing can equal one's initial encounter with an aesthetically satisfying work of art.

In a book on eighteenth-century English literature, Terry Castle touches on the disappointment that plagues literary sequels, and her remarks pertain just as well to film. "Sequels," she says, "inevitably seem to fail us in some obscure yet fundamental way." According to Castle:

> A sequel can never fully satisfy its readers' desire for repetition, however; its tragedy is that it cannot literally reconstitute its charismatic original. Readers know this; yet they are disappointed. Unconsciously they persist in demanding the impossible: that the sequel be different, but also *exactly the same*. Their secret mad hope is to find in the sequel a paradoxical kind of textual doubling—a repetition that does not look like one, the old story in a

new and unexpected guise. They wish to read the "unforgettable" text once more, yet as if they had forgotten it. (133–134)

A handful of sequels have met, and sometimes surpassed, the success of the original texts. However, Castle identifies the peculiarly impractical burden placed on a sequel: An almost inescapable disappointment results from the fact that, at the same time it calls to mind the "charismatic original," a sequel also calls up its absence, fostering a futile, nostalgic desire to re-experience the original aesthetic moment as though it had never happened. Hence, the experience of a sequel differs fundamentally from that of re-watching a beloved movie. Although in both cases we enjoy something reminiscent of our initial pleasure, second viewings of a movie *restore* the original film to us and enable us to relish new insights and details missed on the first viewing, whereas sequels can only *remind* us of the original film whose presence they conspicuously fail to re-invoke.

To compensate for the sensation of absence and loss, the makers of movie sequels tend to supply excessive amounts of whatever audiences seemed to have liked best about the original movies.[4] Most seventies sequels followed this pattern. *Magnum Force* (1973) has far more violence than *Dirty Harry* (1971). Rocky wins in *Rocky II* (1979). *Airport* (1970) depicted the hijacking of a standard jetliner; ten years, three sequels, and dozens of stars later, Universal released *Airport '79: The Concorde*. The shark in *Jaws 2* (1978) is even bigger than the first; *Jaws III* (1983) is in 3-D. The marketing taglines of sequels often emphasize excess and escalation as well: "Where *Willard* ended . . . *Ben* begins. And this time, he's not alone!" (*Ben*, 1972); "The first time was only a warning" (*Damien: Omen II*, 1978); "*The French Connection* was only the beginning—THIS is the climax" (*French Connection II*, 1975); "Now there are three of them" (*It Lives Again*, 1978); "They're back—tougher than ever!" (*Sweeney 2*, 1978); "Buford's back . . . and this time he's out for blood" (*Walking Tall, Part II*, 1975). The escalation of violence and thrills in sequels seems to occur at a rate higher than what has occurred in movies generally, an understandably excessive evolution considering that a sequel must compete not only with other films in its genre but also with the original film it imitates.

THE FLAGRANT DISAPPOINTMENT OF *THE GODFATHER* SEQUEL

Because of the peculiar burden of sequel-making and the damage a failed sequel can do to a filmmaker's career, directors of Hollywood blockbusters often refuse to direct sequels to their own movies. Coppola reportedly refused on six occasions to make a sequel to *The Godfather*. After the first movie, he said:

> I could make five failures, and I'd still be the guy who directed *The Godfather*. There's only one way to undo that fast, and that's to attempt to make another *Godfather*, and fail. If it bombs, then people will look at the first *Godfather* and say it was all Brando, or whatever. If I took my career to an insurance actuary, he'd tell me to lay off the sequels if I wanted to stay healthy. (Cited in Biskind, *Godfather*, 81)

Coppola had joked that the only sequel he would make would be *Abbott and Costello Meet the Godfather*, but when Paramount offered him financing for *The Conversation* (1974) and a million-dollar salary, plus a cut of the gross, to produce, write, and direct a sequel to *The Godfather*, *The Godfather, Part II* began to take shape (see Murray, 53). Coppola also wanted creative control and he got it. The first film had, along with *Love Story* (1970), reversed Paramount's financial slump, and the studio was desperate for another *Godfather*.

After the unprecedented success of the original film, the sequel was bound to disappoint, and, on its release in December 1974, it did. Like most sequels, it showed a profit, but its success came nowhere near that of its predecessor. *Part II* took almost a year to gross as much as the original had in its first month of release, ultimately earning in its first run only a little more than one-third of the domestic rentals of the first movie ($30.7 million as compared to $86.3 million), "considerably less," Jeffrey Chown notes, "than the conventional two-thirds Paramount expected" (104). Prejudiced, perhaps, by their expectations of sequels in general, critics greeted *The Godfather, Part II* almost universally with disappointment and frustration.[5] Moira Walsh's review in *America* was typical: "It is supposedly inevitable that sequels are inferior to the original. Besides, the film runs an impossible 200 minutes without intermission. Over and above its episodic structure, the film's narrative takes various unsettling quantum leaps" (116). Walsh here touches on critics' three main complaints against the movie: too long, too confusing, and inferior to *The Godfather*. John Coleman wrote in *New Statesman*, "It is 25 minutes longer than [*The Godfather*] and about twice as confusing" (669).[6] Vincent Canby hated the movie so much that he wrote two pans of it for the *New York Times*, one of which said that a "thick fog of boredom . . . settles in before the film is even an hour old" ("One Godfather Too Many," II19).

The Academy of Motion Picture Arts and Sciences gave *The Godfather, Part II* six Oscars in 1975—twice as many as the first movie, including another for best picture—but at that point critics still did not recognize the film's virtues. The movie failed to receive any New York Film Critics Circle Awards or Golden Globe Awards, both awarded by the press.[7] Coppola received the National Board of Review's award for best director; however, he won not for *The Godfather, Part II* but for *The Conversation*, which also won the award for best picture.[8] Critics announced their year-end top ten lists about a month after *Part II*'s release, and *The Conversation* made more of those lists than Coppola's *Godfather* sequel: In my own tally of twenty-five major critics' "Best Films of 1974," *The Conversation* came in fourth for the year and *The Godfather, Part II* tied with *The Apprenticeship of Duddy Kravitz* for sixth place.[9] *Part II* even made some "ten worst" lists (see, for example, Thomas, E10). The movie received a few notable good reviews: Pauline Kael called it a "modern American epic" ("Fathers and Sons," 66) and Richard Schickel considered it "a worthy successor" ("Final Act," 73).[10] On the whole, however, critics considered *Part II* a disappointing follow-up to a great American movie, a sequel like any other—a big letdown.

Within a few years of *Part II*'s release, something remarkable happened: The movie's critical stock began to rise, and film commentators started treating it as a classic worthy of praise equal to or stronger than that lavished on *The Godfather*. The 1978 edition of Gerald Mast's textbook, *A Short History of the Movies*, practically ignored the movie, referring to it only parenthetically as one of Coppola's "big commercial projects" (489), whereas his 1981 edition lauded the film (428), and his 1986 edition called it "the best sequel ever made" (445). Robert Bookbinder's 1982 book, *The Films of the Seventies*, considered *Part II* "one of the few film sequels of the seventies that actually improved upon the original" (99). In 2000, David Cook called *Part II* "probably the most distinguished sequel ever made" (186).

After their initial disappointment, many reviewers too came to consider the sequel either nearly as good as or else superior to the original film. Michael Goodwin, film critic for *City* magazine (which Coppola, in fact, published at the time), gave *Part II* a tepid review when it came out, but in his 1989 book about Coppola he admits that he "underrated the film badly" (Goodwin and Wise, 185). The *Village Voice*'s Molly Haskell initially panned the sequel and excluded it from her list of the eleven best movies of 1974, but in 1978, in a survey for James Monaco, she inexplicably lists *Part II* among the ten best movies of the *decade*.[11] Monaco had surveyed twenty of the world's leading critics to determine what they considered the ten best films released between 1968 and 1977. *The Godfather, Part II* and *Nashville* led the list with twelve votes each; *The Godfather* came in third with ten.[12] Hence, whereas in 1975 a survey of critics placed *Part II* sixth for the year 1974, three years later a similar survey ranked it number one (along with *Nashville*) for the past *decade*.[13] Many of Monaco's critics simply grouped both *Godfather*s as one item, perhaps in an effort to sneak in an eleventh pick, but also suggesting a tendency to regard *Part II* not as a sequel but rather as a continuation of the same classic movie. In its 2002 survey, *Sight and Sound*'s prestigious once-per-decade top ten poll of critics lists *The Godfather* and *The Godfather, Part II* together as the fourth best movie of all time, the first time either film has made the magazine's list.[14] To summarize, although initially critics considered *Part II* an inauspicious attempt to capitalize on the success of *The Godfather*, over time most critics began to judge the sequel at least as highly as they did the original film.

To find an explanation for the surprising turnaround in critical opinion, we must look to Coppola and Puzo's inventive response to the burden of sequel-making. Contrary to most sequels, which promise to outdo the pleasures of their predecessors, *The Godfather, Part II* offers ostentatiously *less* of what people seem to have liked most about the original movie. Indeed, like so many Hollywood films of the seventies—*The French Connection* (1971), *The Long Goodbye* (1973), *Badlands* (1973), *The Conversation* (1974), *Chinatown* (1974), and *Taxi Driver* (1976), to name a few—the movie seems designed perversely to frustrate spectator desires and expectations. The sequel has little of the glamour, charm, and excitement of the first *Godfather*, and its protagonist, the new Don Corleone, has little of the glamour, charm, and excitement of the old don. The plot patterning, moreover, lacks the clarity and forward momentum that helped make the first *Godfather* so widely appealing. Despite numerous opportunities to provide the same types of narrative satisfactions that characterize the first movie, *The Godfather, Part II* invites spectators to look back mournfully to the original film and feel the very disappointment with the movie that critics expressed in their initial reviews.

As we will see as we study the film's peculiar mode of narration, spectators of the sequel experience a sense of loss, nostalgia, and deterioration that resonates both emotionally and intellectually with the film's central themes of loss, nostalgia, and deterioration. The felicitous resonance between the experience of the movie and the movie's story line helps account for *Part II*'s singular status among film sequels. *The Godfather, Part II*, in short, makes a success out of what sequels typically do in failure: It does what the original did in a way that is less satisfying.

Before I can demonstrate the justice of the foregoing hypothesis, I must establish the ways in which *The Godfather* sequel, *as* a sequel, lets its viewers down.

PATTERNS OF DETERIORATION

The first two *Godfather* movies parallel each other in many ways, and *Part II* generally appears worse in comparison. None of Michael's entourage in *Part II*, for example, has the liveliness or charisma of the characters who surrounded his father, Vito. Clemenza (Richard Castellano) and Tessio (Abe Vigoda) have both died, and as *caporegimes* (or captains) Michael has Al Neri (Richard Bright) and Rocco Lampone (Tom Rosqui). If you cannot recall them, the reason is that the filmmakers neglected to give them personalities, and Bright and Rosqui seem to have been directed to give the characters as few distinctive characteristics as possible. The actors typically stand in shadows, their faces hidden and backs to the camera. Their chief function in most of their scenes is to open doors and pour drinks for the leads. Michael's *consiglieri*, his adopted brother Tom Hagen, seems even more businesslike than before; in fact, Tom now looks broken, Michael having kept him out of much of the Family's activities. Sonny Corleone is dead and no one in this movie has his fire and charisma. Frankie Pentangeli is a spirited character but antiquated and seems to represent the attitudes and personality of an obsolete world. His raspy Italian inflection and lavish gesticulations are charming but out of place. When Michael's brother Fredo runs into Pentangeli at the celebration of the first communion of Michael's son Anthony, Fredo says, "Seeing you reminds me of New York, the old days." Luca Brasi, loyal to the end, is also dead. In his place, Michael has a nameless, speechless, and charmless bodyguard (Amerigo Tot), whose size and shape vaguely recall Luca. Michael's enemies offer none of the malicious delight of Vito's enemies in the original film. Compare, for instance, sickly, practical Hyman Roth (Lee Strasberg) to the fiery Virgil "the Turk" Sollozzo (Al Lettieri).

Even Michael appears less charming than in the first *Godfather*, having lost his youthful idealism and acquired a sterile, icy manner, like a stolid politician. Al Pacino's understated, lugubrious performance of the heartless

Mafia don (his reaction to the shocking sight of a suicide attack by a Cuban bandit barely registers on his face) contrasts also with the more expressive performance of Marlon Brando in the first movie. Michael shows none of the warmth of the old don, who never treated his family coldly or manipulatively. We can see Michael's likeness to his father, but the comparison invariably makes Michael look worse.[15]

Several events in *Part II* echo those from the original film. Both movies introduce their main characters to us at religious celebrations, for example. *The Godfather* begins at the wedding reception of Michael's sister, Connie, at the Corleone home in New York as the don sits in his study granting favors to visitors. The first scene in *Part II* shows us a flashback of young Vito as he escapes the Sicilian Mafia and immigrates to America, but ten minutes later the movie switches to its first "present day" scene: the first communion of Anthony Corleone. During the celebration at Michael's compound in Lake Tahoe, the don conducts "business," as did his father before him, sitting in his study, receiving visitors. Chown says that in both films "bright outdoor action [is] contrasted through cuts with the dark inner sanctums in which the respective dons conduct business" (106).

Even as the sequel cues spectators to recall comparable scenes from the first movie, it also invites unfavorable comparisons to the more romantic depictions of the Mafia in the original film. The scene of Anthony's celebration, for instance, has none of the familial, ethnic feeling of Connie's wedding. Only respectful Italians visited Vito in his study. Michael's visitors include the aggressively anti-Italian Senator Geary, who tries to bully the don. Later, a garishly dressed Connie and her fiancé, Merle (played by the WASPish Troy Donahue) visit Michael, wanting only money from him, not his blessing. The party scene also reintroduces Fredo, now married to the blonde and drunken Deanna. The band at Anthony's party looks slick, their white coats, bow ties, and bored faces betraying a routine professionalism. Frankie Pentangeli remarks that "out of 30 professional musicians, there isn't one Italian in the group." Professional dancers perform a tango. The entire festivity looks eerily lifeless and business-like. No Johnny Fontanes appear. No family members sing "Che La Luna." Instead, Senator Geary introduces the Sierra Boys Choir, "as a special added attraction," which performs "Mr. Wonderful" on behalf of "Michael Corleon" (the senator mispronounces the name) for having made a "magnificent endowment" to the university; the senator's voice echoes gratingly through a loudspeaker. Whereas, in the first movie, the Corleones seem defiantly against the establishment, in the second they have entered it. At Connie's wedding in *The Godfather*, for example, Sonny remarks on the unwelcome presence of the "Goddamn FBI" and then smashes a reporter's camera, but at Anthony's communion celebration a waiter brings dinner to a police trooper, and Michael and Senator Geary pose for publicity photographs. Later, Anthony, remarking on all the presents he has received, says, "I didn't know the people who gave them to me." The entire event seems less like a family celebration than a corporate function.

Even the murders in *Part II* are a letdown. One could hardly forget the vivid image from *The Godfather* of Captain McCluskey shot in the throat in Louis's restaurant or of Luca Brasi garroted, a knife through his hand, or of Moe Green with a bullet in his eye, blood seeping beneath his spectacles. But how many viewers remember that, in *Part II*, Michael's bodyguard strangles Johnny Ola with a coat hanger (if they remember that Ola is killed at all) or that the same bodyguard is shot by Cuban soldiers? These murders sound graphic, but the narration treats them so indifferently that the result is forgettable. For instance, Ola's death occurs with hardly any buildup or suspense, and, when it happens, the music, cinematography, and mise-en-scène deemphasize the action. The music—a plodding, orchestral clunk, interspersed with piano tinkling—progresses immutably, unaffected by the murder, and the camera centers more on the billowing curtains of the hotel room than on Ola's protracted but half-hearted struggle to stay alive. The murder of Hyman Roth makes a stronger impression but is not much more exciting to watch. The assassination happens at the airport after Israel, Argentina, and Panama refuse "the old man" asylum. When Rocco shoots him, Roth looks ailing and frail, not in the least threatening to anyone. (The most memorable murders in the movie occur when Vito shoots Don Fanucci through the chest, cheek, and mouth and when he disembowels Don Ciccio in Sicily, but both scenes occur in flashbacks, which we will turn to presently.) Both *The Godfather* and its sequel present murder ritualistically, contrasting it with religious ceremony,[16] and, toward the end of each film, Michael stages a series of murders depicted in montage. However, though the murders in *Part II* echo those in the first *Godfather*, none of them matches the first film's more exciting, memorable violence.

The editing of the two films' murder montages most clearly demonstrates the tendency of *Part II*, on the one hand, to call to mind corresponding elements of the first movie and, on the other, to leave out the most narratively and visually exciting components. An elementary comparison of the editing shows that, although both montages last roughly five minutes, the montage sequence in *Part II* combines three scenes (depicting four deaths total) and has an average shot length (ASL) of 9.5 seconds, whereas the comparable sequence in *The Godfather* combines six scenes (depicting eight deaths and the baptism of Connie's son) and has an ASL of 4.4 seconds. The editing in the first *Godfather* gives the sequence tremendous pace, especially toward the end as the ASL decreases (from 5.6 seconds before the murders begin to 2.7 seconds afterward).

The Godfather's murder montage uses graphic matches and other repeated imagery to link the various shots to one another, and most of the matches are characterized by physical movement. A swift panning shot of the priest's hand moving from holy water to the baby's forehead (Figure 3.1) matches a similar shot of a barber's hand, as he moves from the shaving cream dispenser to the face of a Corleone assassin, Willy Cicci (Figure 3.2). Rocco and Neri are both seen preparing guns (Figures 3.3 and 3.4). The image of Neri using a cloth to wipe sweat off his face (Figure 3.5) echoes that of Clemenza making the same gesture as he climbs a staircase (Figure 3.6), and both shots echo nine other shots in the sequence in which characters make gestures over their own or other characters' faces. Clemenza, Cicci, and Don Barzini all quickly move up or down stairs, and five doors fly open dramatically during the forty-five seconds in which the shootings occur. The images of murder are intercut with those of the baptism and edited to the tempo of dramatic organ music, the baptismal liturgy, and the screams of the infant.

By contrast, what unites most of the images and sounds in the comparable sequence in *Part II* is their sluggishness: Roth's feeble walk and the deadpan speech he gives to the press (Figure 3.7); the subtle rise and fall of the lake on which Fredo fishes, his body perfectly still (Figure 3.8); a bloodied Pentangeli motionless in a bathtub (Figure 3.9).

The sequel's murder montage, moreover, offers little of the dramatic tension of the montage in the first movie. Unlike *The Godfather*, the sequel does not heighten suspense with shots of assassins preparing for murder. Except for Moe Green, each victim in *The Godfather* recognizes his imminent death and vainly fights against it. In the sequel, none of the victims resist: Roth simply slumps into the arms of the police, and Neri shoots Fredo from behind. Pentangeli isn't murdered at all. His death is a suicide, a disappointing revelation because ominous music and a brief shot of armed guards outside his prison cue spectators to anticipate that assassins might barge in on him. In fact, both Fredo's and Pentangeli's deaths occur offscreen. The most

FIGURE 3.1. A panning shot of a priest's hand moving from holy water to a baby's forehead . . .

FIGURE 3.2. . . . is matched to a panning shot of a barber's hand moving from a shaving cream dispenser to the face of an assassin.

FIGURE 3.3. Rocco prepares his gun.

FIGURE 3.4. Neri prepares his gun.

FIGURE 3.5. Neri wipes his face with a cloth.

FIGURE 3.6. Clemenza wipes his face with a cloth.

FIGURES 3.1–3.6. Graphically matched shots of physical movement during *The Godfather*'s murder montage.

visually exciting killing in the montage is that of Rocco, Roth's assassin, shot twice by police as he tries to escape—blood trickling from holes in his white jacket, a crowd of people shrieking and ducking to the ground behind him—but his death is a narrative sidebar, unconnected to the narrative's causal progress. Throughout the sequence, repetitive and somber theme music plays, instilling none of the suspense and excitement of the organ's dramatic crescendos in *The Godfather*'s climactic murder montage. Such qualities led

FIGURE 3.7. Hyman Roth's deadpan speech to the press.

FIGURE 3.8. Fredo fishing on a still lake.

FIGURE 3.9. Pentangeli dead in a bathtub.

FIGURES 3.7–3.9. Images of sluggishness during the murder montage from *The Godfather, Part II.*

Frank Rich, in a generally positive review of the sequel, nonetheless to call the sequel's murder montage "a tiresome rehash of the Five-Family wars of *The Godfather*" (57).

At each stage, *Part II* insists upon frustrating expectations established by the first *Godfather*, replacing characters, actions, and scenes with corresponding ones that come across as conspicuously duller and disappointing.

AN AESTHETIC OF FRUSTRATION AND DISAPPOINTMENT

Far from outdoing *The Godfather*, the sequel persistently falls short of the original film, courting spectator disappointment with scenes that seem designed to squander their potentials for suspense and excitement. This frustrating narrative mode, however, enables a positive aesthetic value that film sequels could, but rarely do, exploit. Inviting unfavorable comparisons to the original film, *The Godfather, Part II* anticipates spectators' critical judgment and gives it thematic and emotional resonance. Indeed, the same disappointment and deprivation that critics indicated in their initial reviews of the film reflect those very elements within the story itself. To make this point another way, the experience of *The Godfather, Part II* mirrors prominent aspects of the movie's subject matter: loss, nostalgia, and deterioration.

As the movie cues spectators to contrast the present movie with the previous one, it depicts characters who themselves contrast their lives now with their lives when Vito was don. After he learns of Fredo's betrayal, Michael says to his mother, "Times are changing," a line indicative of a persistent nostalgia among the characters. The most sustained discussion of the "old days" occurs between Tom Hagen and Frankie Pentangeli. As the characters reminisce, a sentimental rendition of the famous theme music from the original *Godfather* plays in the soundtrack.

> HAGEN. You were around the old timers who dreamed up how the Families should be organized, how they based it on the old Roman legions, and called them "Regimes" with the "Capos" and the "Soldiers," and it worked.
>
> PENTANGELI. Yeah, it worked. Those were the great old days. You know, we was like the Roman Empire. The Corleone family was like the Roman Empire.
>
> HAGEN. Yeah, it was once.

The movie gives no indication that Michael has any less power or money than his father did. On the contrary, he seems wealthier and has even more control over the "legitimate" world than Vito had, yet Pentangeli and Hagen see the Family as having deteriorated. It has lost something less concrete than power and money, and, without needing the movie to specify it, we can vaguely understand what Hagen refers to because, prompted by the film's disappointing similarity to its predecessor, we have felt the loss ourselves.

This scene, which occurs late in the movie, depicts one of the sequel's many mournful reminiscences of what has been lost. Indeed, the opening shot of the movie, before the flashback to Sicily, lands on Vito's empty chair. Throughout the film, numerous characters lovingly recall the old don. Michael, for instance, reminisces about his "father's study," and Fredo wishes he could "be more like Pop." Connie recalls her father as she explains a toast made at Anthony's communion celebration: "It means we should all live happily for a hundred years, the family. It'd be true if my father were alive." The death of Vito is an ever-present loss, continually mourned.

Early reviewers of *Part II* recalled the original movie with a sense of loss that almost mimics that of the characters. Paul Zimmerman's mixed review of the movie in *Newsweek* expressed his regret when he recollected the first *Godfather*: "The extended, highly personal coda makes one hungry for the relatively uncomplicated entertainment values of the original. If 'Godfather II' is less satisfying than its predecessor, it is because it refuses to answer this perhaps vulgar but nonetheless real need" (79). In his review, Frank Rich lamented that "[t]he historical relationship of De Niro's Vito and Pacino's Michael . . . is just no match for the Dimmesdale-Chillingsworthesque symbiosis of Brando's Vito and Pacino in the first film" (57). Vincent Canby's pan of the movie began just as mournfully:

> The only remarkable thing about Francis Ford Coppola's "The Godfather, Part II" is the insistent manner in which it recalls how much better his original film was. Among other things, one remembers "The Godfather's" tremendous narrative drive and the dominating presence of Marlon Brando in the title role, which, though not large, unified the film and transformed a super-gangster movie into a unique family chronicle. ("Hard to Define," 58)

Canby's sorrowful remembrances, especially his reference to Brando as *The Godfather*'s dominating and unifying force, sound much like those of Connie, Fredo, and Michael when they think of Vito.

We can observe a similar sentiment in Molly Haskell's devastating review in the *Village Voice* (Haskell, you will remember, first panned the movie and then, in 1978, named it one of the ten best films of the decade): "Brando's absence hangs over the new picture as his presence . . . hung over the previous one" (88). Substitute "Vito" for "Brando" in Haskell's sentence, and it would turn her pan of the movie into a short plot summary. The absence of Brando, for the film's reviewers, emblematizes everything *Part II* lacks: unity, satisfaction, and grandness, the very qualities mourned by the film's characters. I do not mean to suggest that what critics say about *Part II* precisely reflects spectators' experiences of it; however, such consistent critical remarks offer further evidence that the sequel elicits a pervasive nostalgia for the first movie and a disappointment analogous to that expressed in the diegesis. It is striking how closely the nostalgia and disappointment of critics of the film mirror those of the characters in it.

The most conspicuous nostalgia within the film does not come from the mouths of any of the characters but rather from the narration's back-and-forth movement between time periods. The alternations between the grim modern world and the quaint old one also provide the best examples of how *The Godfather, Part II* prompts a nostalgia for the first *Godfather* that emblematizes the nostalgia imbedded in the story: The flashbacks call to mind the original movie at the very moment such segments contrast with the modern story and make the "present day" seem dismal by comparison.

Numerous details in the flashbacks bring to mind the first *Godfather*. The shots of Corleone, Sicily; the introduction of young (fat) Clemenza and young (skinny) Tessio, both of whom have died; even the acting style of Robert De Niro—who, like Brando, won an Oscar for his performance of Vito—all reflect corresponding aspects of the original movie. De Niro studied and mimicked Brando's mannerisms from the first film, such as leaning his head on his fingers and scraping his cheek with his fingernails when he's sitting.[17] Everything sentimental or romantic in *Part II*—Vito's arrival at Ellis Island, his gift of a pear to his wife, his grateful thanks to his employer (the grocer, Abbandando) for behaving like a father to him—occurs in flashback. At one point, Abbandando's son, Genco, asks his opinion of a beautiful stage actress, to which Vito replies, "To you she's beautiful. For me there's only my wife and son." Vito's world is brutal, but it has a romantic feel—an atmosphere accented by the sequence's warm visual tones—and the flashback sequences always clearly distinguish the good bad guys from the bad bad guys.[18]

We know that Coppola wanted to contrast the two narratives in *Part II*. He said, for instance, in an interview for his own *City* magazine: "I thought it would be interesting to juxtapose the decline of the Family with the ascension of the Family: to show that as the young Vito Corleone is building this thing out of America, his son is presiding over its destruction" (Aigner and Goodwin, 36). Indeed, the stories of Vito and Michael parallel each other in several ways, Michael's story always appearing cold by contrast. John Hess points out that the sentimentality of the flashbacks sets up "the audience for the demolition of the sentiments in the following [modern-day] sequence" (82). Indeed, all the romance, charm, and family feeling we associate with the first *Godfather* exist in flashback only.

The final flashback of the film differs from the others and best illustrates the strong correspondence between the nostalgia within the movie and that of the audience watching it. It is the "coda" to which Paul Zimmerman refers in the *Newsweek* review cited above, the flashback that makes him "hungry" for the first film. In a past much less distant than that of the previous flashbacks, the movie depicts the family preparing to surprise Vito on his birthday. Fredo, Tom, Connie, and Michael sit at the dinner table, as well as Sonny, Carlo Rizzi, and Tessio, all three of whom died in the original movie. Michael shocks his family by telling them he has enlisted in the army, like the thirty thousand other men who, as Michael says, chose to "risk their lives for their country" after Pearl Harbor. The scene ends with Michael sitting alone at the table while a surprised Vito, offscreen, is about to come through the door. It then dissolves to a shot of the younger Vito, played by De Niro, leaning out of the window of a train and waving the hand of a small boy, presumably Michael, as they leave Sicily. Not until the shot dissolves to Michael's older, contemplative face does the narration indicate that the flashback signified Michael's own remembrances.

A fitting resolution to the movie, the scene, more vividly than any other, unites the audience's nostalgia for the first movie with the nostalgia of the characters for their own past. The flashback, for one thing, comes closest of all the scenes in the sequel to replicating the milieu of the first *Godfather*. Although these events take place prior to those of the first movie, the flashback projects the same atmosphere of *The Godfather*, largely because the original actors returned to reprise their roles. Coppola pleaded with Brando to return for just the one scene, but that Vito remains just beyond the camera's view emphasizes the sense of irreparable loss. Even the warm classical lighting of the scene (Figure 3.10) seems more like the lighting of the original *Godfather* than that of other scenes from the sequel, which, in the modern-day sequences, typically uses bluish, low-key lighting, often with heavy backlighting (Figure 3.11).

The scene also reintroduces familiar themes from the first movie by showing us a relatively harmonious family, except for the independent and idealistic Michael, and it includes the three Family members—Tessio, Carlo,

FIGURE 3.10. *The Godfather, Part II*: The final flashback's warm classical lighting and the presence of actors James Caan, Abe Vigoda, and Gianni Russo evoke the original *Godfather*.

and Fredo—whom Michael has had killed. Watching it, one can more clearly than ever before contrast the Michael from the first film with the Michael from this one. Finally, once we learn, through the shot of the contemplative Michael, that the flashback is his own reminiscence, the segment becomes expressly about the loss and nostalgia that inundate the modern narrative. Michael looks back wistfully at his past by recalling a moment that most wistfully recalls the first *Godfather*.[19]

Up to its very end, *The Godfather, Part II* seems intent upon reminding viewers of its divergence from its more satisfying forefather, frustrating spectators' expectations that the sequel might deliver the suspense and excitement they enjoyed with the first movie. By emphasizing spectator disappointment over satisfaction, however, and scuttling its potential to give spectators what they presumably went to the sequel for, *Part II* exploits a subtle aesthetic effect available to film sequels, an effect we consider next.

THE GODFATHER, PART II'S DOUBLE IDENTITY

I have focused my analysis of *The Godfather, Part II* so far on a curious commingling of two realities operating in the movie, two realities that operate within every work of fiction: the diegetic reality of the fiction and the non-diegetic reality that the fiction is just a fiction.[20] Works of fiction can mix the two realities and yet continue to preserve their integrity, when, say, figures in a painting look at a painting or actors in a play portray actors in a play. For centuries, artists have exploited the peculiar self-reflexivity of this gimmick,

FIGURE 3.11. A shot from *The Godfather, Part II* with strong backlighting.

perhaps because it offers works of art a felicitous resonance between the diegetic and non-diegetic worlds. When, at the end of *A Midsummer Night's Dream*, the characters watch the performance of a play, they do what we are doing in *our* universe. The two realities of the fiction reverberate, yet the theatrical illusion remains intact.

From Edwin Porter's *Uncle Josh at the Moving Picture Show* (1902) to Woody Allen's *The Purple Rose of Cairo* (1985), filmmakers have exploited the potential for cinema to create a resonance between its diegetic and non-diegetic realities. But the resonance need not be so heavy-handed, and we can speculate about the effects of more inconspicuous manifestations of cinema's double identity as both cinema and diegetic world. Consider, for example, the presence of special effects in science fiction films: Special effects feel appropriate to the genre not only because they allow filmmakers to create futuristic visual imagery but also because special effects are themselves scientific and futuristic. The connection between the science of special effects and their presence in science fiction films offers a narratively superfluous unity that helps to place them fittingly in the cinematic world they inhabit. Or, for another example of an inconspicuous correlation of cinema's two identities, consider how readily Westerns in the 1960s and 1970s—when John Wayne started to seem old and the genre passé—began to depict the passing of the West. Westerns of this period, such as *The Man Who Shot Liberty Valence* (1962), *True Grit* (1969), *The Wild Bunch* (1969), *The Cowboys* (1972), and many dozens more, regularly depicted the death of old heroes or the death of the West itself. The coincidence of the outmoded Western genre and the fading Western frontier gives post-classical Westerns an extra feeling of "rightness," because the two unrelated phenomena seem naturally to belong together. The resonances between the phenomena invite spectators to make passing connections between fundamentally different—in fact, mutually exclusive—universes: the real universe in which we are sitting in a movie theater watching a movie and the diegetic universe depicted on the screen.

All works of fiction enable their audiences to cope with the existence of two realities at once. However, some fictions, such as *The Godfather, Part II*, more fully exploit the potentially subtle and complex relationship between such realities. Taking an inventive approach to sequelization, the film incorporates into its story the nostalgia, disappointment, and sense of loss with which audiences traditionally greet sequels. Because of the fundamental similarity between the degenerative turn from original movie to sequel and the degeneration of the Corleone family that dominates the narrative of *Part II*, the movie encourages spectators to casually correlate two incompatible—but coincidental and analogous—realities. The correlation remains substantively irrelevant to the movie (just as the correlation between the dying West and the dying Western is substantively irrelevant), yet it feels felicitous because disappointment, nostalgia, and loss seem as natural to a sequel as a fading frontier is to a late Western or special effects are to a science fiction film.

I suspect *Part II*'s seductive subtlety led early reviewers to confuse their opinion of what happens in the sequel with their opinion of the sequel itself. It took time, and perhaps some distance from their initial disappointment, for them to recognize the sequel's more subtle, complex, and singular artistic virtues. Although the film's present critical and popular reception indicates that early reviewers misjudged the movie, at the time of the sequel's release they rightly accused the movie of *being* what it is *about*: the disappointing aftermath to the loss of the godfather.

So far, I have argued that the propensity of *The Godfather, Part II* to eschew, rather than intensify, the romance, suspense, and excitement of the original *Godfather* tends to frustrate spectator expectations of the sequel *as a sequel*. *Part II*, I have said, systematically avoids fulfilling the promises of the original *Godfather*. But *The Godfather, Part II* enlists other means of narrative frustration as well, and, to better understand what makes the film exemplary of seventies narration, we must leave our discussion of *Part II* as a sequel and turn to two other narrational strategies, prominent in films of the era, that obstruct the clarity and momentum characteristic of Hollywood narration. The first is the film's convoluted plotting and the second is its tendency to hinder spectator sympathy for its protagonist.

CONVOLUTED PLOTTING

Sometimes *The Godfather, Part II* makes no sense. Many early reviewers criticized the movie as incoherent. Vincent Canby, for instance, wrote, "'Part II' is as stuffed with material as a Christmas goose. It's a mass (sometimes mess) of plots, subplots, characters, alliances, betrayals, ambushes, renunciations, kisses of death, you name it. Much of the time it's next to impossible to figure out who's doing what to whom" ("One Godfather Too Many," II19). Stanley Kauffmann also complained about *Part II*'s incoherence in his pan of the film for the *New Republic*: "Coppola, who wrote [the script] with Mario Puzo, has told how he had to write it in a hurry and how a lot of frantic editing was done after the first previews. That helps to explain the gaps and distentions [*sic*]" (22). I could cite dozens of similar grievances.

As the foregoing reviews testify, *The Godfather, Part II*'s narrative incongruities lead to spectator disorientation; however, they also create intriguing puzzles for spectators to solve and help establish the atmosphere of labyrinthine complexity so central to the film's modern story. An atmosphere of complexity helps sustain interest in the story, as well as our sense that it contains difficult problems that demand attention and deep probing. Although, in some instances, the film's narrative incongruities cannot be fully resolved, their lack of resolution helps to preserve the film's atmosphere of complexity and thematic difficulty, since total resolution threatens to replace intrigue with mastery.

Let's look closely at some of the film's narrative incongruities, which undermine the protocols of classical Hollywood narration in subtle and gratuitous ways. Classical narration is committed to an unambiguous presentation of story information, minimizing spectator disorientation, depicting information redundantly and consistently, and striving, according to Bordwell, for "utmost denotative clarity from moment to moment" (*Narration*, 161–163). *The Godfather, Part II*, by contrast, often disorients spectators by conveying story information that does not fit squarely with previously denoted events. As a result, our understanding of the story contains so many gaps and incongruities that our narrative inferences and predictions fluctuate unstably as the movie develops.

The film's narrative incongruities make it difficult to keep Michael's enemies distinct from his friends. The shooting script makes it clear fairly early on (in a scene Coppola appears not to have shot) that Hyman Roth wants to deceive Michael, but the movie itself is not so generous. It would take a shrewd viewer to know on a first viewing that Roth, not Pentangeli, tries to murder Michael. When Michael tells Roth in Florida that "Pentangeli is a dead man," the movie has offered no reason to doubt him. Michael suspects the presence of a traitor in his family, and his explanation to Roth—that ordering Pentangeli to "lay down" to the Rosato brothers made Pentangeli angry—accords with denoted events. Michael visits Pentangeli in New York and yells at him furiously about the assassination attempt, then adds surprisingly, "It was Roth who tried to have me killed." The film's position on Pentangeli's role in the assassination attempt appears suddenly to have reversed, and the incongruity cues spectators to revise their inferences and predictions or, at the very least, opens up a gap in story comprehension. Far from wanting revenge against Pentangeli, Michael wants to enlist his help, unless Michael is lying.

Cueing spectators to develop false inferences and predictions is nothing extraordinary in Hollywood cinema, particularly in crime narratives, which often incorporate reversals, double crosses, and false friendships. *The Godfather, Part II*, however, repeatedly destabilizes spectator inferences and predictions in erratic ways. For example, later in the film, Michael's faith in Pentangeli is again made suspect when, as the Rosato brothers try to have Pentangeli strangled in a bar, the hit man says, "Michael Corleone says hello." The statement coincides with what the narration originally denoted (that Michael sought revenge for Pentangeli's betrayal) but later negated. Now it seems as though Michael double-crossed Pentangeli. Still later, the movie continues to confuse events when Michael asks Roth who ordered Pentangeli's death. "I know I didn't," Michael says with apparent sincerity. Roth's reply suggests that Roth gave the order, and the movie ultimately leaves us with that impression. In that case, however, then the line of the Rosatos' hit man—"Michael Corleone says hello"—cannot be explained.

The movie, moreover, distributes expositional information broadly across the plot. Fifty-eight minutes elapse between the shooting at Michael's compound and the scene in which Michael questions Roth, and afterward events still remain murky. Spectators find themselves having to rethink story events over a period of time that would tax anyone's memory and analytical abilities, sometimes revising their understanding of events witnessed hours earlier in screen time.

Pentangeli's behavior during the Senate hearings also creates narrative incongruities and gaps because the movie never clarifies why the presence of his brother keeps Pentangeli from testifying. Has Michael threatened the brother? The brother's chumminess with Michael at the hearings suggests otherwise. Perhaps Pentangeli simply cannot bring himself to testify against the Family in front of his own family, an explanation that seems too sentimental for this movie. (Critics have pointed to the Sicilian practice of *omerta*—or the "law of silence"—to explain Pentangeli's sudden silence, but giving it a name does not make it intelligible.) Tom Hagen says that Roth "engineered" Michael's troubles with the government, but what exactly did Roth do other than inadvertently make Pentangeli think Michael tried to have him killed?

The narration, moreover, neglects to subordinate incidental story information to information integral to the causal chain of events, instead relying on spectators' capacity to distinguish between the two. The film sometimes sets out on narrative trajectories that turn into dead ends. In Cuba, for example, Michael tells Fredo that, after the reception at the presidential palace, "they're going to take me home in a military car, alone, for my protection, and before I reach my hotel I'll be assassinated." Michael's lines are poignant, they accord with the earlier assassination attempt at his home, and they seem to introduce a new story line that will have consequences in later scenes. Yet those lines are the first and last we hear on the subject. For all we know, Michael made the whole thing up. Here, the narration has fixated on story information that seems immediately urgent but that ultimately has no bearing on the film's causal progress.

On two other occasions the narration references story elements that seem momentarily important but that lead nowhere. When Michael's wife, Kay, complains, "look what's happened to our son," it sounds as though something has happened to him that we should know about, as though this weren't the only scene to suggest that their son has a problem. When, near the end of the movie, Michael makes an unexplained reference to Tom Hagen's mistress, it seems as though scenes might have been cut out of the film (which is, in fact, the case: In the shooting script, Hagen has an affair with Sonny's widow, Sandra).

(The flashback story contains no such convolutions and ambiguities. Indeed, our cozy knowledge that Vito's is a chronicle of rising power enables us to forecast the outcome of almost every episode, and we know from the first *Godfather*, with god-like omniscience, how his story ends. In contrast to the complexity of Michael's world, the world in flashback seems stable and predictable.)

The movie leaves myriad other questions unanswered, questions about, say, how Fredo could have helped with the assassination attempt on Michael, the relation between Roth and Senator Questadt, Roth's motives in attempting to kill Pentangeli or Michael, Michael's strategy in dealing with Roth and the source of Michael's information about him, and the mysterious deaths of Clemenza and the gunmen at Michael's compound. The movie ultimately suggests that Fredo murders the gunmen but also portrays Fredo as incapable of the strength and viciousness that such murders would require. The reason one might not notice the incongruity in the film's depiction of Fredo is that, when Michael says that the gunmen were "killed by somebody close," the movie has given no reason at that point to suspect the somebody is Fredo.

Throughout much of its three-hour-and-twenty-minute screen time, *The Godfather, Part II* confounds spectators with story incongruities that do not serve any of the film's overt narrative goals. Unlike a conventional mystery film, for instance, *Part II* does not set out to resolve its incongruities as it progresses toward revealed truth (see Bordwell, *Narration*, 158). Indeed, the incongruities remain largely extraneous to the causal progress of the story, wanton impediments to narrative linearity, clarity, and resolution.

We see in *The Godfather, Part II* a model instance of the period's tendency to employ narrative strategies in between those of classical Hollywood and foreign art cinema. The film exploits potentials in the classical crime film (the double cross, the false friendship, the reversal) in ways that confound spectators to an extent rarely seen in classical cinema, prompting spectators to make a series of false inferences and predictions based on causal misunderstandings. The film stretches the potentials of classical narration, generating narrative ambiguities and irresolutions more typical of European and Asian art cinema than Hollywood. Like films of Michelangelo Antonioni, Kenji Mizoguchi, Kon Ichikawa, Ingmar Bergman, or Alain Resnais, *Part II* taxes spectators' memories and analytical capacities, leaves vital story information unresolved, and fixates on events superfluous to the causal chain. Like *The 400 Blows* (1959), *Blow Up* (1966), and *The Conformist* (1970), it delays exposition and distributes key causal factors broadly across the plot, rather than providing them in an order convenient to spectator comprehension.

By gravitating toward art cinema, without abandoning classical narration, ✗ the film gains some distinct aesthetic advantages. Art cinema narration liberates *Part II* from the strictures of familiar plot patterning and adds variety to the film's narrational strategies. At the same time, classical narrative devices stabilize the film's narration and help retain spectators' trust in an underlying unity. Hence, the film avoids the radicalism, experimentalism, and mischievousness of art cinema by anchoring its narration to the classical Hollywood structure. Hollywood's goal-oriented protagonists, cause-and-effect chains, and clear-cut resolutions create parameters for classical films and prevent them from falling into arch unpredictability.

Narrative fictions have parameters that the real world rarely offers. "A narrative has a beginning and an ending," Christian Metz writes, "a fact that simultaneously distinguishes it from the rest of the world" (*Film Language*,

17). However, many of the works of art that our culture considers great admit some of the boundlessness and unpredictability of the real world into their delimited fictional worlds. Disorienting, convoluted, and seemingly pregnant with significances beyond our mastery, *The Godfather, Part II* pulls out large ideas (organized crime, international politics, generational change, corruption, betrayal) and buries them in a convoluted plot that demands deep analytic probing and fails to make the total sense promised by its identity as a classical Hollywood narrative.

Confronted with incongruous story information, spectators likely have a persistent feeling that more remains to be understood about the story than their minds can readily grasp. Humor researchers, as we have already seen, offer us the richest description of the experience of this sort of incongruity.

> In the after-experience of incongruity, we know and feel that something significant has occurred in our mind, but we do not know exactly what it is. We have a tense notion that we know more than we know, and we preserve this uncertain feeling as a means of arousing and sustaining our curiosity for the search. (Schaeffer, 10)

Scholars have described Hollywood as an "excessively obvious" cinema in which causality serves as the narration's prime unifying principle (Bordwell, Staiger, and Thompson, 3). *The Godfather, Part II*, however, succeeds in creating an atmosphere of intrigue, complexity, and thematic difficulty in part by inhibiting story comprehension and derailing causal linearity.

Part II was by no means the only seventies film to gravitate toward narrative convolution. Throughout the period 1970 to 1977, Hollywood films showed a clear penchant for it. Consider, for instance, the pretzel-like narrative structure of *Annie Hall* (1977), which typically links scenes not by chronology and cause-and-effect but rather—like Bergman's *Wild Strawberries* (1957) or Fellini's *8 1/2* (1963)—by character thoughts, memories, and fantasies. *All the President's Men* (1976) links scenes according to chronology and cause-and-effect; however, the film, like *The Godfather, Part II*, often fixates on narrative detours, and some scenes come across as irrelevant to the causal progress of the story. Because the movie is organized around the pursuit of the reporters' leads, many of which amount to nothing (after Bernstein interviews lawyer Donald Segretti, for instance, Deep Throat tells Woodward, "Don't concentrate on Segretti"), the plot feels rambling and often disorienting. Or consider the narrative ambiguities of *The Conversation* (1974) and *Chinatown* (1974) or the puzzling, uncommunicative narration of *THX-1138* (1971), *The King of Marvin Gardens* (1972), and *Mikey and Nicky* (1976).

Nashville (1975) offers another exemplary instance of a seventies narrative intent upon frustrating linear narration through convolution, ambiguity, and disorientation. Many people have told me that they hated the movie until they saw it twice. Indeed, much of the time the narration proceeds as though the audience has already seen the movie. For instance, before we meet Tommy Brown (played by actor Timothy Brown) or hear him sing—that is, before we learn that he's a black singer of white-sounding country music—a scene in which Opal (Geraldine Chaplin) mistakes his African American wife for a member of his entourage makes little sense. Similarly, a joke made by Bill (Allan Nicholls) at the beginning of the movie that politician Hal Phillip Walker "looks exactly like Connie White" (Bill sees a poster of White, who is a country singer, with a Walker sticker pasted on it) will not make full sense until we understand who Connie White is; the movie introduces her fifty minutes later. The uncommunicativeness of the film's narration does not function as a classical retardation device, which, in conventional instances, would delay story resolution in order to retain viewers' interest. On the contrary, the narration's uncommunicativeness threatens to alienate viewers by treating their information needs indifferently.

Nashville, moreover, foregoes traditional transitions between scenes—which a conventional, linear Hollywood movie would link with dialogue hooks and cause-and-effect narration—in favor of surprising thematic connections and contrasts and sudden shifts in narrative focus. Scene changes are not motivated by dangling plot developments, and rarely does a scene in *Nashville* pick up the suspended plotline of the previous scene. Indeed, except for a handful of scenes in which the characters are doing the same thing at the same time—such as the car crash scene, the church montage, and the Parthenon scene—and scenes in which Triplette (Michael Murphy) and Reese (Ned Beatty) work to enlist the various singers in the film for an appearance at a Walker rally, *Nashville*'s plot sprawls out horizontally, instead of building each scene upon the goals, appointments, decisions, accomplishments, and other dangling threads of previous scenes.

Like *The Godfather, Part II*, each of these movies gravitates toward convolution, ambiguity, and disorientation in ways superfluous to the film's causal purpose. The movies frustrate linear narration not necessarily to create suspense or delay resolution but often incidentally, permanently, and for no evident reason except to keep spectators off balance.

The Godfather, Part II, we have seen, obstructs the fulfillment of its promises as both a sequel and a mainstream Hollywood film. *Part II* frustrates spectator expectations by eschewing the narrative satisfactions of the original *Godfather* and frustrates linear narration through plot convolutions superfluous to the story's causal progress. However, we have yet to examine perhaps the most unsettling of all of the film's narrative frustrations: its tendency to obstruct audience sympathy for its protagonist. This tendency, which we find in so many Hollywood narratives of the seventies, is the subject of the final section of this chapter.

THE GODFATHER, PART II's MORALLY INCONGRUOUS PROTAGONIST

Murray Smith has argued that characters, rather than other aspects of a narrative, are the primary means by which spectators "engage" with film fictions. Characters, he says, mediate spectators' "entry into" film narratives because, as narrative devices, characters are so salient (*Engaging Characters*, 18). People take interest in characters because characters are like people: Characters have feelings, goals, and follow behavioral patterns that people recognize as human. A film that forgoes spectator sympathy for its main character (substituting either antipathy or indifference) does so at its aesthetic peril: If spectators do not engage sympathetically with the film's main character, on what basis will they engage with the film? The film industry's emphasis on an actor's "likeability" and the "likeability" of a script's lead character speaks to the commercial value placed on sympathetic main characters.

The Godfather, Part II risks just that sort of aesthetic disaster. *Part II* contains one of the many unsympathetic protagonists from 1970s cinema. Not merely an antihero, such as Bonnie or Clyde, Michael is contemptible, like Popeye Doyle in *The French Connection* (1971), Alex in *A Clockwork Orange* (1971), Kit Carruthers in *Badlands* (1973), and Travis Bickle in *Taxi Driver* (1976). The film, however, maintains a paradoxical sort of audience engagement by directing spectators' responses to its protagonist in two antithetical directions: The narration invites spectators to both deplore their protagonist and at the same time cheer on his most deplorable actions.

Let's first understand how the movie sets about making the character unsympathetic.

Like the sequel itself, Michael is a letdown. The movie, for instance, often cues spectators to anticipate that Michael will behave more decently than he ever does. His dealings with Fredo offer the most illustrative examples since the film sometimes suggests that Michael might act lovingly toward Fredo just before Michael behaves most brutally toward him. Consider the scene in which Michael interrogates and then disavows Fredo after learning of his betrayal: "Fredo, you're nothing to me now. You're not a brother. You're not a friend." Michael looks vicious, Fredo destroyed. Pacino delivers the lines reservedly, pausing between sentences, emphasizing their poignance, and the film accompanies his words with portentous music that underscores the gravity of Michael's speech. Immediately afterward, however, Michael, out of earshot of Fredo, says something to Al Neri that briefly suggests that Michael cares more about his brother than he was willing to admit in Fredo's presence, "I don't want anything to happen to him." The line ultimately turns chilling, however, when, after a pause, the second part of Michael's statement to Neri counteracts the gratifying impression made by the first: "while my mother's alive."

The moment of Michael and Fredo's reunion at their mother's funeral creates an effect almost identical to the one just described. Michael had refused to join the funeral because of Fredo's presence, but Connie seems to have persuaded him to reconcile with their brother. Michael enters the room and clutches Fredo's distraught and grateful face to his belly. The music at that moment, unlike the portentous music in the earlier scene, is romantic, a passionate rendition of themes that appear in many of the flashback sequences. The moment dramatically portrays Michael's forgiveness of his brother. However, even as he is clutching Fredo, the music's mood shifts ominously and Michael gives Al Neri a look with a meaning so terrifying that even Neri looks a little shocked. Fredo is about to sleep with the fishes.

Throughout *Part II*, Michael appears just as ruthless. (Consider, for example, the scene in which Michael, having come upon Kay while she secretly visits their children, slowly closes the door on her pleading face. Michael would have appeared less ruthless had he said something to her, even something mean. The scene did not prepare us for such cold-hearted humiliation.) However, at some of the very moments in which the film portrays him as most contemptible, it simultaneously creates sympathy for his goals and actions. Before we investigate this paradoxical response, let me say a word on what it means to sympathize with film characters.

Murray Smith breaks down the process by which spectators "engage" or "identify" with characters into three distinct cognitive responses to a film's narration. Such responses combine to create what Smith calls a "structure of sympathy": 1) *recognition*, the process by which spectators construct characters out of the perception of film stimuli; 2) *alignment*, a function of spectators' access to characters' actions, knowledge, and feelings; and 3) *allegiance*, a function of spectators' "moral evaluation" of characters (*Engaging Characters*, 84). Allegiance, for Smith, requires both recognition and alignment, but it goes further by causing spectators to morally evaluate and respond emotionally to a character with *sympathy* and/or *antipathy* (85). Smith's categories usefully distinguish between different aspects of viewers' engagement with film characters. For instance, alignment and allegiance, though normally linked in movies, are distinct. A film such as *A Clockwork Orange* mostly aligns narration with a character toward whom audiences have little allegiance. According to Smith, "the most we can say is that the conventional association of alignment and allegiance [in most narratives] . . . primes us to be sympathetic to characters with whom we are aligned" (188).

We can further separate allegiance into two types: 1) allegiance toward the character, and 2) allegiance toward the actions the character performs. We may feel moral sympathy for a character but fault the character's actions, as is the case throughout much of *Detour* (1945), which portrays the protagonist as barely responsible for his own foolish criminal behavior. The opposite can also occur, and *The Godfather, Part II* offers some ideal illustrations. Through scenarios that provoke spectator investment in seeing Michael behave deplorably, *Part II*'s narration exploits the tension between spectators' sympathy for Michael's actions and their antipathy toward the character. Indeed, spectator support for his behavior is often proportionate to the character's moral repugnance.

I want to begin my discussion of the tense coupling of antipathy toward Michael and sympathy for his actions with the last two scenes of the original *Godfather* in which Michael kills Carlo Rizzi and then lies to Kay about it. Both scenes heighten spectators' *alignment* with Michael (by, for instance, restricting narration largely to Michael's point of view and by revealing his knowledge of Carlo's complicity in Sonny's murder) and their sympathetic *allegiance* toward his actions (by enacting revenge against a despicable character and by resolving tension in his relationship with Kay). At the same time, the scenes increase *antipathy* toward the character (by making Michael look cruel, cold, and hypocritical).

It might seem inappropriate to include the first *Godfather* here since we have already seen that the two movies employ very different narrative strategies; however, the last two scenes of *The Godfather* emblematize the entirety of *The Godfather, Part II* in that both films couple antipathy toward Michael with sympathy for his actions. Although Coppola initially had no intention of making a sequel, he has suggested that he built *Part II* upon the ending of the first *Godfather*. For instance, Coppola said, "I felt I was trying to make a harsh statement about the Mafia and power at the end of *Godfather I* when Michael murders all those people, then lies to his wife and closes the door. But obviously, many people didn't get the point I was making. . . . I felt *Godfather II* was an opportunity to rectify that" (Murray, 185). Both the ending of the first movie and several scenes in the sequel elicit moral shock at Michael's wickedness at the very moments in which he accomplishes goals that the film has prompted spectators to support.

When Michael kills Carlo Rizzi in *The Godfather*'s penultimate scene, he retaliates against a character, who, earlier in the movie, humiliated and sadistically beat Michael's sister, Connie. After killing Moe Greene and the heads of the other families, Michael tricks Carlo into admitting he helped Don Barzini kill Sonny. The admission not only offers another good reason to hate Carlo, but it also occasions direct revenge for Sonny's death, once Michael has Carlo killed (a fitting resolution to a story line that the film seemed until this point to have abandoned). But Carlo's murder does not, I propose, increase our overall sympathy toward Michael, only toward his actions. Although he kills a character who clearly had it coming, at the same time he murders his own brother-in-law, just after becoming godfather to the man's child. The murder—Michael watches impassively as Clemenza strangles Carlo in a car, Carlo's boot kicking through the windshield—makes Michael look brutal, hypocritical, and unfeeling, even as it exacts revenge against perhaps the most contemptible character in the movie.

Critics have described the pleasures of *The Godfather* as simple, and in comparison to those of the sequel they are. However, the final scenes of *The Godfather* directly engage some of the potentially unsettling consequences of spectators' allegiance toward the Corleone Mafia throughout the film. For instance, if the film had not included a scene, just after Clemenza kills Carlo, in which Connie accuses Michael of ordering the hit on her husband,

I suspect audiences would not have considered the repercussions of Carlo's murder on her. Indeed, the film might have portrayed Connie as pleased by the death of her abusive husband. Instead, it makes spectators pay for the revenge after the fact.

The final scene of *The Godfather*—the scene that begins with Connie's frantic entrance into Michael's study and ends when Neri closes the door on Kay—heightens the tension between spectator sympathy for Michael's actions and antipathy for the character. After Michael has Connie ushered out, he is left alone with his shaken and doubtful wife.

> KAY. Michael, is it true?
> MICHAEL. Don't ask me about my business, Kay.
> KAY. Is it true?
> MICHAEL. Don't ask me about my business.
> KAY. No . . .
> MICHAEL. Enough! Alright, this one time, this one time I'll let you ask me about my affairs.
> KAY. Is it true?
> MICHAEL. No. [*they embrace*]

The scene is as wickedly manipulative as he is. On the one hand, the film has led spectators to anticipate that Michael might answer her truthfully. Several previous scenes—including Michael's first scene in the movie in which he tells Kay about his father's brutal career—have portrayed Michael sympathetically at moments in which he frankly admits to Kay his family's criminal activities. In this scene, for the first time, he treats Kay with the same tight-lipped callousness that characterizes the way the other Mafiosi treat their wives. But on the other hand, Carlo's murder must be kept secret from Kay because, if for no other reason, she wouldn't understand. She does not know what Carlo has done, and she would not approve of the murder even if she did.

Michael's lie intensifies the conflict between antipathy toward the character and sympathy for his actions: The lie reveals Michael as even colder and more evil than in previous scenes at the same time that it brings the narrative as close as it could come to a satisfying resolution. Michael's hand in the murder of a police captain and half a dozen other men, including his brother-in-law, may be morally offensive, but his lie to his wife is anti-family, unforgivable.

Sarah Kozloff calls Michael's lie "somehow his most shocking action in the film . . . as if he had kicked the viewer in the face" (227). Moreover, Kay's side, the side of decency, has not merely lost; it has been cheated by shameless hypocrisy. At the same time, however, the lie conceals a truth that would only antagonize Kay and prevent narrative closure.

Ultimately, there is no entirely comfortable way for this scene to resolve. If Michael tells Kay to keep out of his business, as he does at first, she will only continue to insist or else exit the scene dissatisfied. If he answers her truthfully, the tension in the scene will only escalate. The lie makes the problem between Michael and Kay go away, a resolution signaled by their affectionate embrace, an embrace that makes Michael look duplicitous even as it brings closure to their conflict.

In *Part II*, spectators' sympathy for Michael's actions remains proportionately tied to their antipathy toward him, as the narration prompts spectators to support actions that make the character contemptible. The scenes of the Senate hearings on organized crime, for instance, mostly portray Michael unsympathetically. The senators on the committee accurately describe his criminal dealings: Michael did indeed kill "a New York Police Captain," he "killed the heads of the five families in New York to consume and consolidate [his] nefarious power," and he does have "control over gambling and narcotics in the state of New York." As he tells the committee of his service in World War II, the film recalls the youthful Michael from the first *Godfather*. However, since the character now has no trace of his previous ideals, it is as though he is talking about a different person altogether, almost a hypocrisy for him even to bring up his former self in his own defense. The rest of his statement reeks with obvious lies, which he delivers coldly and matter-of-factly. The film's spectators saw him become exactly the man he denies being.

The film, however, also portrays the members of the committee as smug and hypocritical, especially Senators Geary and Questadt, who, the film has either shown us or told us, are corrupt. In the moral structure of this film, politicians rank below Mafiosi.[21] Moreover, the narration has "primed" us, in Murray Smith's terms, to support Michael's behavior in the hearing scenes by aligning us in previous scenes with his goals. By contrast, we never have privileged access to the goals and strategies of the senators, whom (except for the corrupt Senator Geary) the film portrays only as antagonists to Michael's objectives, never in scenes as independent characters with whom we might ally. Consequently, when Michael wins, when Pentangeli makes the committee look bumbling and foolish, although Michael again behaves like a shameless hypocrite, it feels like a victory for *our* side.

Several other scenes—such as Roth's murder, Fredo's murder, and Pentangeli's suicide at the end of the film—offer narrative satisfaction in proportion to the degree to which they portray the protagonist as deplorable, but one more illustrative example ought to suffice. Toward the beginning of the movie, the Corleones have a young prostitute murdered in order to gain the compliance of Senator Geary, a character who is as dramatically heavy as he is crooked. Here, the narration constructs a scenario in which the Corleones' unsympathetic behavior has a, in part, just consequence. Because the narration has portrayed the senator as corrupt, arrogant, and bigoted, the film has justified his humiliation; that is, until the camera pans to reveal the shocking sight of a dead, blood-drenched woman, her hands tied to the bed. Because the scene conjoins the senator's humiliation to a brutal murder of an innocent woman, it encourages spectators both to approve the senator's ruin and to blame the Corleones for causing it. Such scenes simultaneously advance and frustrate spectator sympathy by making a satisfying narrative outcome contingent upon the characters' contemptible behavior.

The change in narrational strategy at the end of the first *Godfather* and extending into *Part II* reflects a general change that occurred in Hollywood narration in the 1970s. Most of *The Godfather* maintains a congruous relationship between spectators' allegiance toward the Corleone family and their allegiance toward its behavior by emphasizing the Corleones' more sympathetic qualities, especially in comparison to the film's antagonists; by keeping their unattractive qualities in the background; by allying spectators with their noble goals, such as protecting Vito from assassination; and by further allying spectators with a character who, for much of the movie, both loves his family and rejects its criminality. However, starting shortly before Michael murders the heads of the other Mafia families as he renounces Satan in the church, extending through the murders of Tessio and Carlo, and finally to his repugnant lie to his wife, *The Godfather*'s narration deviates from some of the coherent allegiances that characterize previous scenes in the movie. By 1974, seventies narrative design was firmly established, and *The Godfather, Part II* epitomizes that form. More pervasively than the first film, *Part II* rejects narrative harmony and gravitates toward the various types of narrative frustration one finds in so many celebrated movies of the 1970s: a nagging refusal to fulfill expectations, convoluted narration, and a tendency to thwart viewer sympathy for protagonists.

The Godfather, Part II is, in a variety of ways, an emblem of the principles of narrative perversity studied in the previous chapter. In particular, the film hinders narrative momentum and scuttles numerous opportunities to generate suspense and excitement. It moreover situates its narrative strategies in between classical Hollywood narration and art-cinema narration, whose story convolutions, delayed exposition, and narrative ambiguities and irresolutions serve both to obstruct and enrich *Part II*'s otherwise classical narration. Consequently, the film elicits more uncertain and discomforting spectator responses than those of more conventional Hollywood cinema.

Part II's obstructions of linearity and coherence take the sequel in a direction that the final scenes of the original *Godfather*, looked at in retrospect, seem to foretell. Indeed, such scenes, and the entirety of *Part II*, signal the direction of Hollywood cinema generally in the 1970s, when filmmakers approached the boundaries of classical narration closer than ever before. Tethered to the Hollywood model, whose harmony they both rely on and resist, seventies films stretch out from the model about as far as Hollywood would allow.

CHAPTER 4

GENRE DEVIATION AND
THE FRENCH CONNECTION

In the 1970 war movie *Patton*, our hero delivers a line one does not expect to hear from Hollywood war heroes. Surveying the battlefield after a horrific slaughter of troops, General George S. Patton says, "God help me, I do love it so." The line is not surprising, given what the audience knows about Patton, but it violates conventional expectations of Hollywood war heroes, who traditionally greet the battlefield not with glee but dutifully and reluctantly.

Patton is hardly a traditional war picture, but it is characteristic of seventies genre films, which frequently resisted traditional Hollywood scenarios. Many filmmakers in the 1970s treated genre conventions like a set of outmoded film techniques, the fashion of an older, more innocent generation of filmmakers. The period did produce movies that made little effort to reconceive their genres' conventional topoi: The whodunit *Murder on the Orient Express* (1974), the caper movie *The Sting* (1973), and the musical *Bedknobs and Broomsticks* (1971), for instance, would not have looked much different had they appeared a decade or two earlier. However, movies in the 1970s, with uncommon frequency, played against genre conventions.

In considering the ways in which seventies filmmakers revised the narrative conventions of Hollywood genres, we can divide many of the era's genre-deviant films into two categories: genre breakers and genre benders. A *genre breaker*, such as *Little Big Man* (1970) or *Young Frankenstein* (1974), loudly and self-consciously broadcasts its violation of tradition, inviting audiences to join in the effort to expose, and usually mock, genre conventions. By contrast, a *genre bender*, such as *Chinatown* (1974) or *Taxi Driver* (1976), commits

its violations without advertisement, subtly reworking traditional scenarios without calling much attention to its genre deviance. A genre bender relies on viewers' habitual responses to generic codes, misleading spectators into expecting a conventional outcome. At first, a genre bender seems innocuous and true-to-form, then, like a booby trap, it catches spectators off guard. It therefore generates more unnerving effects than genre breakers, and genre benders tend to come across as more incoherent in their narration.

The French Connection (1971), which we study later in this chapter, perfectly illustrates seventies genre bending. Capitalizing on traditional expectations of Hollywood formulas, the film uses the familiar conventions of the police detective genre in order to cue viewer expectations that it then undermines. The film, however, does not defy genre convention in order to comment on its genre or to give audiences a sense of genre expertise, the way a genre breaker would. On the contrary, by employing and then subverting conventional Hollywood scenarios, the movie creates unsettling narrative ambiguities.

GENRE BREAKERS

Proclaiming their freedom from the strictures of film tradition, many seventies filmmakers self-consciously defied genre conventions. Using their films to call glaring attention to genre constraints—"baring the device," to use Viktor Shklovsky's term—they criticized Hollywood contrivance.[1] Filmmakers, like film scholars, have frequently turned to the Western to stage their commentary about Hollywood, largely because of the genre's tendency to mythologize America's past. Seventies filmmakers exploited the Western's ideological vulnerability by exposing the myth-making strategies that earlier generations of filmmakers often attempted to conceal. John Cawelti has demonstrated the ways in which Arthur Penn's *Little Big Man* (1970) reverses Hollywood myths about cowboys and Indians in order to debunk them: "In [Penn's] film it is the Indians who are humane and civilized, while the pioneers are violent, corrupt, sexually repressed and madly ambitious" (196). Richard Maltby notes that the "self-consciousness" of Sam Peckinpah's *Pat Garrett and Billy the Kid* (1973) "indicates the extent to which it, and other similar movies made in the same period, exposed the conventions by which the genre had operated" (*Hollywood Cinema*, 131). One could say the same about Michael Crichton's *Westworld* (1973), which calls attention to Western conventions by mixing them incongruously into a science fiction story, or Mel Brooks's Western parody *Blazing Saddles* (1974).

These films, along with numerous others, helped establish what amounted to a new Hollywood genre—the genre breaker. Fueled by their difference from previous films of the same genres, genre breakers comment on earlier movies, promoting the notion that Hollywood genres had grown passé. Thomas Schatz identifies this point in a genre's evolution: "As a genre's classic conventions are refined and eventually parodied and subverted, its transparency gradually gives way to *opacity*: we no longer look *through* the form . . . rather we look *at* the *form itself*" (*Hollywood Genres*, 38). It should not be surprising, then, that scholarship about genre breakers largely points out what the movies themselves point out: that Hollywood genre films are deceptive and contrived. William Simon and Louise Spence, for example, argue that Robert Altman's *Buffalo Bill and the Indians* (1976) "employs irony as a self-critical discursive trope to debunk and demystify the central motifs and icons of the genre" (79). Glenn Man says something very similar about Altman's *McCabe & Mrs. Miller* (1971) when he argues that it "demythologizes" the Western hero and represents the "demise" of the Western myth (83). Indeed, Altman himself said the same thing about *McCabe*: "I just wanted to take a very standard Western story with a classic line and do it real or what I felt was real, and destroy all the myths of heroism" (Atlas and Guerin, 20).

Genre breakers parallel a kind of film scholarship that Rick Altman calls an "ideological approach" to genre, which "characterizes each individual genre as a specific type of lie, an untruth whose most characteristic feature is its ability to masquerade as truth" (29). They have attracted exhaustive scholarly treatment and tend to be critical favorites because they do what film scholars and critics do: they comment on film.

Genre breakers bring spectators inside the inside joke about Hollywood. By inviting us to notice the difference between the film predicted by the genre and the film we are watching, a genre breaker helps us to feel movie-literate. So, for example, when viewers watch a genre-breaking Hollywood whodunit, such as *The Last of Sheila* (1973) or *Murder by Death* (1976), they feel they know something about Hollywood and about whodunits. Unlike *Murder by Death*, *The Last of Sheila* does not outright parody the whodunit, but it bares its device by conspicuously violating an unspoken convention of genre filmmaking that the characters do not acknowledge that the scenario they are experiencing has, in the past, been the subject of movies. *Sheila* creates genre irony when characters remark that their situation has a Hollywood quality, encouraging audiences to feel mastery over the conventions the film exposes.

Seventies musicals offer a paradigm of seventies genre breaking. The seventies might seem an odd time for a genre that is partly distinguished by its fancy and exaggerated cheeriness because the period is usually characterized by such gritty films as *Badlands*, *Dog Day Afternoon*, and *Taxi Driver*. For this very reason, however, the musical genre suited seventies genre breaking. The 1970s, moreover, fell close enough to the prime of movie musicals that audiences understood when movies of this period "quoted" classic musicals. In fact, studios in the late sixties and early seventies, emboldened by the successes of *My Fair Lady* (1964) and *The Sound of Music* (1965), were still putting out films—such as *The Happiest Millionaire* (1967), *Doctor Dolittle* (1967), and *Bedknobs and Broomsticks* (1971)—in the style of Hollywood's "golden era" musicals, although with little commercial success. Seventies filmmakers, exploiting the fact that the public already considered the genre passé, found musicals a convenient critical tool for exposing Hollywood artifice.

Martin Scorsese's *New York, New York* (1977) contains a sequence that shows Liza Minnelli starring in a 1940s Hollywood musical, *Happy Endings*. The conspicuous artificiality of the film within the film, in which the main character marries her true love and becomes a Broadway star, contrasts the depressing "realism" of the larger story, in which the lovers fail to unite. The disparity between the stories emphasizes the artificiality of the musical's narrative topoi. In *Alice Doesn't Live Here Anymore* (1975), Scorsese made reference to Hollywood musicals in order to contrast their artificiality with "real life." The film opens with a sequence from Alice's childhood—a sequence with a look and feel reminiscent of old Hollywood musicals—then startlingly cuts to the present day as Alice and her teenage son listen to loud contemporary rock music, signaling a shift from movie fantasy to harsh reality.

For a generation of American filmmakers fascinated with calling attention to the artifice of cinema that their predecessors normally tried to mask, the movie musical's convention of "breaking into song" provided an opportunity to mock Hollywood.[2] Rather than trying to conceal the artificiality of the convention, a film such as *Bugsy Malone* (1976) calls conspicuous attention to it. A cast of children play the parts of gangsters, and, although the child actors speak in their own voices, when they open their mouths to sing, we hear the deep, mature voices of adult singers, voices that contrast conspicuously with the images and sounds of the children. *All That Jazz* (1979) represents, through hallucinations, the deathbed scene of its main character, Joe Gideon (Bob Fosse's semi-autobiographical filmmaker and Broadway choreographer).

In a setting that looks like a surreal mixture of hospital room and Hollywood soundstage, Gideon imagines his family and friends talking to him through a series of musical performances. When his family and a cast of dancing chorus girls burst into the 1923 song "Who's Sorry Now?"—performed in the fanciful style of a Busby Berkeley number—the film associates Gideon's fantasy with the fantasy of the musical genre itself.[3]

At least one non-musical film of the seventies also uses songs to ridicule Hollywood. When the theme song to Robert Altman's *The Long Goodbye* (1973) frequently resurfaces within the diegesis—on car stereos, as supermarket Muzak, on characters' doorbells, and in almost a dozen other unlikely places—the film mocks the artifice of film scoring. Not surprisingly, *The Long Goodbye* also mocks the conventions of its principal genre, the private detective film. The role of Philip Marlowe (previously played by such rugged actors as Humphrey Bogart and Robert Mitchum) is here played by Elliott Gould, known for his uptight roles in intellectual comedies.[4] Like earlier Marlowes, this one makes wisecracks, but he mumbles them under his breath, behaving more like a snotty private dick than a witty one. At one point, Marlowe, parodying the stock dialogue of old private eye movies, says to a policeman interrogating him, "Is this where I'm supposed to say, 'what is all this about?' and he says, uh, 'shut up. I ask the questions'?" Altman himself said that he was "making a film in Hollywood and about Hollywood, and about that kind of film" (Wexman and Bisplinghoff, 365), a notion most clearly evidenced at the end of *The Long Goodbye* when the soundtrack ironically plays "Hooray for Hollywood" (which also opens the movie). Here, Altman encourages audiences to laugh smugly at the wry comment on the story and on movies themselves.

GENRE BENDERS

In order to appreciate the variety and complexity of genre deviation in the 1970s, we must turn to a more diverse and subtle group of genre films, a group I call "genre benders" because they twist genre conventions without cracking them open. Like genre breakers, they play with genre expectations, but they are not flagrantly self-conscious and ironic, they do not encourage us to look at the form itself, and they are less likely to expose the ideologies embedded in their genres. In fact, genre benders deny us the ideological mastery that genre breakers congratulate us for having gained. Genre benders more subtly exploit habitual responses to generic conventions as they set us up for their unconventional outcomes. As a group, they tend to be more ambiguous and to create effects far more disconcerting than those of genre breakers.

The best way to understand seventies genre bending is to examine some exemplary case studies. *Chinatown* (1974) offers us a textbook example. Traditionally, private eye films portray the detective as smarter and savvier than anyone else in the movie. In keeping with that tradition, *Chinatown*'s Jake Gittes (Jack Nicholson) behaves with the brash confidence characteristic of a Hollywood private eye; however, the movie recurrently exposes how little he understands. Gittes even says at one point, "I'm not supposed to be the one who's caught with his pants down." Like *The Long Goodbye*, *Chinatown* violates the conventions of the private detective film. However, whereas Altman's film self-consciously calls attention to our expectations of the genre, *Chinatown* uses those expectations against us so that, by failing to satisfy them, it catches us off guard in an unnerving way. Usually as surprised by Gittes's ignorance as he is, viewers are suckered into trusting his hunches because, according to the genre, they are supposed to be trustworthy. *The Long Goodbye* pokes fun at the private detective genre by self-consciously highlighting the artificiality of its conventions, but *Chinatown* surreptitiously changes the conventions' function in the narrative.

In "*Chinatown* and Generic Transformation," John Cawelti says that the film perverts traditional private detective formulations in order to bring "its audience to see the genre as the embodiment of an inadequate and destructive myth" (194). But Cawelti overstates the self-consciousness of the film's genre deviation and ends up giving the movie a message about the private detective genre that I doubt the film delivers. Whereas I am suggesting that *Chinatown* combines genre conventionality with genre deviation in order to make spectators falsely predict the outcome of several scenes, Cawelti argues that it does so as a means of "ironically commenting upon the generic experience itself" (194). For Cawelti, because the film is genre-literate— portraying the insufficiency of the traditional private eye—*Chinatown* must also be critiquing its genre and, in the process, educating viewers about the myth of the Hollywood private detective. For Cawelti, *Chinatown* is a genre breaker, encouraging viewers to adopt its derisive attitude toward private eye conventions and offering its audience mastery over the ideologies that manipulated previous filmgoers.

However, far from teaching audiences about private eye conventions, *Chinatown* keeps them largely in the dark. Whereas *The Long Goodbye* never prompts spectators to anticipate conventional results from its private detective (whom Altman portrays largely as a loser), *Chinatown* follows enough private eye conventions to lead viewers to believe that Gittes might succeed in the traditional role. Jack Nicholson gives his character the pluck and confidence characteristic of the classical private detective, traits we don't see in *The Long Goodbye*'s Elliot Gould, who—typical of the actor's earlier roles, such as *Bob & Carol & Ted & Alice* (1969) and *Getting Straight* (1970)—offers a more casual, carefree performance, delivering many of his lines with the same sort of ironic mumble he developed working with Altman on *M*A*S*H* (1970). Although *Chinatown* often reveals Gittes's shortcomings (his misunderstandings, a puerile wit, and an occasional lack of poise, principles, and judgment), the character also shows traditional private eye ingenuity (impersonating a government official by swiping the man's business card, determining the time a suspect moves his car by putting a watch under his tire, breaking the rear light of Mrs. Mulwray's car in order to more easily tail her) and exhibits several of the private eye's other traditional characteristics (self-assurance, self-reliance, a cool toughness, and a useful capacity to move through all levels of society). Such traits instill trust in his ability ultimately to solve the larger problems, despite the film's intermittent violations of that trust. Gittes's ignorance and ineptitude are surprising again and again, up to and including the point at which he fails in his task to expose corruption, bring his suspect to justice, and restore order to the city.

Hence, we can learn much more about the private detective genre from Cawelti's essay about *Chinatown* than from *Chinatown* itself because the essay contains a far more overt critique of the genre than can be found anywhere in the film. I doubt that, even at the film's end, audiences learn any lesson about private detective films. If Cawelti were right, then once viewers recognized the ending's irony they would feel a sense of mastery. But *Chinatown*'s ending is unnerving. More likely, *Chinatown* causes viewers to distrust their *own* ability to grasp events than to distrust the traditional private eye hero or, as Cawelti says, to view the genre "as the embodiment of an inadequate and destructive myth" (194).

Reworking genre conventions is, in itself, nothing special. Stephen Neale notes that all genre films exhibit genre variation because all both fit within their genres and differentiate themselves from earlier films in the same genres. "If each text within a genre were, literally, the same," Neale says, "there would simply not be enough difference to generate either meaning or pleasure. Hence there would be no audience. Difference is absolutely essential to the economy of genre" (49–50). A film like *Chinatown*, however, does not simply stretch the limits of genre deviation; it exploits audience familiarity with its genre to create uncomfortable ambiguities, employing genre conventions for purposes of deception. Spectators, unwittingly manipulated by conventions familiar to them, cannot trust the genre cues because the ones they lean on customarily are, in this movie, not entirely reliable. So, although all genre films deviate from tradition, as Neale says, only genre benders manipulate genre conventions in ways that intensify the films' ambiguity and unnerving effect. The effect of genre-bending films, therefore, is the opposite of that of genre-breaking films, which give one a sense of mastery by making one feel overly familiar with a genre. Genre benders make one feel inadequate and uncertain because, as *Chinatown*'s Noah Cross says to Jake Gittes, "you may *think* you know what you're dealing with, but, believe me, you don't."

Although few are as generically ingenious as *Chinatown*, several other movies of the period bend their genres in similarly inventive ways. Consider two seventies caper movies, *Thunderbolt and Lightfoot* (1974) and *Dog Day Afternoon* (1975). Although *Dog Day Afternoon* was marketed primarily as a "true crime" film, it employs several caper movie conventions: an urban setting, an emphasis on speed and timing, a bank as the target of the crime, the individualism of our protagonists set against impersonal societal institutions, and a noble motive on the part of a sympathetic criminal hero.[5] The narration, however, frequently injects ordinary concerns into its extraordinary central event, concerns that have no business in a caper movie. What if the hostages have to go to the bathroom? What if the criminal protagonist is bisexual? The genre deviations add an air of authenticity to the depiction of this real-life event, not because it is more authentic to have a bisexual bank robber (although Sonny Wortzik's real-life prototype was indeed bisexual) but because of the random departure from convention. For instance, just as the heist has begun, one of the robbers decides he can't go through with it, and, when Sonny asks him for the keys to the getaway car, the robber replies, "Well, how will I get home?" Whereas conventional genre use helps us predict narrative outcomes, such unexpected and unconventional intrusions of everyday life keep us from getting ahead of the movie, which, at such moments, seems to reflect the randomness of reality.[6]

Thunderbolt and Lightfoot behaves more like a typical caper movie and was marketed as one (the poster for the film read, "He has exactly seven minutes to get rich quick!"). The narration, however, includes elements that do not comfortably fit the genre. For instance, although the protagonists score a big heist, it is not the heist they spent the entire movie meticulously planning. At the end of the movie, one of the robbers dies unexpectedly, not from a gun wound but from a brain hemorrhage, the result of a kick to the head that at the time seemed causally incidental. During the last fifteen minutes of the film—as the character slowly grows paralyzed, first stumbling, then lisping, then passing out and dying—the rules of the universe seem to have changed because nothing like this has ever happened in this kind of movie before.

Leo Braudy alludes to something like genre bending in *The World in a Frame*, and his description helps explain how genre films can use genre to catch audiences unaware. "The genre film," Braudy says, "lures its audience into a seemingly familiar world, filled with reassuring stereotypes of character, action, and plot" (110). Consequently, he says, genre films can make us complacent, an easy target for manipulation. When we encounter a familiar genre cue—town drunk, "I'm just two weeks from retirement," "boil water and tear up some sheets"—we anticipate, out of habit, a limited number of corollary outcomes. But if what follows falls outside the range of traditional generic probabilities, as it does with genre bending, audiences can grow uneasy. If we have never seen the conventions used this way before, we have no way of confidently knowing what to expect. According to Braudy:

> Genre films can exploit the automatic conventions of response for the purposes of pulling the rug out from under their viewers. The very relaxing of the critical intelligence of the audience, the relief that we need not make decisions—aesthetic, moral, metaphysical—about the film, allows the genre film to use our expectations against themselves, and, in the process, reveal to us expectations and assumptions that we may never have thought we had. (110)

Indeed, it can be aesthetically exciting, although potentially disconcerting, when a genre film surprisingly switches from traditional genre use to genre bending, such as when *Thunderbolt and Lightfoot* exploits our cozy familiarity with caper movie scenarios and kills off one of our protagonists in a disarmingly unconventional way.

Ultimately, Braudy, like Cawelti, emphasizes genre films' educational potential, justifying their aesthetic value, for instance, by suggesting that they "reveal to us expectations and assumptions that we may never have thought we had." Braudy stresses genre films' ability to teach viewers about movies (*His Girl Friday* is "a reflection on the importance of women reporters in many other films of the period" [115]), about society (genre films may contain a "radical critique of the values of the society that produced them" [180]), and about themselves ("self-conscious uses of genre can reveal our previous assumptions in a new perspective" [115]). However, when a seemingly conventional scenario ends up violating its own generic probabilities, the violation does not necessarily enlighten us. Rather, the genre benders I consider here largely succeed in keeping us in the dark, always one step behind the narration in our understanding of the story's progress. In fact, as I demonstrate when we turn to *The French Connection*, genre bending often works below the level of conscious detection, exploiting accustomed responses to coded stimuli without letting spectators know they have been so manipulated.

GENRE DEVIATION IN THE 1970S

Genre breaking and genre bending represent opposite responses to the same phenomenon: the feeling, prevalent in the seventies, that Hollywood genres had grown fatigued and that their conventions had worn out their efficacy. The artistic cautiousness of so many sixties genre films—and the commercial failure of so many expensive ones, particularly musicals and epics such as *The Bible* (1966), *Camelot* (1967), *Star!* (1968), and *Battle of Britain* (1969)—accelerated the growing feeling of genre exhaustion. At the same time, however, the industry relied on genre and encouraged genre film production as a form of risk reduction. The financial risks of producing increasingly expensive films for a shrinking audience required stories that had proven appeal and films that could be readily marketed and replicated as sequels, as is the case with many genre films. Moreover, the new generation of directors and screenwriters did not disdain genre filmmaking. On the contrary, enamored with American film history, many of them (including Allen, Altman, De Palma, Fosse, Friedkin, Peckinpah, Penn, Polanski, Scorsese, Schrader, and Towne) showed keen interest in genre filmmaking, albeit of an unconventional sort.

So although the genre system still flourished in Hollywood, many seventies filmmakers sought to challenge its traditions. Seventies genre breakers responded to genre exhaustion by sharing in audience's weariness with film tradition, standing back from the conventions and saying, "You can't manipulate us anymore." Such films were, in effect, sounding genre's death knell. Genre benders, by contrast, responded by using the same old conventions to subtly manipulate audiences in novel ways, breathing new life into dying tropes. The first response seems almost inevitable, given genres' customary progression from classicism, to exhaustion, to parody. The second response, however, is not. Although it necessarily relies on a precedent period of classical genre use, genre bending can appear any time a skilled filmmaker sees an opportunity to exploit spectators' complacent acquiescence to film tradition. One would expect to see genre bending, therefore, during a period in Hollywood, such as the seventies, when audiences were both tired of conventional pictures and excited about cinema's possibilities.

As the foregoing remarks testify, seventies filmmakers did not invent genre-bending. Films such as *The Searchers* (1956), *Vertigo* (1958), and *Psycho* (1960), for example, also rely on our habitual responses to genre conventions in order to mislead us in subtle and unnerving ways. However, when seventies filmmakers turn to genre bending, they generally refrain from resolving the inconsistency between conventional and unconventional genre use, sustaining uneasy and relatively unresolved narrative incongruities. Whereas earlier genre benders periodically reconcile the conflict between convention and deviation so as not to make the films inordinately disharmonious, seventies genre benders increasingly intensify the conflict, straining our ability to resolve story information that the films insist on presenting as deeply incongruous.

A brief look at *Taxi Driver* and *The Searchers* will help distinguish seventies genre bending from that in other periods. The protagonist of *Taxi Driver*, Travis Bickle, is in part modeled after the heroes of some Westerns, private detective movies, and police detective movies of the 1940s and 1950s: a character who takes the law into his own hands in order to save an innocent girl from forces corrupting her. Scriptwriter Paul Schrader and director Martin Scorsese both acknowledged that they patterned Travis in part after John Wayne's Ethan Edwards from *The Searchers*, and we see in both characters a mixture of honorable savior and brutish murderer. In John Ford's Western, two cowboys search for a young girl, Debbie, captured by Comanche Indians. Wayne plays racist Civil War veteran Ethan Edwards, who grows insanely violent when he encounters Indians, firing at a tribe, for instance, as they collect their dead after a fight and shooting at a herd of buffalo with the obsessed intent of starving the Indians to death ("At least they won't feed any Comanche this winter"). He even wants to kill his niece Debbie because she "ain't white anymore." To complicate matters, Debbie does not want to be saved, preferring to stay with the Indian community that captured her. Such incidents call into question the objectives of the film's hero, who appears (at moments that are mostly unconventional for the

Western) vicious, brutish, and foolish and (at more conventional moments) noble, admirable, and exceedingly capable.

Taxi Driver's protagonist shows some of the same dissonances between generically conventional and unconventional behavior that characterize the protagonist of *The Searchers*, but the film continually turns up the volume on the dissonance. For one thing, Robert De Niro is not John Wayne. De Niro's Travis is strange, a social freak who turns to vigilantism to try to give purpose to his lonely life. However, even as the narration reveals Travis's perspective as distorted and disturbed, it uses a variety of generic conventions to ally spectators with the character: voice-over narration, his desire for romantic love, his efforts to save an abducted girl, a montage sequence of meticulous preparation and training, and a climactic shootout with a group of malignant foes. As his actions become more bizarre and unpalatable (starting when he takes his love interest to a pornographic movie and ending with his murderous rampage), the narration increasingly challenges spectators' sympathy for Bickle and ultimately denies spectators much access to his thoughts, until, by the end of the film, his motivations might be incomprehensible. The kind of behavior that Hollywood genre films have taught us to consider satisfying and wholesome (such as an effort to save an innocent girl from a life of crime and degradation) here seems deeply unsettling and even depraved.[7]

In *The Searchers*, both in the end and numerous times along the way, conventionality and resolution supplant the film's deviations from tradition, sometimes flattening out the interesting complications the film has raised. For instance, at the film's conclusion, Debbie changes her mind about wanting to be saved, and Edwards decides to rescue her, instead of shooting her. *Taxi Driver*, by contrast, continually intensifies the incongruity between the film's generically conventional and unconventional elements, and, in the end, genre deviance wins out. Indeed, far from reinforcing stability and resolution, the film's epilogue aggravates the instability and irresolution of the climax when it reveals that the media views Travis's bloodbath as an act of heroism and that he seems not to have worked his depravity out of his system.

We can see now the ways in which seventies genre bending points us to larger narrative patterns in seventies cinema and illustrates the narrative principles we began studying in Chapter Two. Seventies genre benders exploit unrealized potentials in the Hollywood paradigm, mining it for irresolutions, incongruities, and uncertain and discomforting effects that previous generations of Hollywood filmmakers often attempted to avoid. At the same time, such films depend on the paradigm for stability. They challenge the standard practices of Hollywood genre filmmaking, but they rely on those same practices for their very foundation and structure, more like the classical French genre films of the mid-fifties—e.g., *Touchez pas au grisbi* (1954), *Rififi* (1955), and *Bob the Gambler* 1956)—than the more eccentric French art films of the sixties, such as *Breathless* (1960) and *Shoot the Piano Player* (1960), which allude to American genre cinema but forego its stabilizing structure. Finally, genre benders show a perverse tendency to integrate narrative devices (e.g., *Taxi Driver*'s creepy, dissolute protagonist) counterproductive to their own generic purposes (e.g., a climactic shootout with gangsters and pimps). To use the formulation from Stephen Booth with which we began this book, genre benders flirt with disaster at the same time that they wed themselves to the reliable order and purpose of the classical Hollywood model.

Scholars have given little critical attention to genre bending because the films do not form a tight group and because their uses of genre, more subtle than those of genre-breaking films, are also more difficult to demonstrate persuasively. However, these very qualities make them worthy of closer consideration. Consequently, we should analyze in some detail the narration of one exemplary genre bender from the seventies in order to understand the peculiar narrative mode of seventies genre bending. The 1971 blockbuster *The French Connection* offers us a perfect case study. Normally regarded as the supreme example of the police detective film (sometimes called the "cop movie," "*policier*," or "police thriller"), the film is in fact a poor representative of the genre that critics have generally supposed it to epitomize. *The French Connection* is famous for its action scenes, but its use of police detective film conventions is far more complex than film criticism has previously acknowledged and more complex than the film's flashy veneer would lead one to predict.

THE FRENCH CONNECTION AND THE POLICE DETECTIVE FILM

The back of *The French Connection*'s video box reads as follows: "An action-packed thriller culminating in the biggest narcotics seizure of all time and the capture of all the smugglers . . . except one." (The ellipsis is the box's own, not mine.) The video box description makes the movie sound like any other movie one might find in the "Action" section of the video store. By emphasizing the size of the narcotics seizure, the description highlights the success of the detectives, not the failure that is the ultimate focus of *The French Connection*'s narration. The video box neglects to mention, for instance, that, while police captured all but one smuggler, most of them, the film tells us, subsequently went free. The description even manages to make the escape of the main drug smuggler sound, through a strategically placed ellipsis, like an exciting turn in the story, rather than the detectives' most glaring blunder. The box misrepresents the film, ignoring those aspects of *The French Connection* that do not fit within the police detective genre or distorting them until they sound as though they do.[8]

Like most video box descriptions, this one illustrates moviegoers' affection for genre. The writer of the blurb recognized that many filmgoers prefer action movies that seem already familiar. Genre promises an experience similar to ones we have enjoyed in the past, and it makes what's new and potentially unusual appear already normal and comprehensible. Genre instills confidence in one's ability to predict outcomes. Like any other ritual, genre tells us where we are and where we are going.[9]

The French Connection exploits spectator confidence in generic promises by surreptitiously doctoring the police detective formula. The film cues spectators to do what the back of the video box does: restrict the movie to its genre's boundaries. In the end, however, the narrative moves so far beyond those boundaries that it undermines efforts to limit the movie to the dimensions of its generic mold. The narrative works like a joke: It sets up perceivers by appearing to head in a familiar and appropriate direction, but it ends somewhere off the mark it seemed to have been shooting for. And like a joke, the narration, as we will see, has been surreptitiously preparing spectators for its ending all along. *The French Connection* cues spectators to draw conclusions that the film's genre and narrative patterning have made improbable.

Before discussing the aspects of the film that make it unusual for its genre, we must first look at the similarities between *The French Connection* and other police detective films. Doing so will allow us to see that, prior to its conclusion, *The French Connection* works in many ways like a traditional genre film. I modify that point when I examine the film's surreptitious deviations from its genre, but it can stand provisionally.

Gene Hackman plays Popeye Doyle, a violent renegade cop. Doyle leads the police department in arrests but is nonetheless distrusted and resented by a department overly concerned with regulations and not concerned enough with the business of catching criminals. Working mainly on instinct, Doyle is rough, uncompromising, and obsessively committed to his case.

My description of Doyle could apply to the lead character of just about any police detective film released either before or after *The French*

Connection, including the other major police detective film released the same year, *Dirty Harry*. Harry Callahan (Clint Eastwood) is, like Doyle, violent and headstrong, a renegade and a racist. According to a fellow officer, "Harry hates everybody—limeys, micks, hebes, fat dagos, niggers, honkies, chinks. You name it." He is in constant conflict with his superiors about his disregard of regulations and excessive use of force. The most genre-typical exchange in *Dirty Harry* occurs between Callahan and the district attorney (the movie's spokesperson for the rule of law) shortly after Harry apprehends a murderous psychopath:

> D.A. Where the hell does it say you've got a right to kick down doors, torture suspects, deny medical attention. Where have you been? Does Escobedo ring a bell? Miranda? I mean you must have heard of the fourth amendment. What I'm saying is that man had rights.
> HARRY. Well I'm all broken up about that man's rights . . .
> D.A. This rifle might make a nice souvenir, but it's inadmissible as evidence. . . . It's the law.
> HARRY. Well then the law is crazy.

Drawing attention to the legal system's inefficiency in prosecuting criminals, the scene endorses Harry's vilification of "the law." Constitution or no Constitution, Harry has a point.

Most police detective movies made just prior to 1971 followed the same formula. In *Madigan* (1968), Richard Widmark also plays a rough, unscrupulous police detective, who, according to Chief Inspector Charles Kane, nonetheless holds "more departmental citations for heroism and excellent service" than any other badge in the department. Kane has the following conversation with Police Commissioner Russell after Madigan allows a murder suspect to escape:

> RUSSELL. Damn that Madigan. He was bound to get caught in a ringer sooner or later.
> KANE. Madigan's a good cop, Tony. Doesn't always go by the book—
> RUSSELL. I like the book, Charlie.

Constantly in conflict with his superiors, Madigan searches resolutely for the murderer, using any means, legal or not, to track down the criminal he has lost.

Steve McQueen's title character in 1968's *Bullitt*, while a good deal more wholesome than Callahan and Madigan, displays many of the same qualities. Detective Bullitt is nonconciliatory, uncompromising, and determined to catch his criminal. He has impeccable instincts about crime, doesn't play by the rules, and periodically ignores his superiors' orders. Midway through the movie, Captain Bennett tells him to "play it by the book from now on." Bullitt, of course, plays it his own way, and runs into the same conflict with his superiors that we see again and again in *Madigan* and *Dirty Harry*. In all of these movies, the detectives' instincts are always right and their superiors' always wrong, although the films' spectators are the only ones who know it.

The conventions of the police detective genre extend back to the police *noir* films of the 1950s. Detective Sergeant Walter Brown, for instance, from *The Narrow Margin* (1952), Detective Sergeant Mark Dixon from *Where the Sidewalk Ends* (1950), and Detective Wilson from *On Dangerous Ground* (1952) display the thriller cop's characteristic roughness—they are tough cops who get results. Wilson's superior frequently bawls him out for his brutal tactics: "Make up your mind to be a cop, not a gangster with a badge." Detective Sergeant Bannion from *The Big Heat* (1953) exhibits all the traits of a full-blown thriller cop of the sixties and seventies: He is rough, stubborn, lawless, and insubordinate, his intuitions invariably right. After he barges into the home of the city's main mobster, Bannion engages in the following exchange with Lieutenant Wilks:

> WILKS. What makes you think you can walk into Lagana's house and slug his bodyguard? . . .
>
> BANNION. I'm trying to tell you that nothing dirty happens in this city without Lagana's OK.
>
> WILKS. I'm not interested in your theories, not when they affect my job. You're just begging to go back into uniform, pounding a beat out in the sticks.

Lieutenant Diamond in *The Big Combo* (1955) exhibits the same character traits as Bannion and has the identical relationship with his superior. Captain Peterson bawls out Diamond for arresting the city's biggest mobster and all his hoodlums—"Ninety-six false arrests!"—and then closes the case. But Diamond is a fanatic, like Bannion, obsessively driving at the case anyway until all of the hoodlums are dead or arrested.

Whereas the straight-laced police officers of many late forties police detective films—such as *The Naked City* (1948) and *He Walked by Night* (1948)—display a chummy camaraderie with their superiors, by the late sixties, the tension between the cop and his superiors had become generic orthodoxy. That tension became so integral to the genre that *They Call Me Mister Tibbs!* (1970) includes it despite the fact that the story contains no motivation for it: Captain Marden screams at the upstanding Tibbs for the flimsiest of reasons, as though merely to satisfy the generic requirement. The convention remains active in police detective films today.

The dialogue from the earlier police detective films is too heavy-handed for *The French Connection*, but the formulas imbedded in the dialogue are not. Doyle's immediate superior, Simonson (played by Eddie "Popeye" Egan, the real-life detective on whom Doyle is based), distrusts Doyle. Theirs is the stock relationship of the genre. When Doyle and his partner, "Cloudy" Russo, want to wiretap a suspect, Simonson cites the rule of law: "The first thing you know you'll wind up in an entrapment wrap, the both of ya." FBI agent Mulderig, who is teamed with Doyle and Russo, also challenges Doyle continually and holds a more personal grudge: "I know Popeye. His brilliant hunches cost the life of a good cop." Mulderig takes every opportunity to get in Doyle's way, coming across as more despicable than any of the criminals because his attacks on Doyle are so personal.

Whereas Simonson and Mulderig distrust Doyle, *The French Connection*'s narrational devices endorse Doyle's instincts by aligning spectators with him. An early scene, in which Doyle and Russo visit a nightclub, helps demonstrate that alignment. When Doyle sees someone spreading money around the club, he becomes suspicious. "That table is definitely wrong," he says. Like Doyle, the narration is itself suspicious of the people at the table and cues spectators not to trust them. The shots of Doyle and Russo sitting at the bar are steady, but those of the table use a shaky, handheld camera that makes the characters look suspect. We peer at the characters through Doyle's eyes without hearing them (Figure 4.1). Instead, we hear eerie, high-pitched music along with Doyle and Russo's banter ("Dig the creep that's coming to the table now." "That's Jewish Lucky. He don't look the same without numbers across his chest"). The subjective cinematography and sound conform to Doyle's appraisal of the characters: Like him, we know the table is "definitely wrong"; we can feel it. Doyle appears, at least at that moment, a generically suitable police detective.

FIGURE 4.1. *The French Connection*: Popeye Doyle's POV shot makes people at a table look "definitely wrong."

One scene most tellingly illustrates *The French Connection*'s use of police detective film conventions. The scene has all of the genre's fundamental elements: a headstrong cop working on instinct, obsessing over his case, trying to convince his reluctant superiors to let him continue an investigation that spectators know is worthwhile. In those respects, the scene is pure formula. Simonson wants to scrap the case: "If there was a deal, it's gone down by now." Doyle won't accept his supervisor's judgment: "I know the deal hasn't gone down. I know it. I can feel it. I'm dead certain." Agent Mulderig sparks a fistfight when he butts in, "The last time you were dead certain we ended with a dead cop." It's a cheap shot, spoken spitefully, and, what's more, an earlier scene has already revealed to us that Mulderig and Simonson are wrong, that the criminals have put off the exchange and are planning to kill Popeye. Simonson yells at Doyle, "No collars are coming in while you two guys are running around town jerking off. Now go back to work! You're off special assignment!" The last line alone tells us the film's genre.

Anyone who has not seen *The French Connection* is probably wondering at this point why it is considered exceptional among police detective films. The story, as I have described it, seems formulaic, and one famous car chase cannot sustain a film's reputation for distinction. I said earlier that, aside from its surprising ending, in many ways *The French Connection* works as a standard police detective film. However, although much of *The French Connection* follows police detective film convention, several incidents throughout the film disrupt the generic simplicity of the story and distinguish the film from conventional police thrillers. "Incidents" is the right word because the movie treats these story elements as though they are merely incidental. Like its hero, the film remains fixed on its goal: catching criminals. However, like all genre benders, the film strategically combines genre convention and genre deviation in ways that cue spectators to falsely predict narrative outcomes. Ultimately, the film builds its conclusion on the deviations, giving them a retrospective impact that they did not carry initially. Such deviations merely hint at a narrative pattern that becomes fully realized only at the film's conclusion.

To explain the effect of such incidents, I want to return to the scene that culminates in Doyle's removal from the case because my description omitted one aspect that makes the scene unusual. The scene is set at the site of a car crash superfluous to the main narrative. The characters barely mention the crash, which is precisely what makes its inclusion strange.[10] Visiting the site simply to talk to Simonson, Doyle seems completely indifferent to the bloody, dead teenagers pulled from the cars around him. He doesn't even notice them. *We* notice because the film inserts six brief shots of the bodies (Figures 4.2 and 4.3), but the narration pays only slightly more attention to them than Doyle does. For the most part, the camera follows the main story line—Doyle's argument with Simonson and Mulderig—occasionally interspersing shots of the shocking setting. Although the deaths are extraneous to the causal chain of the story, and hence less central to the narrative than Doyle's unjust dismissal from the case, it seems strange that neither Doyle nor the movie itself seems to care about those dead accident victims.

That scene is one of many that prompt questions about the ethics of the film's hero and the ethos of the film itself. Several other scenes insert similarly minor events that run contrary to police detective film convention, which traditionally proceeds to its climactic conclusion virtually undisturbed by spectators' ethical misgivings. Immediately after the car crash scene, one of the French criminals shoots at Doyle from a rooftop. The sniper accidentally

FIGURE 4.2.   FIGURE 4.3.

FIGURES 4.2–4.3. *The French Connection*: brief shots of crash victims whom Detective Doyle does not notice.

(and incidentally) hits a woman pushing a baby carriage. The woman falls, Doyle tells bystanders to leave her, but the narration never attends to her or comments on her death: no shots of her body, no paramedics, no weeping child, no parents identifying the body at the city morgue. She is completely out of the picture. The narration abandons the woman and moves forward into arguably the most gripping car chase ever filmed: a chase (again incidentally) that depicts Doyle as a maniac (Figure 4.4), recklessly smashing cars and speeding through intersections, and that culminates when he shoots his unarmed suspect in the back (Figure 4.5). Like the dead bodies in the car wreck scene, the mother's death and Doyle's mania do not serve the main story line and are therefore of less consequence than the chase, which dominates the narration.

FIGURE 4.4. Doyle screams maniacally during *The French Connection*'s famous car chase.

FIGURE 4.5. *The French Connection*: The car chase culminates when Doyle shoots his unarmed suspect in the back.

To a certain extent, the narration allies spectators with Doyle, who gives only fleeting attention to events outside his primary goal of catching criminals. In that respect, the film exploits the parallel between Doyle's drive to solve the case and spectators' drive to resolve the narrative. But the narration gives slightly more attention to outside events than Doyle does. Indeed, although the narration, like Doyle, focuses primarily on the business of catching the French drug smugglers, it nonetheless disturbs that fanatical interest with incidental story elements that seem superfluous to, and incongruous with, the story's causal chain and generic identity.

The most disturbing sight of all is Doyle himself, a lecherous, reckless, slovenly, lawless, foul-mouthed drunk who seems to enjoy beating up people. Moreover, he is a terrible racist, and not an indiscriminate racist like Harry Callahan, who "hates everybody," including "honkies." Doyle hates blacks. "Never trust a nigger," he says to Russo, recently stabbed by a black suspect. Doyle harasses dozens of African Americans in the movie, shaking down an entire bar, for instance, just to make contact with one informant. The most troubling aspect of his racism is that the movie never condemns him for it. The racism is not exaggerated and does not seem to interfere with his police work. Except for one tame comment by Doyle's partner (Russo's reply to Doyle's "Never trust a nigger" is "He could have been white"), none of the film's characters seems to notice his bigotry.

Actor Gene Hackman does not temper the character's disturbing traits; he emphasizes them. In his first leading role in a major film, Hackman gives a confident, physical performance of a man who too much enjoys the powers afforded him by his dirty job. Although Hackman lends Doyle the actor's natural charisma, he also instills the character with a gruff, abrasive energy: drumming his fingers, banging on tables and cars, smacking his chewing gum even as he's drinking, rubbing his face, chomping food, running his tongue along the inside of his bottom lip. The actor never stays still. And his movements have nothing gentle or refined about them. Doyle's manic energy only heightens when he converses with other characters, whom he generally treats impatiently, as though he's trying to move conversations forward as fast as possible. When other characters don't respond quickly enough, he shouts, even at his supervisor, or bangs his hand into them. The ease with which he harasses characters he doesn't like, a crooked smirk on his face, the salacious look he gives young women wearing leather boots, and the delight he appears to take in beating suspects give the impression of a heartless operator.

Doyle differs from the clean-cut Bullitt or even "Dirty" Harry Callahan, who, though equally unscrupulous about the law, seems more honorable than Doyle. Harry may be a brute and a renegade, but *Dirty Harry* does not allow spectators to feel so disturbed by Harry's antisocial qualities. Besides, unlike Doyle, Harry seems to hate what he does. His adversary, moreover, behaves so vilely that he must be stopped, and only Harry has the gumption to do it. *Dirty Harry* portrays the Bill of Rights as merely a document that interferes with effective law enforcement. *The French Connection* prompts spectators to question not only the protagonist's tactics but also his commitment to the public good.

Questions about Doyle's ethics do not fit within the parameters of the police detective genre, a genre that might allow for mild disapproval but rarely overt condemnation. Since the narration does not confirm such questions by depicting characters who similarly question Doyle's behavior, and since our impression of the character results in many ways from nuances of Hackman's portrayal, rather than from more explicit story information (the film does not portray Doyle as corrupt, for instance), one's concerns about Doyle are likely to feel personal and individual. We can see such concerns in the film's critics, many of whom feel they must convince others that Doyle is *really* a bad cop, despite the fact that no one seems to disagree.

One critic of the film literally thought that he was the only one bothered by Doyle's uglier traits. An editorial for the *New York Times* says that *The French Connection*

> is merely a celebration of authority, brutality and racism. . . . It is true that police practices across the country are racist, but there is a vital difference between demonstrating this fact, which the movie does not, and approving it, which it does. I saw the film in a Southern city, and the white audience responded enthusiastically to the scenes of Doyle roughing up black people. (Epps, II15)

The author believes he was alone in his reaction, and perhaps he was. (Still, it's hard to imagine how the author would have known if there were like-minded spectators in the audience with him.) But, in any case, there is a clear discrepancy between how he feels about the movie (troubled by the racism and brutality) and how he feels the movie *wants* him to feel (celebratory). Even if those white southerners displayed as much enthusiasm as the author says, he is in any case taken in by the subtlety of the film's manipulation, a subtlety that leads him to condemn the movie as racist. The author wants *The French Connection* to be as obvious as a genre-breaking film, in which case it would not only advertise its position toward police violence but also congratulate the audience for sharing it.

The French Connection uses genre convention (which allies spectators with the protagonist's goals) and genre deviance (which prompts questions about the protagonist's tactics, values, and character traits) in ways that create ideological incongruities in the film's narration, incongruities that help account for some of the urgent denunciations of the film's hero. Attacks on Doyle are not unwarranted, just suspiciously adamant, suggesting that the commentators do not trust that other spectators saw in the movie what they did. Whereas genre films, as Braudy says, generally "make us one with a large mass audience, often despite our more articulate and elitist views" (113), genre benders, because of their ambiguity, can make us feel our experiences are idiosyncratic. *The French Connection* panders to our sense that we are more observant, more sensitive, and more moral than the mass of viewers around us.

We can see such elitism exhibited in Michael Shedlin's 1972 *Film Quarterly* essay on *The French Connection*. Shedlin puts distance between himself and the viewers manipulated by the film's "subliminal message" that authoritarian police are good and necessary (4). However, it is difficult to understand how a police detective film that ends by discrediting the detective can be seen, as Shedlin writes, ultimately to reinforce "the heroism of the authorities it seems to be criticizing" (3). Shedlin fails to recognize that his responses to Doyle are entirely typical, evidenced in part by the film's reviewers, who, whether they praised the film or panned it, regularly remarked on the racism and brutality of the detective.[11] Indeed, as far as I can tell, and I've looked very thoroughly, no commentators on the movie endorse Doyle or his methods. Shedlin goes on to argue that audiences view Doyle's "fascism, homicidal compulsion and white supremacy" as "minor character flaws" that serve only to make Doyle "someone we can identify with" (4). Shedlin does not include himself in the "we" who identify with Doyle and provides no evidence that other spectators do. Indeed, such character traits evidently *impede* viewers, including Shedlin, from identifying with the protagonist.

In a more recent critique, the blurb on *The French Connection* in the *Time Out Film Guide* also accuses the film of endorsing the ideology of its protagonist: "The film maintains no critical distance from (indeed, rather relishes) its 'loveable' hero's brutal vigilante psychology" (Pym, 307). "Loveable" is in quotes presumably because, like Shedlin and the *New York Times* commentator, the author thinks the movie encourages spectators to delight in Doyle. The only thing we can say for sure, however, is that the movie encourages spectators to think that *other* spectators delight in him.

THE FRENCH CONNECTION'S DEVIANT CONCLUSION

The ending of *The French Connection* plays a subtle joke on spectators, unpredictably altering the film's narrative trajectory. The final scenes denote that Doyle's righteous battle with the drug smugglers is not the ultimate concern of the film. In the end, the narrative becomes *about* all the troubling elements that have interfered with a conventional depiction of a police detective protagonist, the very elements that distinguish *The French Connection* from most films in its genre.

During the climactic shootout, Doyle and Russo follow the chief French smuggler, Alain Charnier, into an abandoned warehouse. Doyle says confidently, "Frog One is in that room," and we have no reason to doubt him. He sees a figure moving in the shade and fires several rounds. The two detectives move toward the dead body, which is, in fact, that of Agent Mulderig. Shocked, Russo says, "You shot Mulderig." Reloading, Doyle replies, "That sonofabitch is here. I saw him. I'm gonna get him," and he runs into another part of the warehouse and disappears. A single shot rings out and the screen turns black. That shot does not conclude the movie, but we should pause here to examine the death of Agent Mulderig.[12]

Mulderig is perhaps the most offensive character in the film, continually hounding Doyle for causing the death of a fellow officer; however, his death proves him absolutely right about Doyle's trigger-happiness. To Russo's dismay, Doyle is indifferent to the accidental shooting: Instead of lamenting Mulderig's killing, or even noticing it, Doyle reloads his gun and goes after Charnier. Although the film has never shown Doyle caring much about anything except catching criminals, his callousness about shooting an FBI agent is the most vicious instance of his disinterest in outside events.

The change in the narration's depiction of Doyle is bolstered by the change in cinematography during the scene of Mulderig's death. Before Doyle kills Mulderig, the narration aligns spectators with their protagonist by restricting itself to shots of Doyle's pursuit and shots of the surroundings accessible to his point of view. The camera tracks him as he heads determinedly toward the room in which he thinks Charnier is hiding (Figure 4.6). As in the earlier scene in the bar, his point-of-view shots make the room appear suspicious: The camera slowly zooms in on the room as eerie music is heard on the soundtrack.

The cinematography after the killing makes Doyle himself look suspicious. A medium close-up now centers attention on Doyle's facial expression, emphasizing his astonishing indifference to his mistake, rather than on the pursuit of Charnier (Figure 4.7). Low-key lighting, which casts heavy shadows across his face, and a slightly low angle make him look peculiar. Moreover, he no longer looks certain of Charnier's whereabouts, scanning the room, rather than purposefully pursuing him. As Doyle, now swirling around wildly, races to find the criminal, the camera does not track with him anymore or provide his point of view. Instead, the camera remains stationary as he moves farther away (Figure 4.8), until he disappears around a corner and we hear the off-screen blast. For the first time in the film, the cinematography seems in tune with one's misgivings about Doyle.

Immediately after that gunshot, pictures of the captured criminals appear on the screen, along with captions indicating that most of their cases were dismissed or their sentences reduced or suspended. We then see a photograph of "Frog One" smirking—a still shot from the scene in the subway station in which he wittily evaded Doyle—with the following caption: "ALAIN CHARNIER was never caught," and, "He is believed to be living in France" (Figure 4.9). The last picture is of Doyle and Russo, and their caption reads: "Detectives DOYLE and RUSSO were transferred out of the Narcotics Bureau and reassigned." The screen fades out and the credits roll.

FIGURE 4.6. *The French Connection:* The camera tracks with Doyle as he searches for Charnier.

FIGURE 4.7. *The French Connection*: A medium close-up of Doyle emphasizes his indifference to his accidental killing of an FBI agent, and low-key lighting and a slightly low angle make him look peculiar.

FIGURE 4.8. *The French Connection*: After Doyle accidentally kills FBI agent Mulderig, the camera remains stationary as Doyle swirls around wildly and withdraws from the scene.

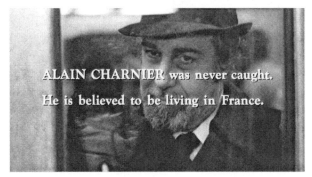

FIGURE 4.9. *The French Connection*: A still shot shows a smirking "Frog One."

On the one hand, the closing captions could inspire a generically conventional lamentation for the inefficiency of the courts, the ineptitude of which allows the criminals to go free. Only two of the criminals, Lou Boca and Henri Devereaux—the definition of "small potatoes"—serve any time in prison, the toughest sentence going to Devereaux, whom the movie portrays as a naive pawn in Charnier's criminal conspiracy. But on the other hand, the courts alone are not to blame, especially since the police never caught Charnier. That failure is clearly Doyle's, and, taken together, the captions—which come at the point in the film when, according to police detective film convention, the detective is vindicated—contribute to the impression that Doyle has bungled the job. That Doyle has killed another officer during the seizure makes his failure not just flagrant but fatally negligent. *Dirty Harry* ends when Callahan kills his suspect and triumphantly throws his badge into a river. At the end of *The French Connection*, Doyle and Russo are reassigned in disgrace.

The ending of the movie capitalizes on the fact that the stock virtues of a generic police detective have a darker side. In Doyle, these virtues emerge ambiguously as character flaws, the cause of his failure as a cop. His energetic pursuit of crime and disregard of the law are linked to his brutality. His determination and obsessive commitment to his case emerge as fanaticism and callous indifference to victims. His instinctive, shoot-from-the-hip temperament leads him to accidentally kill a fellow officer. The movie teaches spectators to trust Doyle's instincts, despite his flaws, and then presents him as untrustworthy, exposing finally the inadequacy and harsh indifference of the detective we mistook for our hero. The only consolation is that the police seized the heroin, poor recompense for the trouble, expense, and loss of life. The movie does not even mention the seizure (unlike the video box blurb, which emphasizes it, trying arduously and speciously to make the detectives look triumphant). Whereas all along the narration had largely allied spectators with Doyle against his critics, the end of the film largely allies spectators with the critics against Doyle. For probably the only time in police detective film history, the detective's critics, it turns out, knew better than the audience.

Common sense says that *The French Connection*'s conclusion would cause spectators to recognize that they have been wrong about the movie all along. Common sense might also lead one to assume that, by the end, the film has taught spectators something about the myth of the infallible Hollywood police detective. Common sense is wrong. Because the film has surreptitiously prepared for its disturbing conclusion, the ending does not come as an ironic revelation but rather as an extension of troubling incidents that have appeared throughout the movie, albeit only on the periphery of the screen. At the end, such throwaway incidents seem to define our hero; however, they do so only in retrospect since, at the time, they were extraneous, even impertinent, to the film's main narrative. The non-formulaic ending is certainly unexpected, but the film has prepared us for it because Doyle has from the beginning behaved with the same callousness, impetuousness, and fanaticism that he exhibits at the film's end. The shift in spectators' understanding of the story feels appropriate because the ending draws on story information already available to spectators. Moreover, even though the ending prompts spectators to reevaluate the portrayal of their protagonist, the film has all along depicted Doyle ambiguously, an ambiguity that no doubt elicits the adamant condemnations expressed in some critics' reviews.

The French Connection does not overtly challenge its genre's assumptions or critique the police detective film's often glorified portrayal of police brutality. Unlike genre-breaking movies, which comment on genre by self-consciously calling attention to it, *The French Connection* exploits the ambiguities of the police detective film's standard tropes without ever advertising the ways in which it has altered them. Indeed, if the movie did have something to say about its genre, then presumably audiences would hear it, but all the evidence suggests that this genre bender never makes viewers aware that it has used their generic expectations to manipulate them. Whereas genre breakers invite viewers to share in the joke about genre, *The French Connection* uses genre to play a joke on viewers themselves, a joke so subtle that, though they fall for it, they don't seem to get it.

CHAPTER 5 CONCEPTUAL INCONGRUITY
AND *THE EXORCIST*

hat follows is a conceptually tidy ending common in action movies of the past two decades or more, an ending so familiar and specific that I am surprised I haven't seen it parodied:

The protagonist (let's say the protagonist is female) and the villain (let's say the villain is male) have met in their final confrontation, and the villain finds himself at the protagonist's mercy with a gun pointed at him. The villain then makes a taunting remark, such as, "You don't have the guts" or "I'm unarmed and the law says you can't shoot me" or "You won't do it because you know you'll have to live with it for the rest of your life." The protagonist buys the villain's argument: "You're not worth it," she says, or "The killing stops here." Then, to the consternation of the audience, she throws down her gun or lowers her guard. Predictably, the villain pulls a concealed weapon from his sock. The protagonist is then *forced* to kill the villain, or perhaps another lead character (sometimes the movie's spokesperson for pacifism) unexpectedly appears to finish the job. Before the villain dies, the camera establishes his surprised recognition of defeat.

I first took notice of this scenario in 1994 when I saw three movies with the same ending (*Surviving the Game*, *The Lion King*, and *The River Wild*), but the scenario serves as the climax to countless movies for more than twenty years—including *Lethal Weapon* (1987), *Hook* (1991), *Bad Boys* (1995), *Copycat* (1995), *The Jackal* (1997), *The Postman* (1997), *U.S. Marshals* (1998), *Blue Streak* (1999), *Double Jeopardy* (1999), *Rush Hour 2* (2001), *Spiderman* (2002), *The Count of Monte Cristo* (2002), *Enough*

(2002), *Hellboy II* (2008)—and it also appears in studio-era films, such as *My Darling Clementine* (1946) and *Wagon Master* (1950). The scene's defining factor is that the hero does not wish to shoot the villain (unlike, say, Harry Callahan from *Dirty Harry* [1971], who, though he gives the villain a chance to stay alive at the end, clearly wants to kill him).

This popular ending to recent action films strategically avoids the potential for ideological incongruity imbedded in a story in which both heroes and villains use violence to resolve problems. Whereas, in movies, violence often provides the quickest and most satisfying means of making problems go away, it also threatens to ally the hero ethically with the villain. Consequently, action movies generally construct scenarios in which violence emerges as the protagonist's only effective solution to narrative urgencies. The scene I describe offers violent revenge and moral justification at the same time. The ending establishes, once and forever, an ethical distinction between the protagonist and the villain, avoiding the implication that they come from the same mold. At the same time, it enacts the revenge the film has predicted ever since the villain started behaving villainously. The scene is wonderfully logical, even brilliant, the first few times.

We saw in Chapter Two that conceptual incongruities in a film can take several forms: *moral* or *ideological incongruities*, which indicate a discrepancy between different ethical beliefs or belief systems contained in a movie; *factual contradictions*, when story information contradicts other story information; *logical inconsistencies*, which denote inconsistencies in a story's underlying system of principles or in the inferences one derives from them; and *characterological inconsistencies*, when characters behave in ways inconsistent with their previous characterizations. Whereas Hollywood film-makers, in order to avoid ambiguity, normally try to harmonize potential incongruities in a film's ideology, facts, logic, and characterizations, many seventies filmmakers present story information that threatens to undermine their films' conceptual coherence. Unlike the hero-villain scenario described above, for instance, films of the seventies often resist establishing their heroes' ethical superiority, capitalizing on the potential for moral incongruity present, but often unexplored, in traditional Hollywood scenarios. The seventies certainly produced plenty of movies with coherently defined heroes and villains—e.g., *Bedknobs and Broomsticks* (1971), *The Sting* (1973)—yet the period also saw a lot of movies in which the hero and villain were the same character, movies that refrain from clearly defining their moral attitude toward their protagonists. *Carrie* (1976) exploited the conflict between righteous and deviant teenage rebellion that was present, but more tempered, in earlier high school films, such as *Rebel Without a Cause* (1955) and *Blackboard Jungle* (1955). *A Clockwork Orange* (1971) and *The Godfather, Part II* (1974) intensified the incongruity between attitudes of celebration and condemnation toward criminal protagonists found in so many studio-era crime films. *Taxi Driver* (1976) intensified ideological incongruities inherent in films, such as *Stagecoach* (1939) and *The Big Heat* (1953), in which protagonists take the law into their own hands.

As such cases suggest, the roots of seventies conceptual incongruities can be found in Hollywood's own past. We have already identified the influence of foreign art films on the narrative strategies of seventies cinema, but Hollywood itself also contributed sources for its own narrative change. So before we examine a seventies case study of conceptual incongruity, we should understand something about the genealogy and evolution of conceptual incongruity in Hollywood, from its more muffled expression in movies from the studio era—first in crime films and later in horror films—to its more disquieting revival in more recent Hollywood cinema. By looking at studio-era films alongside seventies and post-seventies films, we can see not only the development of narrative perversity in Hollywood cinema but also the lasting impact of seventies narration on contemporary American film. I want to focus in particular on the endings of movies because, emblematic of larger trends, endings point us to the chief quality that contemporary Hollywood narrative gained from the 1970s: the ability to create and sustain conceptual incongruities without the pressure to resolve them.

HOLLYWOOD ENDINGS: BEFORE AND AFTER THE 1970S

More so than films of the studio era, seventies films, at the moment of conclusion, refused to resolve or cloak the incongruous ideas generated by their narration. Studio filmmakers generally guided their films toward harmonious, usually upbeat, endings, often smoothing over conceptual incongruities generated along the way. In contrast, seventies filmmakers created a trend in films—*Mean Streets* (1973), *The Long Goodbye* (1973), *Thunderbolt and Lightfoot* (1974), *Taxi Driver* (1976), and *Network* (1976) are but a few examples—that conclude with moments that are at the same time narratively decisive and pointedly irresolute in the ideas they provoke.

Although the tendency in contemporary Hollywood narration, as in the studio era, is toward conceptual resolution, conceptually unresolved endings have grown more widespread, even somewhat traditional, since the 1970s. We saw in Chapter Three that, in *The Godfather*'s final moments, Michael's lie to Kay makes him look hypocritical and ruthless at the very moment it unites the two characters, resolves the tension in the scene, and solidifies his successful achievement of his objectives. Many more-recent Hollywood films similarly prompt the spectator to evaluate their endings based on incongruous ideas. At the conclusion of *The Silence of the Lambs* (1991), for example, Hannibal "The Cannibal" Lecter's witty closing line, "I'm having an old friend for dinner," upsets the possibility of conceptual coherence. On the one hand, the joke comes at the expense of one of the most repugnant characters in the movie: Chilton, the psychiatrist, a character whom the movie never punishes properly until the end. William Paul points to the moment's narrative closure when he says that it allows Lecter to take the revenge against Chilton that FBI agent Clarice Starling herself cannot take and that it "rids society of one of its undesirable members and forwards the good work of the FBI," providing "an odd reassurance that the safe social order we desire has been preserved" (428). On the other hand, the ending's "odd reassurance" also raises a troubling conceptual incongruity: The ending undermines Starling's success even as it comes during a party celebrating the FBI's achievement. In the process of stopping one serial killer, the FBI has unleashed another.

In numerous contemporary American films, the protagonists seem to both win (i.e., achieve their objectives) and lose at the same moment. At the end of *The Talented Mr. Ripley* (1999), our protagonist gets away with murder, but his success comes when circumstances force him to kill the only character in the film who offers him love and a chance of happiness. The triumph of the two hit men at the conclusion of *Pulp Fiction* (1994) is threatened by our foreknowledge that one of them will soon die. Although the end of Terry Gilliam's *Brazil* (1985) shows our protagonist arrested and tortured because of a bureaucratic error, the film has something of a happy ending because, having gone insane, the protagonist enters the idyllic fantasy world he has been dreaming about since the opening credits, blithely oblivious to his dreadful circumstances. All of these endings—like those of *Thelma and Louise* (1991), *Starship Troopers* (1997), *Memento* (2000), and numerous other post-seventies American films—are compelling for the same reason the ending of *The Godfather* is compelling: A decisive narrative resolution precludes the possibility of a decisive conceptual resolution.

Before the 1970s

We can trace the conceptual incongruities in cinema of the "New Hollywood," which most scholars define as the film industry since the late 1960s, back to the studio era. Working within the largely felicitous and harmonious "classical" mode, studio-era filmmakers often incorporated into their movies conceptual incongruities that, although less disconcerting and pointed than those one finds in seventies and post-seventies cinema, still tested the conceptual harmony and resolution of the classical model. One can find such moments in any number of studio-era movies, but crime films offer some of the most illustrative examples because the genre, with its paradoxical interest in celebrating and condemning criminals, comes closest to displaying the kinds of incongruities we see in New Hollywood cinema.

Conceptual incongruities in studio-era crime films resulted partly from the fact that studio filmmakers, under pressure from the industry's Production Code Administration (PCA) and state and municipal censors, sometimes contorted crime narratives in order to ensure exhibition. The PCA, according to Stephen Prince, protected studios from regional censors by providing prompt feedback about potentially objectionable material in their scripts and finished films (see Prince, *Classical*). Consequently, the Code (written in 1930 but not fully enforced until July 1934, when most of the studios agreed to abide by its provisions) regulated the depiction of some of the standard subject matter of the crime genre, such as illicit sex, criminal behavior, violence, and vulgarity.

James Naremore notes that PCA intervention often resulted in incongruities in Hollywood cinema's portrayal of ideologically controversial material because the activity of censorship usually "manifests itself as a slight incoherence or displacement" in a film's narrative, and one can see in such displacements "many of the things that censorship was trying to repress."[1] Indeed, regional censorship and PCA regulation sometimes led to complex ideological inconsistencies within crime films that sought to abide by Code provisions—"the sympathy of the audience should never be thrown to the side of the crime, wrong-doing, evil or sin"; evil should not be "made to appear attractive or alluring" or good "to appear unattractive"—even as the films exploited audience's delight in crime and criminals. *The Roaring Twenties* (1939), for instance, spends far more narrational attention, and star power, aligning spectators with the goals of the film's bootlegging, murderous gangsters (played by James Cagney and Humphrey Bogart) than with those of the G-men trying to jail them. *Pickup on South Street* (1953) pits a crooked underworld against a ring of Communist spies, whose inherent moral corruption contrasts with the crooks' potential redemption and industrious efforts to profit within moral limits. Such films, like many from the PCA era, construct scenarios that tacitly elicit sympathy for criminals while overtly denouncing their crimes.

Although pregnant with possibilities to create the kind of pointed and irresolute conceptual incongruities one finds so often in seventies cinema, studio-era crime films almost invariably smoothed over their ideological incongruities with conventionally harmonious climaxes or epilogues. Such films sought ideological resolution partly because of PCA regulations but mostly because Hollywood narrative norms, especially as they manifested in the studio era, insisted upon it. Richard Neupert refers to this type of resolution in Hollywood cinema as "ideological" closure (73), and Murray Smith similarly identifies classical Hollywood's insistence upon "moral resolution" (*Engaging Characters*, 213).

It's tempting to hold the Code chiefly responsible for the ideologically conventional endings of studio-era crime films, since the weakening and ultimate eradication of the Code in the late sixties coincides with the emergence of a series of prominent Hollywood movies—*Bonnie and Clyde* (1967), *The Graduate* (1967), and *The Wild Bunch* (1969)—that conclude with moments of pointed ideological incongruity. Moreover, as demonstrated in my study of film endings, the years 1966 (when Hollywood abolishes the Code) and 1968 (when it replaces the PCA with the Classification and Rating Administration [CARA]) also mark the beginnings of a period in which the endings of the top ten movies of the year tended to show an above-average degree of irresolution (see Graph 2.1 in Chapter Two).

However, narrative norms during the studio era had at least as much influence as the PCA on Hollywood's tendency to create ideologically resolved film endings. The endings of most "pre-Code" crime films of the period 1930–1934, for all the fuss critics make about their presumed ideological subversiveness,[2] abide by most of the same ideological and narrative strictures found in PCA-era films.[3] For instance, the three biggest gangster pictures of the pre-Code period—*Little Caesar* (1930), *The Public Enemy* (1931), and *Scarface* (1932)—despite the controversies surrounding them at the time of their release, all end by punishing the gangster with death, an ending typical of the Code years 1934–1967 as well as the pre-Code period.[4] Moreover, by the 1950s, Hollywood had difficulty enforcing the Code because of a 1952 Supreme Court decision (*Joseph Burstyn Inc.*

v. Wilson) that afforded films First Amendment protections of free speech. Furthermore, the 1948 Paramount case had forced studios to divest their holdings of movie theaters. The divestment allowed theaters to show films without Code seals of approval, including independent films over which the studios had no control. Hence, studios enforced the Code strictly for fewer than twenty years, yet the standard practice of creating ideologically resolved endings lasted much longer, forty years or more. Finally, scenarios that did not threaten to violate Code restrictions generally offered ideologically neat resolutions as well. Studio-era Westerns *Red River* (1948), *Fort Apache* (1948), and *The Searchers* (1956) construct morally ambiguous scenarios that would not trouble the PCA (which gave Westerns more latitude anyway),[5] yet the films paste over their ambiguities with closing moments of felicitous, gratuitous, and narratively under-motivated harmony. Studio-era filmmakers felt all sorts of pressures to end their films with conventional, harmonious resolutions; the Code was merely one of them.

Whether for normative, ideological, or regulatory reasons, crime filmmakers of the studio era tended to wipe over their films' often complex ideological incongruities sometime before the closing credits. *The Woman in the Window*'s (1944) it's-all-been-a-dream epilogue supplies a clumsy example of a regular trend. *Angels with Dirty Faces* (1938) pairs Pat O'Brien and James Cagney as good and bad father figures, respectively, to the neighborhood kids of Hell's Kitchen. The film creates some complex ideological incongruities as we witness the mutual respect that the two men have for one another and as Cagney's character, although a resolute criminal, seems to have a positive influence on the boys. However—whether spectators think Cagney's gangster really goes "yellow" on his way to the gallows or, as O'Brien's priest asks him to, just feigns it[6]—*Angels With Dirty Faces* ultimately rejects the viewpoint of the criminal in favor of the priest.

Studio-era gangster movies worked hard in their concluding moments to deny the ambivalence with which they presented their protagonists, and one does not have to look very far to see the filmmakers struggling to find an ideologically harmonious resolution. *White Heat* (1949)—also starring Cagney, in his first gangster role since 1939's *The Roaring Twenties*—seems to both revile and delight in gangster Cody Jarrett's good-natured attitude toward crime and violence. Consider, for instance, the odd amusement of his response to the complaints of an escaped convict, whom Jarrett has locked in the trunk of a car, that it's "stuffy": Jarrett, blithely eating a chicken leg, says, "Stuffy huh? I'll give you a little air," and fires several rounds into the trunk. The presence of undercover cop Hank Fallon, who befriends Jarrett and infiltrates his gang, further complicates the film's attitude toward Jarrett. The moment when Jarrett discovers Fallon's real identity creates some sympathy for the gangster, who clearly liked Fallon, and Jarrett's hysterical reaction at the moment of discovery makes him look hurt by the betrayal: Laughing wildly, he says, "I treated him like a kid brother."

Nonetheless, compared to New Hollywood gangster movies in which cops go undercover, *White Heat* contains a far more ideologically straightforward depiction of police and criminals, particularly at its conclusion. In its last few scenes, the film seems intent upon avoiding the potential moral ambiguity of a situation in which a cop earns the affection of a likable criminal. Fallon never shows remorse about befriending Jarrett, and his transition back into the role of policeman is immediate and untroubled. *White Heat* concludes on a note of complacent ideological resolution after Jarrett dies in a fiery blaze: "Cody Jarrett," Fallon says smugly, "finally made it to the top of the world, and it blew up right in his face."

It would be more efficient for my argument if all studio-era crime films harmonized their conceptual incongruities with conventional resolutions, but rarely does film history provide the convenient distinctions that film scholars want from it. Films such as *The Maltese Falcon* (1941), *Detour* (1945),[7] *The Asphalt Jungle* (1950),[8] and *Kiss Me Deadly* (1955)[9] portray their cops, private detectives, and criminals with an uncommonly irresolute attitude. Such films, though memorable, are relatively rare in the studio era. The seventies, by contrast, gave us legions of them. Moreover, even in such studio-era outliers, the ideological incongruities in the behavior of the protagonists help to establish mysteries and dilemmas pertinent to the films' stories, whereas in comparable seventies films, such incongruities often seem counterproductive to the narratives in which they appear, superfluous incongruities that threaten to hinder, not further, narrative progress. American films of the 1970s often seem intent upon preventing—by way of narrational devices irrelevant to, often impediments to, narrative logic—conceptual harmony and closure.

After the 1970s

The morally ambiguous depictions of police in *Dirty Harry* (1971), *The French Connection* (1971), *The New Centurions* (1972), *The Offense* (1972), *The Seven-Ups* (1973), and *The Choirboys* (1977) made it more normal for

Hollywood crime movies to portray law enforcement in inconsistent ways, so that today films such as *White Heat* seem quaintly innocent in their straightforward depiction of police. In light of seventies cinema, for instance, the clean-cut portrayal of Fallon looks like a missed opportunity. Writing in 1998, one film scholar complains, "Rather than introduce a complex G-man caught in the inner circle of a gang, Fallon's motives remain nothing more than an abstract belief in crime fighting" (Yaquinto, 82). The story this scholar wants to see occurs only in the New Hollywood. The undercover cops in *Cruising* (1980), *Donnie Brasco* (1997), and *In Too Deep* (1999), for instance, become disturbingly compelled by the criminal world they infiltrate, and, unlike *White Heat*, *Reservoir Dogs* (1992) relishes, rather than dodges, the moral and emotional implications of its undercover cop's predicament. In *Reservoir Dogs*, a policeman, Freddy (Tim Roth), infiltrates a gang of thieves and develops a close relationship with one of the criminals, Larry (Harvey Keitel). Their relationship grows increasingly distressing when, at the end of the film, Larry mistakenly defends Freddy against the other gangsters, who suspect the policeman's true identity; Larry kills two of them to protect Freddy and is himself shot. At the end of the film, Freddy confesses, "Larry, I'm sorry, I'm so sorry. I'm a cop." Would the studio era have depicted a policeman, particularly at the plot's conclusion, sincerely apologizing to a criminal for being a policeman? To their very end, such films aggravate, rather than soften, their conceptual incongruities.

After seventies films heightened many of the incongruities in Hollywood narration as much as the classical framework would allow, the narrative incongruities that sometimes stunned viewers in the seventies became some-what traditional, a readily available alternative to the notorious "Hollywood ending."[10] Although most contemporary Hollywood films, especially at the moment of closure, continue to emphasize the harmony and resolution typical of studio-era filmmaking, numerous others ride in the wake of seventies cinema, which popularized less conceptually coherent stories than one nor-mally finds in Hollywood cinema. Largely as a consequence of seventies cinema's assault on ideological resolution, post-seventies Hollywood crime movies regularly develop incongruous attitudes toward their protagonists. Films such as *48 Hours* (1982), *Angel Heart* (1987), *Goodfellas* (1990), *Menace II Society* (1993), *Se7en* (1995), *The Usual Suspects* (1995), *Set It Off* (1996), *LA Confidential* (1997), *Payback* (1999), *Insomnia* (2002), *Mr. and Mrs. Smith* (2005), *Casino Royale* (2006), *The Departed* (2006), *Shoot 'Em Up* (2007), *A Quantum of Solace* (2008), and countless others demonstrate the lasting influence of seventies conceptual incongruity on New Hollywood cinema.

We turn now to the Hollywood genre whose conceptual incongruities rival those of the crime film: horror. In particular, we examine *The Exorcist* (1973), the phenomenally successful horror film, based on the best-selling novel by William Peter Blatty. The film offers us a model case study of conceptual incongruity in mainstream seventies cinema. Capitalizing on conceptual incongruities already present in the horror genre, *The Exorcist* integrates and concentrates them at precisely those moments when they most threaten the logic and closure of classical Hollywood narration.

THE EXORCIST AND THE SEVENTIES BLOCKBUSTER

Part of a horror film boom that occurred between 1971 and 1974, *The Exorcist*'s success towered above that of its peers.[11] Upon its release, it quickly became one of Hollywood's most profitable movies, earning $71.7 million in U.S. and Canadian rentals by the end of 1975. Still one of Hollywood's highest-grossing films, it has an all-time domestic gross of $233 million, making it the third highest-grossing movie of the 1970s, after *Star Wars* (1977, $461 million) and *Jaws* (1975, $260 million). In dollars adjusted according to ticket price inflation, it is the ninth highest-grossing movie of all time.

The Exorcist is sometimes regarded as the pinnacle of Hollywood high-budget exploitation cinema: a movie financed and designed to exploit spectators' interest in sensationalist story material. In the seventies, mainstream Hollywood entered exploitation filmmaking like never before, and sensationalist films such as *Billy Jack* (1971, Warner Bros., $32.5 million in domestic rentals), *Shaft* (1971, MGM, $7.1 million), *The Towering Inferno* (1974, 20th Century Fox/Warner Bros., $48.8 million), *Jaws* (1975, Universal Pictures, $129.5 million), *The Omen* (1976, 20th Century Fox, $28.5 million), and *Carrie* (1976, United Artists, $15.2 million) often dominated *Variety*'s weekly box office reports.

Hollywood's turn toward exploitation cinema was part of a general trend toward blockbuster filmmaking in the seventies. As the decade progressed, the average negative cost of a mainstream film had risen so greatly—from $1.97 million in 1972 to $9.38 million in 1980, a 376 percent increase in eight years—that movies geared to smaller audiences had increasingly little chance of recuperating their costs and were priced out of the market. The studios responded to production cost inflation, and to declines in theatrical attendance, by making fewer films (thereby creating "product shortages"), making films with easily marketed story lines ("high concepts"), and promoting them with such saturation that people would regard the film as an important and unique cultural experience (an "event film").

Paramount's blockbuster profits with *Love Story* (1970, $48.7 million in rentals) and *The Godfather* (1972, $86.3 million) had, in a time of industry instability, given the studios a clearer strategy for financial success. This strategy became known as the "blockbuster syndrome": the tendency of the studios to put the large majority of their investments into a small handful of films and their promotion in the hopes of reaping windfall profits from at least one of them. "By this kind of logic," Cook writes, "only films that were carefully packaged and laden with 'proven' elements, like pre-sold properties (best-selling books [novels], hit plays, popular comic strips) and bankable stars had a reasonable chance of becoming top-echelon blockbusters" (14). The rest of the studios' output, the smaller-budgeted films, were financed merely as hedges against loss and in the hope that one of them would turn unexpectedly into a hit as well, as was the case with *M*A*S*H* (1970, 20th Century Fox, $36.7 million in rentals), *Woodstock* (1970, Warner Bros., $16.4 million), *American Graffiti* (1973, Universal Pictures, $55.3 million), and *The Rocky Horror Picture Show* (1975, 20th Century Fox, $3.5 million upon its initial release but another $40 million by the end of 1979).

Although Warner Bros. executives regarded *The Exorcist* in some ways as a prestige picture for the studio,[12] they conceived and marketed it primarily as a high-concept mainstream exploitation film, its sensationalist aspects emphasized both in the film and in its promotion in order to ensure cultural attraction.[13] The film became a "cultural phenomenon of large proportions," according to Cook, because of its "lurid depiction of a demonically possessed 12-year-old girl in assorted acts of cursing, urination, vomiting, and masturbation with a crucifix" (226). High-concept blockbusters, particularly mainstream exploitation films such as *The Exorcist*, do not normally lend themselves to the pointed conceptual incongruities that help characterize seventies narration. Indeed, conceptual incongruities threaten to undermine high-concept filmmaking, which, by its nature, relies on simple premises rather than complex or incongruous ideas. However, *The Exorcist*'s director, William Friedkin, has always seen himself as an artistic daredevil, and his film contains a variety of elements that seem to serve no other function than to undermine the film's conceptual logic. Since *The Exorcist* depicts such brazen images and language, one might infer that the movie's exploitative portions constitute the majority of one's experience; the most memorable scenes contain vomiting, cursing, violence, and other grotesque behavior. However, *The Exorcist* is not mere exploitation: As this chapter will testify, the film's conceptual incongruities stimulate more intellectual activity than its high concept would predict and than commentators on the film generally recognize.

In order to demonstrate the ways in which the film's narration generates incongruous ideas, we should first understand the initial reception of *The Exorcist* in 1973, especially the critical response to the film's concept and to its most blatantly exploitative elements, many of which do not function as straightforwardly as critics suggested. Although commentators purported to account for the unprecedented success of the movie, in their zeal to explain the hoopla surrounding *The Exorcist*'s release, they overlooked some of the movie's more subtle qualities. Such subtleties often undermine the high concept and exploitative elements that commentators on the movie have reacted to, both in 1973 and now.

THE EXORCIST RECEPTION

William Friedkin directs the kind of movies that many critics and moviegoers say they hate: His movies don't *suggest* violence and gore; they show it. His inclinations therefore suit the modern horror film, a typically explicit genre (particularly since the 1970s) that gathers much of its potency from the conflict between two opposing inclinations: the desire to see and the desire not to see what the screen depicts. At some point, horror films are likely to exploit what Noël Carroll calls the spectator's "curious admixture of attraction and repulsion" to shocking imagery (*Philosophy of Horror*, 161). The explicitness of the genre has helped to place it at the bottom of the movie genre bin. Aside from pornography, no genre is more denigrated and despised than horror, "dismissed with contempt," Robin Wood says, "by the majority of reviewer-critics, or simply ignored" (77).

Not surprisingly, reviews of the shocking and explicit *The Exorcist* were mostly damning. One would expect a publication such as *The Christian Century* to moralize: "In addition to being repulsive with its scenes of mutilation and vomiting, *The Exorcist* is also a commercially exploitative motion picture" (Wall, 91–92). However, the tone of its review was no more preachy than that of other publications, many of whose critics considered the film a disgrace. *Film Quarterly* called it a "sickening exhibition," and "the trash bombshell of 1973, the aesthetic equivalent of being run over by a truck" (Dempsey, 61–62). Vincent Canby considered the movie "a chunk of elegant occultist claptrap" (46). In Pauline Kael's review, she said about Friedkin, "He has himself said that Blatty's book took hold of him and made him physically ill. That's the problem with movie makers who aren't thinkers: they're mentally unprotected. A book like Blatty's makes them sick, and they think this means they should make everybody sick" ("Back to the Ouija Board," 61). Some regional authorities disapproved as strongly as the critics. The district attorney's offices in Boston and Washington, D.C., considered the movie obscene and gave it an "X" rating, even though the Motion Picture Association of America (MPAA) rated it "R." After the film's release, church groups staged burnings of Blatty's novel. For twenty-five years, Great Britain banned the movie on television and home video, even in a cut version such as the one that appeared on American TV.

Despite such vigorous disapproval, the culture could not get enough of the movie. Moviegoers stood in line for hours to see the film for the second and third times. Newspapers reported incidents of fainting and vomiting throughout the country, and many theater managers said they kept smelling salts to awaken the faint-hearted and cases of kitty litter to absorb the vomit of filmgoers sickened by the movie. One manager, Frank Kveton, said, "My janitors are going crazy wiping up the vomit." Some viewers fled the theaters, and managers sometimes had to replace doors and curtains damaged by unruly crowds. "I've never seen anything like it in the 24 years I've been working in movie theaters," said H. Robert Honahan, division manager for Berkeley's ABC/Plitt theaters. "We've had two to five people faint here every day since this picture opened" (Woodward, 61). Exorcism and demonic possession emerged as popular dinner table topics, "challenging the energy crisis and Watergate tapes for the public attention" (Glynn, 65). News publications reported that some viewers confronted priests after seeing the movie, demanding an exorcism (see, for example, Woodward, 63).

I have found more contemporary articles about *The Exorcist* than about any other film I researched for this book. The movie elicited editorials from all sorts of directions—from psychologists, sociologists, film critics, and theologians—most of them trying to answer the same question: Why would *The Exorcist* create such a furor? Commentators offered plenty of answers. Several editorials suggested that in an atheistic age people are looking for meaning and a clear distinction between right and wrong. Others believed that moviegoers were simply titillated by the gore. Further explanations pointed to the movie's mixture of sexuality and violence, to humans' innate fear of evil, to a trendy fascination with the occult, to rising violence in society, and to the age-old theme of the struggle between good and evil. An editorial in *Social Policy* read: "It may express people's uncertainty about how to explain their society to themselves, and their desire for simpler and less ambiguous explanations of the deplorable state of today's world" (Gans, 72). *Newsweek* interviewed several experts to explain the phenomenon. Jungian analyst Dr. Thayer Greene wrote: "Modern consciousness has become so rationalized that the reaction to this kind of movie is a compensatory up thrust of irrational forces." Los Angeles psychiatrist Judd Marmor said: "In times of great insecurity, people turn to mystical explanations, including astrology, witches and demon possession." William Peter Blatty—who wrote the book and screenplay and who also produced the movie—offered another explanation: "Do you know what I think has all those people—and they are mostly men, you know—shaking and fainting in that movie? I think that they are making the unconscious connection between that repulsive monstrosity on the screen and the moral evil in their lives" (Woodward, 64).

Some of these explanations seem more ludicrous than others, but none answers why *The Exorcist*—as opposed to the many other horror movies distributed at the same time—elicited the phenomenal response that it did. Hollywood released three other movies about possession just before Friedkin's: *Crucible of Terror* (1971), *The Possession of Joel Delaney* (1972), and *Night of the Devils* (1973). Only *The Possession of Joel Delaney* earned rentals large enough ($473,490 in its first run, mostly as part of a double feature with *Hannie Caulder*) to make the cutoff for *Variety*'s top fifty films of the week, and it did not come close to recuperating its negative cost of $1.3 million.[14] All told, about 150 horror movies found distribution in the United States and Great Britain between 1971 and 1974. One can assume that many or all of them pit good against evil, combine sexuality and violence, and involve the supernatural or the occult in a shocking and disturbing way. In fact, the very factors identified by critics of *The Exorcist* appear in most Hollywood horror movies from any era, since such factors define not just this one horror film but the genre itself. If the response to *The Exorcist* resulted from the film's treatment of some popular themes of the culture, then at least some of these other horror movies should have created the same frenzy.

More recent scholars continue to look at social issues when they comment on the movie. In 1999, one scholar wrote that the film's setting in "Georgetown, Washington, in 1973, parallels the kind of exorcism that is determined to be necessary in Washington at the time due to the Nixon administration's surveillant [sic] propensities" (Miller, 91). A lengthy article in *History Today* about the 2000 re-release of the movie—which grossed $67 million worldwide, making it one of the most profitable re-releases in history[15]—says that *The Exorcist*'s success during its initial release resulted from the fact that it "touched on issues that were all too alive for the world of 1973," such as the Vietnam War, "inter-generational conflict," "campus dissent," "the breakdown of the family," Thalidomide babies, and the legalization of abortion (Cull, 46–51). The author's analysis, however, fails to account for why the movie would earn a hugely profitable nationwide re-release twenty-seven years after these hot topics were hot. Presumably, no one in the year 2000 went to see *The Exorcist* because of an interest in Thalidomide babies. Hollywood produces a lot of horror movies and exploitation product. Why re-release this one and not others? In explaining the public's astonishing mania for the film, commentators have turned mostly to *The Exorcist*'s subject matter and cultural context, rather than turning, as I propose to do, to the film's peculiar mode of narration.

CONCEPTUAL INCONGRUITY IN *THE EXORCIST*
AND THE HORROR GENRE

The Exorcist advertises one kind of experience—loud and straightforward—yet it delivers an experience more complex than the one promised by its identity as a mainstream Hollywood horror film. I do not pretend to account entirely for the *Exorcist* phenomenon, but I hope my analysis will help explain some of the film's persistent attraction by focusing on one key narrative strategy: its tendency to generate incongruous ideas. The film's narration, I plan to show, cues spectators to understand, evaluate, and respond emotionally to what they perceive on the basis of ideas that threaten the coherence of the film's fundamental themes. This peculiar narrative strategy adds variety to the film's otherwise uncomplicated "high" concept and excites spectators to perform more cognitive activity than is commonly recognized by film commentators, who mostly regard the film as merely blatant, visceral, and sensationalist.

Commentators have identified *The Exorcist*'s most fundamental theme as a war between good and evil waged over the body of an innocent twelve-year-old girl, Regan MacNeil (played by Linda Blair). In the prologue, set in Iraq, the film visually establishes the opposing combatants in this war when it depicts Father Merrin (Max von Sydow), the aged exorcist himself, standing opposite a statue of a demon (Figure 5.1). Friedkin said about this shot, "[The demon] faces Father Merrin in a symbolic face-off between good and evil," but the shot makes the idea obvious enough without the director's commentary.[16] Indeed, *The Exorcist* establishes the moral polarities in the most easily distinguishable terms: the Catholic Church and the devil himself. The Church stands for goodness and impassive strength, whereas the devil stands for evil and grotesque violence. The film's narration, however, frequently generates ideas and emotions that violate what would seem to be an easy distinction.

The poster shot of Father Merrin's arrival at the MacNeil household—a poster that Friedkin himself helped design—provides a visual emblem of the incongruity I am describing. Some critics have remarked that the shot of Merrin as he stands in the fog is the film's most heavy-handed use of traditional horror film imagery: mist, backlighting, an antique lamppost on an abandoned street (Figure 5.2). However, as Mark Kermode notes, the traditional imagery is reversed: "Merrin (the messenger of good) is depicted as a dark, brooding presence, seemingly threatening the brightly lit house," while Regan's room projects a ray of light (90).

A moment after the shot, when Regan's mother, movie actress Chris MacNeil (Ellen Burstyn), opens the door for the exorcist, the film plays high-pitched eerie music and depicts the priest's menacing silhouette, which looks like that of a vampire (Figure 5.3). Ominously backlit, Merrin says, "Mrs.

FIGURE 5.1. Director William Friedkin said that, in this shot from *The Exorcist*, the demon "faces Father Merrin in a symbolic face-off between good and evil."

FIGURE 5.2. *The Exorcist*'s most famous shot reverses traditional horror film imagery by depicting Father Merrin as a dark, threatening figure.

MacNeil," with a voice so hoarse and foreboding that he sounds like a demon himself. As the piercing music fades, Merrin steps into the light and genially introduces himself. In a matter of seconds, he transforms from a threatening figure into a comforting priest (Figure 5.4). At such instances, Father Merrin briefly evokes the evil whose virtuous opposition he represents, and the film's depiction of him momentarily collides with his identity as a "good" character.

The phonetic (and etymological) resonance between the first name of Father Damien Karras (Jason Miller)—who assists Father Merrin in the exorcism—and the word "demon" also threatens to disrupt the clarity of the devil/church distinction that the movie relies on in order to make sense. Even the movie's ominous-sounding title evokes the same kind of horror evoked by the titles of other horror movies, which almost invariably refer to their films' evil menaces, not, as in this case, to the movie's figure of goodness.

Rounding out the symbolic mix-up, the demon, too, refuses to appropriately signify its side of what should be a simple moral juxtaposition. *The Exorcist* is a story of a little girl (good) who is possessed by the devil (evil). The movie, however, often makes it difficult to distinguish the devil from the girl because Regan is both the tormented and the tormentor. In the middle of the film, when her behavior is still fairly mild, she spits in the face of a physician trying to give her an injection and curses, "You fucking bastard!"

FIGURE 5.3. Father Merrin ominously backlit.

FIGURE 5.4. Father Merrin steps into front lighting.

FIGURES 5.3–5.4. A single shot from *The Exorcist* in which Merrin transforms from a threatening figure into a genial priest.

At that moment, she looks like a rotten kid, not demonically possessed. Later, the narration depicts Regan at the same time more sympathetically and more despicably, in many instances creating radical and abrupt transformations in its depiction of the character, similar to the transformation of Father Merrin when he steps into the light of the MacNeil home. During the exorcism, the priests alternately abuse the demon and comfort the girl, strapping her down on the bed one moment and soothingly pulling up her covers the next. After a scene in which Regan projects vomit onto Father Karras, her stomach displays the words, "Help me." Regan is both evil and its innocent victim, both revolting and sympathetic.

These types of conceptual incongruities (good mixed with evil, sympathy with revulsion, incongruous characterizations, irrational ideas) can be found in numerous earlier horror movies. Horror regularly represents its good and evil figures as opposing versions of the same thing, an idea evidenced most forcefully, according to Wood, in the doppelgänger motif, which, he says, "reveals the Monster as normality's shadow" (80). Horror films other than *The Exorcist*, moreover, incorporate conceptual incongruities, often at the very heart of their narratives since monsters, ghosts, and other unnatural beings violate our sense of an orderly universe. Carroll points to the mixture of "disgust tinged with sympathy and care" in the audience's emotional response to the title character of *The Fly* (1958) (*Philosophy of Horror*, 40). He notes that even Dracula (*Dracula*, 1931), a prototypical evil monster, has his sympathetic moments, when, for instance, the character says, "To die, to be *really* dead, that must be glorious" (208). In many horror films—the Jekyll and Hyde movies, Frankenstein movies, King Kong movies, Invisible

Man movies, Wolf Man movies, and some vampire movies, especially recent ones—the difficulty of distinguishing good from evil becomes an explicit theme. Often the monster, who might generate more sympathy than the representatives of normality, is blamed for society's ills or for humans' moral weakness or vanity.

The Exorcist's Regan, as both twelve-year-old girl and demon, emerges out of a long line of what Carroll calls "fusion figures," which he defines as "a composite that unites attributes held to be categorically distinct and/ or at odds in the cultural scheme of things in *unambiguously* one, spatio-temporally discrete entity" (*Philosophy of Horror*, 43). In other words, a fusion figure is a monster that has traits of two normally separate beings, such as Frankenstein's monster (who is both living and dead and is made from many bodies), the Body Snatchers (human and alien), and the Alligator People (need I explain?). These "categorically impossible beings" (206) are perfect vehicles for exploring conceptual incongruities because not only do they combine normally distinct categories, but they also enable filmmakers to exploit ambivalent emotional responses (fear and curiosity, disgust and sympathy) to such figures.

Although many horror films temper ambivalent emotional responses to fusion figures by making their monsters uniformly repulsive and threatening (the 1956 and 1978 *Invasion of the Body Snatchers*, for instance), others exploit the genre's underlying conceptual incongruities in order to intensify spectator ambivalence. In *Cat People* (1942), for instance, Irena (played by Simone Simon), a cat-woman fusion figure, becomes an object of sympathy because she herself worries that she is a monster. She refuses sex with her husband, not to torment him but to protect him because she fears her passion will cause her to turn into a cat and kill him. Critic Roger Ebert says about the film, "It has the same kind of uneasy sympathy for Irena that Anne Rice has for her vampires. It's not much fun, being a cat woman" (Ebert). Similarly, *Frankenstein* (1931) frequently emphasizes the monster's sympathetic qualities through moments that make it look innocent, even childlike; through scenes in which Dr. Frankenstein's assistant, Fritz, torments the monster; and, in the scene of its destruction, through shots of a hysterical mob that burns it to death with as little moral hesitation as one shows when setting logs in a fireplace. The depiction of the monster's frantic response to the flames surrounding and eventually engulfing it (its high-pitched screaming and whimpering and frenzied attempts to escape the firestorm) seems specifically designed to prompt pity.

The Exorcist's conceptual incongruities exploit those that already infuse the genre, incongruities that the film concentrates and, most crucially for our purposes, makes narratively and conceptually inappropriate. *Frankenstein* employs conceptual incongruities that advance narrative causality (the monster's innocence leads it accidentally to kill a child) and the film's themes (the monster's miserable death demonstrates the wretched consequences of Frankenstein's efforts to, as the prologue says, "make a man after his own image, without reckoning upon God"). The same may be said of the monsters in *The Fly* (1958), *The Invisible Man* (1933), *King Kong* (1933), and the many other horror films with sympathetic monsters. Similarly, the irrational ideas at the heart of *Dracula*, *The Wolf Man* (1941), and *Cat People* (whose stories of supernatural events suggest worlds governed by forces beyond reason) provide crucial elements in the films' cause-and-effect chain.

By contrast, *The Exorcist*'s conceptual incongruities often hinder narrative logic and threaten to play havoc with the film's stable and brazenly simple conceptual basis: a straightforward combat between good and evil. The devil, for instance, does not come across as Merrin's doppelgänger (not unless one considers all combatants doppelgängers), nor does the film invite spectators to feel conscious sympathy for the devil or antipathy toward the exorcists. Still, *The Exorcist*'s narration generates incongruous concepts and iconography (the devil is ominous and so is his opposition), some of which result in incongruous imagery (priests burning Regan's legs with acidic holy water, then kindly tucking her into bed), characterological inconsistencies (a malevolent, repulsive girl is a helpless victim), and irrational ideas (the frightening arrival of the exorcist signals relief from our fears). The story justifies its conceptual incongruities: The priests, for instance, must harm Regan's body in order to save her, and Regan's vile behavior results from her possession, not her character. However, the film's potent images and language cannot help but evoke thoughts and emotions antipathetic to the film's themes.

The conceptual incongruities reach their greatest concentration at the film's climax, which generates a persistent run of incongruities that impede linear narration and conceptual closure: Ideological incongruities, factual contradictions, and logical and characterological inconsistencies permeate the scene. Consider, for example, Karras's successful effort to exorcise the demon from Regan. After Merrin's fatal heart attack, Karras kneels on top of Regan, strangles her, and hits her hard (the sound effects make Karras's punches sound brutal), exhibiting the kind of violence previously associated with the demon. No matter how much one tells oneself that Karras is attacking the devil, one cannot ignore the sounds and images of a furious priest strangling a twelve-year-old girl and punching her hard in the face (Figures 5.5 and 5.6).

Then, when the demon complies with Karras's demand to leave Regan and enter him ("Take me!"), the scene, Paul observes, depicts something wholly illogical when a point-of-view shot through Damien's hands reveals that, again, he intends to strangle her (Figure 5.7): "Damien possessed by the Devil again wants to attack Regan, which is precisely what Damien had been doing when not possessed. What's the difference?" (309). *The Exorcist* advertises a straightforward combat between good and evil; however, the narration often depicts good and evil in almost precisely the same terms.

The image of Karras attacking Regan creates only some of the many conceptual incongruities in the movie's climax. Indeed, the scene pervasively

FIGURE 5.5.   FIGURE 5.6.

FIGURES 5.5–5.6. *The Exorcist*: Father Karras brutally punches and strangles Regan.

FIGURE 5.7. *The Exorcist*: While possessed by the demon, Father Karras intends to strangle Regan, just as he did when he was not possessed.

violates the belief systems that the film has relied on throughout the exorcism scenes. The scene, for instance, reverses the principles previously established for fighting the devil. Earlier in the movie, Father Merrin determines both the wrong method of combat (emotional responses to the devil) and the right one (ritualistic focus).[17] When, in an earlier scene, Father Karras reacts emotionally as the demon speaks to him in the voice of his dead mother, Merrin chastises the agitated priest. At another point, Karras is so dumbfounded by the demon's power to raise the bed that he stalls the exorcism by failing to give the liturgical response Merrin demands ("The response please, Damien!"). The lesson is clear: Emotion is the devil's province and must be overruled by Catholic ritual. The demon looks bothered, for instance, when the priests recite the Catholic Rite of Exorcism. When Merrin and Karras repetitiously chant at her levitated body ("The power of Christ compels you"), she slowly descends. In the climax, however, the film's conceptual logic abruptly changes. After the demon causes Father Merrin's fatal heart attack, Karras does precisely what Merrin had warned him not to do: He responds with vulnerable emotion, without ritual, speaking to the demon directly. Using language that sounds like a milder version of the curses Regan hurls at the priests, he shouts, "You son of a bitch! Take me! Come into me! God damn you!" Yet, unlike all of the other instances in which Karras exhibits emotion in front of the demon, this one works. He achieves what Merrin did not—he drives the devil out of Regan—upsetting the film's confident distinction between right and wrong behavior. Emotion succeeds where ritual failed. Without ever acknowledging the incongruity, the narration abruptly establishes a new conceptual logic.

The incongruities mount when the devil obliges the priest by entering his body, at which point Karras leaps out of Regan's window, taking the demon with him. The question remains: Did he beat the devil or did the devil beat him? According to Blatty, "Fifty per cent of those who've seen the film think the demon is taking Karras out the window, and that it's a triumph of evil over good. But it's an act of love, not one of despair. It's clearly a triumph for Karras" (Woodward, 66). Even if we are among the fifty percent who saw Karras's act the way Blatty wanted us to see it, the ending is still logically inconsistent. For one thing, Karras has killed himself, not the devil. Second, contrary to Church doctrine, the Catholic priest's final victorious act is suicide. Furthermore, Karras's "act of love" does not express his personal triumph as "clearly" as Blatty says. In the end, the movie suggests that Father Karras commits a selfless act and thereby achieves a kind of martyrdom. The sacrifice points to a growth in his character, a testament to the faith he had admitted to losing. One film scholar calls Karras's act a "redemption" (Clagett, 137), another "the restoring of his faith" (Segaloff, 150). However, the film has always portrayed Karras as deeply self-sacrificing, tormented about his dying mother, and guilty about not giving more. Karras complains about being "unfit," but he never behaves that way. The climax of the movie treats his sacrifice as though it signified a renewal, but in the end, Karras transforms into exactly the man he has been all along: a saint.

More than a decade before *The Exorcist*, horror filmmakers had already begun to conclude their films with narrative devices that resisted conceptual resolution and story closure. In the classical horror film of the 1930s, 40s, and 50s, good generally triumphed in a definitive climax, but, starting in the 1960s, the open and unhappy ending begins to prevail. These days, horror filmmakers *customarily* create open, unhappy endings, often with a scene of victory over the monster, followed by an epilogue that shows the monster, or its double, readying for another assault.

Scholars often regard *Psycho* (1960) as the turning point between the closure typical of the classical period of the genre and the irresolution characteristic of modern horror. Stephen Prince, Isabel Cristina Pinedo, and William Paul all see closure as dominant in horror's classical period and consider the 1960s the moment when the genre began to favor open and unhappy endings. Prince says, "Things have changed in the modern period, with *Psycho* (1960) being one of the threshold films that mark a separation between eras. . . . As that film ended with the shot of Norman's (and Mother's) grinning face, Hitchcock suggested that madness and chaos endure because they are not explicable" ("Introduction," *Horror Film*, 4). Indeed, the final scene of *Psycho* uses a variety of narrative and stylistic devices that resist closure. A creepy sense of continuing threat results from the strangely barren mise-en-scène of Norman's cell in the final scene, the off-center framing, Norman's to-camera gaze, the dissolve between Norman's face and the decomposed skull of his mother, and the abrasive-sounding voice-over of the mother, which, we are to understand, emanates from the mind of the male character we are watching. Moreover, Norman's attention to the fly on his hand gives the narration a bizarrely incidental fixation right at the film's concluding moments, undoing the arduous efforts, of the immediately previous scene with the psychiatrist, to wrap things up.

Finally—and I have never seen anyone remark on this particular conceptual incongruity in the vast scholarly literature on the film—the mother's voice-over narration in this last scene gratuitously contradicts the explanation the psychiatrist has just given for Norman's behavior. The psychiatrist said that he "got the story from the mother" (meaning Norman's mother personality), who, he says, admitted to committing the crimes, an admission that accords with the scenes of murder and attack depicted in the film. But in this final scene, when *we* listen to the mother, she says that she told the psychiatrist that Norman committed the crimes: "It's sad when a mother has to speak the words that condemn her own son, but I couldn't allow them to believe that I would commit murder." Scholarly silence on this peculiar and trivial contradiction suggests that it gains little traction in spectators' consciousness, yet I suspect the moment has briefly puzzled many spectators of the film who, right at the moment of closure, find themselves having to reconcile a gratuitous incongruity in the narration.

As the genre progressed in the 1960s, the conceptual incongruities mounted, as did the genre's resistance to closure. Paul believes that *The Birds* (1963), for instance, "took the move against closure even further [than *Psycho*] by ending *in the middle* of a suspense sequence, absolutely refusing to resolve the immediate concerns of the narrative." He reports that "audience reaction at early previews led to a 'The End' title over the final shot. . . . People kept sitting in their seats, waiting for the next scene" (412). Pinedo sees lack of closure as the defining characteristic of the "postmodern" (by which she means after *Psycho*) horror film. "The classical horror film constructs a secure universe characterized by narrative closure," she says. "In contrast, violating narrative closure has become de rigueur for the postmodern genre. The film may come to an end, but it is an open ending" (99). Films such as *Rosemary's Baby* (1968) and *Night of the Living Dead* (1968) helped make the unhappy, unresolved, or ambiguous ending common practice in the genre. We had hints of this type of open ending in studio-era horror, such as in the Val Lewton horror unit at RKO, whose films, including *Cat People* (1942), *I Walked with a Zombie* (1943), and *The Body Snatcher* (1945), often concluded with an lingering sense of continuing horror. Compared to the modern horror film's open endings, however, such endings seem resolute. As Pinedo describes the difference, "open-ended narratives are dominant in the postmodern, but *emergent* in the classical genre" (100).

The Exorcist, like many horror films since *Psycho*, resists narrative closure, but here one finds it difficult to pinpoint the source of the ominous feeling of open-endedness typically reported by viewers and in scholarship about the movie. (Blatty fought with Friedkin about the ending and said about it, "Even the audience that understood the climax of *The Exorcist* wanted to walk out and cut their throats. You feel depressed" [Clagett, 124].) One reason for finding it difficult to identify the source of the open-ended feeling is that the narration does not foreground the ending's conceptual incongruities (for instance, the change in the narration's attitude toward emotional confrontations with the demon, the oddity of a priest punching a girl, the fact that Karras tries to strangle Regan both before and after his own possession), incongruities that never become the narration's primary concern.

Moreover, like *Psycho*'s ending, this one cues ambivalent attitudes, not because the story lacks closure (which would be a traditional form of ambiguity by this point in the genre's history) but rather because the film subtly cues spectators to evaluate the ending in antithetical ways. In the most blatant respects, the film ends positively—the demon is successfully exorcized— while more subtle narrational devices run counter to this conclusion. For instance, the characters who defeated the devil (Merrin and Karras) are no longer in the film, offering us no figure with whom to share the triumph. The characters who remain do not look triumphant: Chris says Regan "doesn't remember any of it," and the two of them are cutting their losses and getting out of town; Karras's friend, Father Dyer, looks heartbroken. All in all, there is little reason to feel triumphant. The demon managed to kill Chris's director and friend, Burke Dennings, as well as two priests, briefly possessing one of them. The movie gives no indication that the MacNeils have grown from the experience. It is unclear what Father Karras, the one character who seems to have learned from the event, has learned. In any case, he died learning it. Moreover, the narrative devices the film uses to signal closure[18] draw spectators' attention not to the success of the exorcism but to aspects of the plot that evoked horror and failure. In the last few shots of the movie, the narration depicts the stairs and window where Dennings died and Karras leapt to his death. Meanwhile, a rendition of the film's haunting theme music, "Tubular Bells," briefly reemerges in the soundtrack, "cut short," Kermode says, "by the crashing orchestral stabs which accompany the red-on black credits. With one final aural jolt, the movie spits its audience back out into the world, startled and disoriented, unable to recover their composure, with no time to reflect on the horrors they have seen or draw any reassurance that everything is indeed 'going to be all right'" (84).

I am not arguing that evil actually wins in the end of the movie. Rather, good wins because, in this film, victory has all along meant exorcising Regan's demon.[19] However, the film's positive ending does not accord with some of the ideas and emotions the narration evokes. At the end of classical horror films, such as *Dracula* (1931) and *The Thing* (1951), typically good triumphs. At the end of New Hollywood horror films, such as *Rosemary's Baby* (1968), typically evil triumphs. At the end of *The Exorcist*, again good triumphs, but it doesn't feel that way.

Although *The Exorcist* is clearly extraordinary among horror films of this period, it offers a model illustration of the principles of narration that characterize seventies cinema generally. The film, as we have seen, exploits unrealized potentials within Hollywood cinema through subtle modifications of classical narrative and genre devices. In doing so, it prompts more uncertain and discomforting spectator responses than those of more typical Hollywood films. Furthermore, like so much seventies cinema, it emphasizes irresolution, particularly at the moment of climax. And the film's narration tends to integrate conceptual incongruities counterproductive to its overt narrative purpose, incongruities that hinder narrative linearity, momentum, and closure and that threaten to play havoc with the film's fundamental themes.

Why would such popularity—arguably the most manic in film history—attach to such a perverse form of narration? Where is the aesthetic pleasure in such peculiar entertainment? Let's look past the film's sensationalist subject matter and cultural context, which do not help us distinguish *The Exorcist* from other mainstream exploitation product of the period, and speculate on the pleasure afforded by the film's conceptual incongruities, which complicate plot patterning and excite creative mental activity unavailable to spectators of more conceptually harmonious Hollywood narratives.

The Exorcist's conceptual incongruities add a layer of variety and unpredictability to a film that would otherwise be highly straightforward—an uncomplicated, albeit visceral, narration of a classic struggle between good and evil, rendered in the form of big budget exploitation cinema. Amid the film's explicit gore and brazenly simple "high" concept, its underlying conceptual incongruities stimulate spectators to fabricate connections among discordant ideas and story events, liberated from the inhibiting forces of story logic, linear plotting, and conceptual coherence. As long as *The Exorcist* does not present concepts so blatantly illogical and incongruous that spectators would not mentally repair the breaches—that is, as long as the film's conceptual incongruities remain somewhere beyond the range of detection by our processes of strict logical reasoning—then the film has enabled in spectators a potentially thrilling kind of mental activity, one predicated more on imagination than on precise logic. If spectators understand, for instance, that a malevolent tormentor is also an innocent and pitiable figure, that the ominous appearance of Father Merrin is a hopeful sign, that by punching Regan Father Karras is curing her, that strangling Regan is both a priestly and demonic act, that passionate emotion is wrong *and* correct, and that Merrin's heart attack, Karras's suicide, and the general horror of the film's final moments denote a successful exorcism, then the film has prompted spectators to understand concepts that do not, on their face, make sense, incongruous concepts that require creative distortion in order to resolve. Such mental activity is more playful than rigorous problem solving, more of the nature of free association than logical reasoning.

I would not go so far as to say that spectators value *The Exorcist* mostly for its conceptual incongruities. I imagine that a lot of its value to spectators comes precisely from the explicit shock that critics of the film deplore. As critics have also noted, it has better acting and better visual and sound editing than most exploitation cinema of the seventies, as well as a bigger budget. Such qualities alone, however, would not suffice to draw audiences to the film decades after its initial release. Critics normally regard *The Exorcist* as one of the sensationalist "event films" of the seventies: a highly marketed, highly anticipated, high-concept thrill movie (such as *The Towering Inferno* [1974], *Earthquake* [1974], and *Jaws* [1975]), designed to draw crowds eager to participate in a cultural happening. I propose that spectators leave *The Exorcist* having had an experience more cognitively eventful than the film's shocks, thrills, and thematic substance can account for.

In the preceding chapters, I have argued that the defining narrational modes of films of the period are: 1) their refusal to satisfy narrative promises in conventional ways, 2) unsettling deviations from genre norms, and 3) conceptual incongruities. Some of the most celebrated Hollywood films from the 1970s precariously risk incoherence by undermining the simple harmonies we tend to associate with Hollywood cinema, even as such films are stabilized by classical structures that prevent them from collapsing into disorder.

Yet more remains to be understood. We don't yet know the limits of narrative incongruity in mainstream seventies cinema or what narrative incongruity would look like if it were unlimited by Hollywood's strict norms of narration. The extremes of narrative incongruity is the subject of the final part of this book.

PART III

Incongruity's Endpoints

How far can filmmakers take the narrational strategies characteristic of the 1970s? In Part III, we examine the work of two filmmakers, Martin Scorsese and John Cassavetes, who persistently tested the limits of seventies modes of narration. Scorsese worked mostly in Hollywood, exploring the farthest boundaries of classicism through daring narrative and stylistic incongruities. His films epitomize the manner in which seventies filmmaking integrates narrative incongruities into the classical Hollywood model. Cassavetes, very early in his career, mostly abandoned Hollywood filmmaking, fully indulging his perverse inclination to employ narrational strategies counterproductive to the linear progress of his stories. Cassavetes's films offer us a vision of radical narrative perversity, unstabilized by classical structures, and reveal aspects of seventies narration that mainstream American films restrain. His unpopularity during the 1970s illustrates the commercial risks of narrative perversity, especially when taken to its extreme end point.

CHAPTER 6 INCONGRUITY AND UNITY IN MARTIN SCORSESE'S *TAXI DRIVER*

Martin Scorsese shot the low-budget exploitation film *Boxcar Bertha* (1972)—his second feature film and the first for which he was paid as director—for independent producer Roger Corman at American International Pictures (AIP). Scorsese, proud of some of his work on the film, showed it to his friend and mentor, John Cassavetes.[1] According to Scorsese, Cassavetes said to him, "You spent a year of your life making a piece of shit. You're better than that stuff, you don't do that again" (Kelly, 68). Scorsese took his friend's advice and began pre-production on *Mean Streets* (1973), but his experience working with Corman taught the young director a skill from which Scorsese would continually profit during the 1970s and 1980s: how to give a professional look to a low-budget film. Most valuably, Scorsese learned to storyboard almost every shot in a film before beginning principal photography, a practice he has used on most of his features. The director's penchant for elaborately preparing his films in pre-production allows him to shoot quickly (and to quickly eliminate shots on the set, if time constraints make it necessary to do so) and has endeared him to his editor, who largely re-assembles the shots that Scorsese already pre-assembled on storyboards before production.

The polished appearance and lavish visual effects in Scorsese's relatively low-budget films in the 1970s resulted also from technological advances in cinematography at the time, particularly from improvements in film stock and lens technology and from the introduction of small, lightweight cameras.[2] Michael Chapman, Scorsese's director of photography on both *Taxi Driver* (1976) and *Raging Bull* (1980), was particularly pleased to be able to use on those films the newly invented Zeiss Super Speed lenses, the precision of which allowed him to "expose confidently, knowing I would get exactly what I hoped for."[3] Scorsese and Chapman also took advantage of the small and relatively lightweight Arriflex 35BL camera, introduced by Arnold & Richter in 1972, which allowed the filmmakers, without ballooning production costs, to create complex point-of-view shots and smooth tracking shots, to quickly reorient the camera in the middle of a shot, and to use makeshift rigs in order to, Scorsese said, "get the cameras flying the way I wanted" (Kelly, 139).[4]

Technological advances, Scorsese's skill at making glossy films on a small budget, and his alliance with a bankable star, Robert De Niro (who has frequently foregone his standard salary to work with Scorsese), helped the director obtain funding for projects that Hollywood executives would normally consider too financially risky. Without the burden of having to justify big budgets by generating even bigger profits, Scorsese had the freedom to develop his unusual talents as a filmmaker and, in the process, created some of the most artistically progressive films in contemporary Hollywood cinema. A steadfast experimenter—whose movies (including *Mean Streets*, *Taxi Driver*, and *Raging Bull*) have often been appreciated more in retrospect than at the time of their release—Scorsese regularly tests the limits of classicism through daring narrative and stylistic incongruities.

Taxi Driver has been a recurrent example throughout this book because it offers such extreme, and therefore illustrative, instances of the modes of narrative perversity examined in Part II: narrative frustration, genre deviation, and conceptual incongruity. Consider the scene—a textbook example of all three narrative modes—in which Travis Bickle shoots and kills a gunman robbing a New York market. Exhibiting the kind of narrative frustration we saw in Chapter Three, the scene seems intent on avoiding the suspense and thrills that normally accompany scenes in which Hollywood protagonists use violence to stop armed robberies in progress. The narration builds some suspense when a medium shot shows a robber pointing a gun at the owner of the market, as Travis, in the background of the shot, draws his own gun (Figure 6.1).

The shot—which both communicates Travis's intentions to the audience and reveals the gunman's ignorance of Travis's presence—seems primed to exploit the scenario's potential for Hollywood-style action, if, for instance, the robber recognized that Travis had the jump on him and responded violently. In a more typical Hollywood movie, the deadly face-off between the two characters would generate excitement, but here it comes across coldly. The

FIGURE 6.1. A shot from *Taxi Driver* seems primed to exploit the robbery scene's potential for action and excitement.

moment of confrontation, quick and un-suspenseful, begins when—rather than delivering the kind of sharp, confident line that spectators often hear during comparable moments in Hollywood crime movies ("Go ahead, make my day"; "Yippee-ki-yay, motherfucker")—Travis quietly says to the robber, "Hey. Hey." It ends just two seconds later when the robber, whom Travis shoots only once, slumps down dead before firing a shot. A moment such as this seems designed to frustrate spectator expectations of a satisfying confrontation, squandering its potential for thrills, suspense, and spectator satisfaction.

We can also note how the scene, like the genre benders analyzed in Chapter Four, exploits conventional genre devices in order to create unsettling and unresolved incongruities in the film's narration. The scene relies on our habitual responses to generic conventions (an armed hoodlum threatening an innocent victim; our protagonist, prepared but untested, forced into a confrontation in which he must demonstrate his mettle through violent action) in order to set us up for its unconventional outcome. The face-off scene would be familiar to spectators from a variety of movies released just prior to *Taxi Driver*—including *Billy Jack* (1971), *Dirty Harry* (1971), *Straw Dogs* (1971), *Shaft* (1971), *Deliverance* (1972), *Walking Tall* (1973), and *Death Wish* (1974)—in which a character initiates a violent confrontation in order to save another character from a hoodlum or gang, a frequent scenario in films of the early seventies. Like any genre bender, the scene begins true to form: We hear the hoodlum demanding money of the store owner and watch Travis at first considering what to do and finally reaching for a pistol hidden in his pants. However, the movie neglects to fully deliver on its generic promise, preferring instead to portray a scene far more unnerving than the one predicted by its genre. Even compared to other seventies movies in which protagonists save people from hoodlums, *Taxi Driver*'s use of the scenario is extremely unconventional: Whereas generically similar scenes tend to glamorize vigilante killings, this one creates disconcerting conceptual incongruities of the sort we studied in Chapter Five.

The scene comes across as conceptually incongruous largely because the narration's attitude toward the killing seems oddly inconsistent. Robin Wood notes this quality in the movie, saying that "the central incoherence of *Taxi Driver* lies in the failure to establish a consistent, and adequately rigorous, attitude to the protagonist" (53). Indeed, the movie seems both to condemn and to side with Travis's actions. On the one hand, his reaction to the killing makes him look callous: Travis is more concerned with how to deal with his un-permitted gun than with the killing itself, and earlier scenes in which he glares at black characters gives the shooting of the thief, who is black, a racist undertone. On the other hand, he does come to the defense of a crime victim. Moreover, his reaction to the shooting seems sympathetically confused and afraid. After the killing, De Niro wrinkles his forehead anxiously, turns his body in several directions, and continues to point the gun at the obviously dead body, leaving the impression that Travis, clearly frightened by the event, doesn't know what to do with himself. The film's ambivalent attitude toward the killing impedes efforts to form a coherent moral judgment of Travis's action.

Perhaps the most frustrating, generically unpredictable, and conceptually incongruous moment occurs after Travis leaves the scene, and the narration lingers on in the market. For no reason pertinent to narrative causality, the owner of the market—who, for a brief period, the film identifies primarily as an innocent victim of a robbery—viciously and inexplicably beats the dead body of the robber with a metal bar, a kind of "primal therapy" taken to an absurd extreme. Moments such as these indicate the extent to which Hollywood could take the narrative perversities characteristic of seventies storytelling.

STYLISTIC INCONGRUITY

So far, this study has focused chiefly on narrative patterning in seventies cinema, but many seventies filmmakers—including Scorsese, Stanley Kubrick, Robert Altman, Woody Allen, and others—also display a daring penchant for idiosyncratic stylistic patterning that strains their works' classical foundations. As David Bordwell notes in his study of film narration, stylistic patterns have the potential to gain such prominence in a film that, more than mere ornamentation, they become a shaping narrative force. According to Bordwell, for instance, Alain Resnais's *Last Year in Marienbad* (1961) "elevates various stylistic features to the level of intermittently dominant structures" and that films such as Robert Bresson's *Pickpocket* (1959), Jean-Luc Godard's *My Life to Live* (1962), and Volker Schlöndorff and Jean-Daniel Pollet's *Méditerranée* (1963) highlight film technique to such an extent that it threatens to "deform" other narrational devices (*Narration*, 278). Distinctive stylistic patterning is far more characteristic of European and Asian films than Hollywood, which discourages conspicuous and idiosyncratic stylization. By the standards of classical Hollywood cinema, films such as *Taxi Driver*—which, as we will see, integrates bold stylistic patterning—risk aesthetic disaster for a classical film, diverting spectator attention away from plot patterning and onto film technique. In *Taxi Driver*, Scorsese creates idiosyncratic stylistic devices so pervasive and bold that they become a form of narration in themselves, cueing spectators to frame hypotheses and draw inferences based on patterns in the film's style.

We can see Scorsese's penchant for idiosyncratic stylistic patterning displayed in his very first feature, *Who's That Knocking at My Door* (1968). In a sequence, depicted entirely in slow motion and without diegetic sound, that contributes nothing to narrative causality, we see several male characters clowning around at a party while the Ray Barretto song, "El Watusi," plays on the soundtrack. At first, the song's upbeat, Latin tempo accords with the playful boys-will-be-boys atmosphere, but the imagery and music increasingly jar with one another as the characters start to play with a handgun. When an unnamed character jokingly aims the gun at a boyish-looking character at the party, Sally Gaga (Michael Scala), the sequence, one of the more memorable and stylistically eccentric in the film, becomes downright frightening. The editing juxtaposes shots of the men at the party pointing and laughing at the situation before them (Figure 6.2) with those of the distraught kid, dragged by the neck by a man pointing a gun at his head who looks maniacal enough to shoot him (Figure 6.3).

Shots of the gunman make him look increasingly fearsome, and those of Sally reveal his growing terror and desperation. Although the tone of the scene transforms—as the narration draws attention increasingly to the bawling

FIGURE 6.2.   FIGURE 6.3.

FIGURES 6.2–6.3. *Who's That Knocking at My Door*: A character "playfully" points a gun at the head of a distraught young man, as other characters at the party laugh and look on from a safe distance.

Sally, who, if he isn't shot, appears traumatized by the joke—the tone of the music remains consistent throughout, so that, by the end of the five-minute sequence, the soundtrack goes pointedly against the depicted action. Michel Chion calls this type of film music "anempathetic" because, rather than participating "in the feeling of the scene," the music exhibits "conspicuous indifference to the situation, by progressing in a steady, undaunted, and ineluctable manner'" (8–9). "El Watusi" plays out with detached inevitability, even as the situation for the kid grows more terrifying.

Mean Streets (1973), Scorsese's third feature, contains a moment that similarly juxtaposes upbeat music with dangerous-looking narrative action when the film's characters enter into a barroom brawl as the audience hears the 1961 Motown hit, "Please, Mr. Postman," on the soundtrack. The lightheartedness of the sequence results largely from the Marvelettes' rendition of the song; watching the sequence without sound makes the fighting look far more menacing. The jaunty tempo, doo-wop backup, and female vocals jar with images of angry fighting men and threaten to make the scene ridiculously discordant.

The use of "Please, Mr. Postman" in *Mean Streets* causes the sequence to move in two stylistically disparate directions at once; the same holds true for "El Watusi" in *Who's That Knocking*. Neither sequence, however, comes across as noticeably dissonant because other stylistic elements within the sequences help to harmonize the disparities between the soundtrack and the images and draw together the incongruent devices. For instance, "Please, Mr. Postman" joins with the dance-like camera movements and sometimes cartoonish depiction of fighting to create a playful tone that helps to assure us that no one will get seriously hurt. And while the steady, upbeat tone and tempo of "El Watusi" is at variance with the growing terror of the kid threatened with the gun, the cinematography of the scene, like the music, remains stylistically unvarying, mechanically indifferent to the ever-more disturbing situation the camera records. Indeed, "El Watusi" sets Scorsese's roving, slow-motion camera to music and accords with the scene's long pans and long dissolves. Such unities keep in check the scenes' tendencies toward stylistic incongruity.

The remainder of this chapter focuses on the visual style of *Taxi Driver*, particularly the ways in which the film's stylized cinematography and mise-en-scène both sustain and restrain the film's tendencies toward formal incongruity. The chapter sets out to demonstrate two chief points: 1) that *Taxi Driver*'s incongruous stylistic devices jeopardize the film's organic unity, while various harmonizing elements provide continuities from shot to shot and throughout the film that hold together the film's incongruous parts; and 2) that such devices generate narratively superfluous and potentially distracting visual patterns that rival classical narration, competing with it for prominence and threatening to draw spectator attention away from plot patterning.[5] *Taxi Driver*'s eccentric formal devices illustrate the manner in which a talented seventies stylist, such as Scorsese, can create stylistic and narrative incongruities that are relatively extreme for Hollywood cinema but that nonetheless integrate with classical narration.

TAXI DRIVER: REINED REALITY AND MODIFIED HALLUCINATION

Scorsese managed to obtain funding for the bleak, grotesquely violent, and seemingly un-commercial *Taxi Driver* because of a fortuitous combination of events. Many of the individuals committed to making the film recently had important successes in Hollywood, affording them some clout in the film industry. Scorsese had just made the popular *Alice Doesn't Live Here Anymore* (1975); scriptwriter Paul Schrader had just sold his screenplay for *The Yakuza* (1975) for $300,000; and Robert De Niro had just won an Oscar for his portrayal of Vito Corleone in *The Godfather, Part II* (1974).[6] De Niro would accept $40,000 to play *Taxi Driver*'s lead, reportedly turning down another picture that would have earned him half a million (Pye and Myles, 210). In addition, *Taxi Driver*'s independent producers, Michael and Julia Phillips, had recently had an enormous commercial success with *The Sting* (1973). Committing $1.3 million to the project, which included the script and actors' salaries (a tiny budget for a film with a major star shot on location in New York City), Columbia Pictures got a hot combination of filmmakers at a bargain price.

To shoot the movie, Scorsese relied on the low-budget film techniques he learned directing for Corman. "Because of the low budget," Scorsese said, "the whole film was drawn out on storyboards, even down to medium close-ups of people talking, so that everything would connect" (Thompson and Christie, 54). The director's extensive storyboarding enabled him to create a visual unity from shot to shot, scene to scene, and throughout the film as a whole, so that each shot not only connected to the shots around it but also contributed to the film's overall visual style.

Reviewers of *Taxi Driver* often described the film's style in incongruous ways. Some reviewers considered the film intensely realistic, an impression created by shots of filthy Manhattan, sweltering in the heat of the summer, the often documentary-like mise-en-scène and cinematography, as well as the performers' acting styles. One reviewer referred to De Niro's "stunningly dimensional" performance, which fleshes out "the surface dynamics of [the character's] madness into all-too-believable flesh and blood" (S. K., 7). Another complimented the actor's "totally convincing" work and Scorsese's "naturalistic direction" (Bartholomew, 35), and another the film's "frighteningly plausible case history" (Murf., "Taxi Driver," 3). Reviewers said that events in the film take place "as haphazardly as in life" (Gow, 30) and that "the sophisticated use of lighting, color, camera angle and editing make the city streets so real that a viewer can feel fear even before violence occurs" (Lauder, "Hell," 467).

But reviewers also recognized in *Taxi Driver* an almost baroque stylization at variance with the film's powerfully realistic effect.[7] From the movie's first shot of a taxicab driving through mist (Figure 6.4)—a shot that would better open a stylized horror movie—to the abstract expressionism[8] of the film's closing credits (Figure 6.13), *Taxi Driver* integrates numerous anti-realistic film styles. Film scholar Robert Kolker noted the stylistic incongruity: "'Realism' and expressionism work against each other, creating a strong perceptual tension that can be felt throughout [Scorsese's] work" (166).[9] A reviewer at the time of the film's release referred to Scorsese and cinematographer Chapman's "admirable mix of reined reality and modified hallucination" (Gow, 30). And Scorsese himself said, "The overall idea was to make [*Taxi Driver*] like a cross between a gothic horror and the New York *Daily News*" (Thompson and Christie, 54).

When viewed side-by-side, the film's stylistic devices sometimes baldly clash with one another. For instance, if one saw just the scenes of playful banter between the campaign worker, Betsy (played by Cybill Shepherd), and her coworker, Tom (comedian Albert Brooks), and the scene of murderous carnage near the end, one would have a hard time placing them within the same film. *Taxi Driver*, however, integrates both types of scenes through a variety of visual motifs.

The following analysis of *Taxi Driver* examines first the film's potpourri of realistic and anti-realistic devices and, second, the means by which the movie unifies its stylistically disparate parts. Afterward, we seek to understand the aesthetic function of the film's distinctive stylistic patterns and the ways in which Scorsese integrates them into classical narration. Finally, we examine some historical factors that encouraged Hollywood in the seventies to relax its restrictions on the idiosyncratic expression of a director's style.

STYLISTIC INCONGRUITY IN *TAXI DRIVER*

Various elements within *Taxi Driver* violate the realism of the film's portrayal of an alienated psychopath who drives his taxi through the seediest streets of Manhattan. By "realism," I mean a seemingly objective presentation of events through the classical use of cinematography, editing, mise-en-scène, and sound devices.[10] Although *Taxi Driver* mostly adheres to classical realism, it also peppers scenes with highly stylized elements, such as expressionistic and abstract distortions. For instance, when Travis enters a pornographic theater, the theater itself looks realistic and the movie *sounds* realistic, but

FIGURE 6.4. *Taxi Driver*'s opening shot draws on stylized horror film imagery.

the image of the pornographic movie displays the two-tone fuzziness of a Rothko painting and looks so vaguely biomorphic that we cannot make out a single figure (Figure 6.5). The imagery inside Travis's taxicab generally looks realistic, but the images of the streets outside his windows suggest an expressionistic blur of lights and shapes (Figures 6.8–6.10).[11] The smoke that billows from the New York streets sometimes looks exaggerated and yellowed, giving such scenes an ethereal quality.

Taxi Driver also violates classical principles of "objective" cinematography. By "objective," I mean cinematography that is not restricted by the perspective of any of the characters, is generally communicative, and is not noticeably self-conscious. For instance, often the film cuts to a slow-motion shot in the middle of an otherwise conventionally filmed scene. *Taxi Driver* frequently inserts self-conscious point-of-view shots, such as in the scene in which Travis, talking to another cabbie, fixates on a group of African Americans on the sidewalk. A shot of Travis talking on the telephone conspicuously and inexplicably tracks to Travis's right in order to film, for twenty-five seconds, an empty hallway (Figure 6.6), as though the film were temporarily directed by Antonioni. (Scorsese said about the shot, "I guess you can see the hand behind the camera there" [Thompson and Christie, 54].) During the "You talkin' to me?" scene, the film noticeably violates continuity with a jump-cut that quickly repeats a shot of Travis turning toward the camera. And, after his murderous rampage at the end of the film, the policemen who arrive on

FIGURE 6.5. *Taxi Driver*: The pornographic theater Travis enters looks realistic, but the image of the pornographic movie looks like an abstract expressionist painting.

the scene stand, for twenty-five seconds of screen time, with a strange stillness that violates the norms of realistic blocking (Figure 6.7).

The last scene, the epilogue in which Betsy reemerges in the film as Travis's fare, emblematizes the film's visual incongruities. The scene incorporates several conflicting film styles, from classical realism to abstract expressionism, even within single shots. The stylistic incongruities in the scene intensify increasingly until, by the end of the film, the images create striking contrasts.

At the scene's beginning, the stylistic incongruities remain fairly muted. We first see medium close-ups of Travis through the front windshield of his cab, a long take, shot in a realistic style, except for the occasional images of blurry colored lights reflected on the windshields behind and in front of him (Figure 6.8). The film then cuts to a close-up of Betsy, seen through Travis's rearview mirror, sitting in the backseat (Figure 6.9).

FIGURE 6.6. *Taxi Driver*: a self-conscious twenty-five-second shot of an empty hallway.

FIGURE 6.7. *Taxi Driver*: Policemen stand with a strange stillness that violates the norms of realistic blocking.

FIGURE 6.8. A shot of Travis contains blurry colored lights reflected on the windshields behind and in front of him.

FIGURE 6.9. A soft focus shot of Betsy's face in Travis's rearview mirror accentuates her classical beauty and displays abstract shapes inside and around the mirror's frame.

FIGURES 6.8–6.9. *Taxi Driver*: Contrasting images of Travis and Betsy in his taxi.

Like the shots of Travis, the image of Betsy looks realistic, although it uses a softer focus, accentuating her classical beauty, her hair billowing as though blowing in wind. More incongruous, however, are the blurry, abstract images inside and around the mirror's frame, crisscrossing colored lights and shapes moving in various directions. Whereas Betsy, as seen through Travis's point-of-view shots, appears romanticized, the world around her looks crazed and out-of-control. The lights that drift around her face reflect the repetitious, itinerant roving of the taxi and give the scene a modern, urban expression. The film repeatedly cuts between the classical shots of Travis and the simultaneously more romantic and more abstract expressionist shots of Betsy. And, although the scene is edited in a conventional shot/reverse-shot pattern, the set-up in the taxicab offers a realistic excuse for the awkward, noirish blocking in which the two figures face the same direction, communicating without looking directly at each other, their conversation mediated through Travis's rearview mirror (Figure 6.9).

The next series of shots in the scene intensifies the stylistic mix. As the taxi pulls up to Betsy's destination, the movie provides two extreme close-ups of Travis's eyes in his rearview mirror (e.g., Figure 6.10) that look jarringly different from the shots of Betsy. The close-ups have the same abstractions surrounding the mirror's frame but none of the ethereal beauty of the earlier shots. Instead, the images look haunting and ominous, the eyes canted and creepy, as though in a horror movie.

The sequence's most incongruent mix of styles comes at the end of the scene during a whip pan from a shot of Betsy to a shot out of Travis's front

FIGURE 6.10. *Taxi Driver*: a haunting shot of Travis's eyes.

window. As Travis pulls away from the curb, we see Betsy in a reverse tracking shot, filmed as though through the back window of Travis's cab (Figure 6.11). The camera then quickly whip pans from this image of Betsy, through the inside of the cab, until it faces the front of the cab, where we see the back of Travis's head, his face in the rearview mirror (brightly and strangely lit through no evident light source), and the streets of New York out of the front windshield (Figure 6.12). During the whip pan, the world seems to have dramatically changed in incongruous ways, a transformation signaled by the dramatic change in film styles. The shots of Betsy out of Travis's back window use soft focus and dim, diffused light, imbuing the evening scene with the kind of overcast realism of turn-of-the-century American Naturalist street scenes and portraits, such as those by Whistler, Eakins, and Sargent. The shots out of Travis's front windshield, however, look high-contrast and use extremely hard, low-key lighting, giving the New York streets a distinctly modern appearance; blurry urban lights and shapes dot the screen. Whereas the shot of Betsy through the rear windshield makes the world look benign and normal, the images seen through Travis's front windshield, obscured and abstract, make the world look strange and ominous. The image, moreover, now has a coarse look, the high-contrast and grainy dense blacks created by pushing the Kodak Ektachrome E.F. film stock an extra stop. Travis, moreover, seems to have driven, in the time it takes to whip pan, from New York's Upper East Side all the way to Forty-second Street.

Soon thereafter, in the final shots of the movie, *Taxi Driver* fully indulges its inclinations toward abstract expressionism: In images of New York streets, filmed as though through Travis's windshield, we can make out shapes of people, signs, and buildings, but many of the images appear as high-contrast

FIGURE 6.11. A reverse tracking shot of Betsy uses soft focus and diffused light to create a naturalistic portrait of a benign city.

FIGURE 6.12. A high-contrast shot from inside Travis's taxi uses hard, low-key lighting to portray a threatening and obscured image of New York.

FIGURES 6.11–6.12. Two images from *Taxi Driver*, separated by a whip pan, display incongruous visions of New York.

abstractions of color and shape that dissolve into one another and reposition chaotically (Figure 6.13). The shapes and colors move into the frame from all directions, layered on top of one another, the composition dynamic and hectic because the picture does not offer a single area of intensity but rather encourages viewers to shift their focus throughout the frame. This image of the city, an ominous modern landscape of lights and shapes, is the visual antithesis of the one we saw as the taxi pulled away from Betsy's curb not ten seconds earlier, as though the film had whip-panned from Betsy's comfortable Manhattan into Travis's crazed vision of the city. The strangeness of the film's final images, especially when presented so quickly after the more classically realistic images of Betsy, creates a frenzied impression of Travis's world.

Such incongruous visual devices threaten to undermine the film's organic unity; however, *Taxi Driver* does not come across as an incoherent film. As we see in the next section, the film develops patterns of images, ideas, and idiosyncratic cinematography devices that help to structure and harmonize its visual style. Rather than relying solely on classical narration to provide structure and harmony, the film develops its own patterns of eccentric stylistic devices that keep incoherence in check and rival classical narration for formal dominance. Using visual style as an organizing principle, the movie employs a mode of narration normally associated with foreign art-house directors, such as Alain Resnais, Yasujiro Ozu, Jacques Tati, and Robert Bresson. This mode, which Bordwell calls "parametric narration," appears very rarely in Hollywood cinema, although we see it exhibited in the films of some of the seventies boldest film stylists.

STYLISTIC UNITY IN *TAXI DRIVER*

When scholars note a stylistic pattern, they generally seek to establish its meaning. The critical penchant for detecting meaningful patterns results in part from a history of literary and film criticism that has encouraged scholars to assume that observations about an artistic work must somehow support a *critical interpretation* of it. In *Making Meaning: Inference and Rhetoric in the Interpretation of Cinema*, David Bordwell offers what has become film studies' most prominent condemnation of critical interpretation. (Previous theorists have offered even more far-ranging condemnations, most notably Susan Sontag in *Against Interpretation*.) Bordwell distinguishes between activities of *comprehension* and activities of *interpretation*. Whereas comprehension, according to Bordwell's definition, involves "apparent, manifest, or direct meanings," interpretation involves "implicit" meanings (ones that go beyond what the film says explicitly) and "symptomatic" meanings (disguised meanings that "the work divulges 'involuntarily'") (2, 8–9). Although deeply wary of interpretation, Bordwell sees it as inevitable. He says that "a thoroughgoing rejection of interpretation is likely to sway virtually no reader" and that "a criticism that ignored implicit or symptomatic meanings [i.e., interpretations] could not comprehensively account for artworks' construction or effects" (258).

Unlike Bordwell, I believe that criticism that avoids interpretation *can* account comprehensively for artworks' construction and effects (inasmuch as such an accounting is at all possible), but I define "interpretation" somewhat differently. Whereas Bordwell draws a distinction between "comprehension"

FIGURE 6.13. *Taxi Driver*: The final credit sequence displays high-contrast abstractions of color and shape that reposition chaotically, depicting an ominous and frenzied modern landscape.

and "interpretation," I want to distinguish between two types of activity, both of which we call "interpretation." The first is the perceiver's act of constructing meaning (explicit, implicit, symptomatic, or whatever kind of meaning) when perceiving or thinking about an artwork. Such activity is indeed inevitable; we do it all day long when perceiving or thinking about the world. The second is the act of constructing "critical interpretations" (or "readings"), which attempt to *change* people's understanding of an artwork's meaning—a process of interpretive interference. Unlike the first type of interpretation, critical interpretation is an effort to decipher meanings that the critic believes perceivers should catch in the future, an effort to make the work mean something different to people from what it meant to them before.

As an example, consider the comments of Robert Kolker who, observing *Taxi Driver*'s repetition of items of food and drink, says that the "junk food Travis is always eating [is] superficially filling but empty and finally destructive," and who later, noting the repetition of high-angle shots in the movie, says that they are "meaningful immediately or prepare for meaning later in the work" (197, 202–203). In both examples, the repetitions, according to Kolker, function ultimately to generate narrative meanings that viewers seem not to have caught. However, such repetitions might have all sorts of other functions; meaning is only one kind of artistic effect. "We must first be willing to assume," Kristin Thompson argues, "that a film's form is not limited to its narrative and our activity as viewers is not aimed simply at a constant interpretation of all elements in terms of the meaning they create" (*Breaking*, 250). Film scholars repeatedly practice the interpretation of texts but, as a group, are far less practiced at discussing cinema's non-meaningful effects.

My line of argument raises the question: What *is* the function of patterns in an artwork, if not to generate meaning? The remainder of this chapter will answer that question as it examines patterns of stylistic devices in *Taxi Driver*. The chapter does not attempt to change one's understanding of *Taxi Driver*'s meaning. Indeed, I do not presume to convince readers to experience *Taxi Driver* in any way that differs from how they already do. My analysis of the film may emphasize my critical or aesthetic biases or may be flat-out wrong, but it is not a critical interpretation: It does not attempt to decipher the film in order to change the way people experience it. Rather, as in all of the chapters of this book, here I am examining some of the film's surface qualities in order to understand their aesthetic functions and ultimately to persuade readers that such qualities account for much of the aesthetic value placed on so many Hollywood films of the 1970s.

I offer my distinction between interpretive and non-interpretive criticism in preparation for the following discussion of stylistic patterns in *Taxi Driver*. Far from justifying my observations by pointing to the significance behind the patterns, I want to show that the value of the film's patterns rests precisely in their *in*significance within the causal chain of the narrative. The patterns create extra-significant systems of coherence, systems that contribute to *Taxi Driver*'s aesthetic value without contributing much or anything in the way of theme, characterization, or story causality. As we will see, the film's stylistic patterns help to organize and harmonize *Taxi Driver*'s incongruities and encourage spectators to link various elements of the film that barely connect narratively, thematically, or in any other meaningful way. Using devices that often deviate from Hollywood norms, *Taxi Driver* develops idiosyncratic stylistic patterns that supply the structure and harmony normally supplied by classical narration alone.

But before we try to understand the functions of *Taxi Driver*'s stylistic patterns, we must first identify their presence in the film. And if I am to demonstrate that such patterns serve aesthetic functions that differ from those one typically finds in a Hollywood film, we must identify not only their presence but also their peculiarity.

Non-signifying patterns operate, at some level, in all movies. We could note the repetition of scenes in *The Big Sleep* (1946) in which a character is killed after opening a door, or of scenes in *The Searchers* (1956) in which Captain Reverend Clayton is interrupted in the midst of performing a ceremony, or of scenes in *Pulp Fiction* (1994) in which characters eat each other's food or drink each other's drinks. Shots of characters riding in convertibles repeatedly appear in *Touch of Evil* (1958), as do shots of flowers in *Frankenstein* (1931) and of stairs and cars in *Psycho* (1960), which also features repeated uses of voice-over narration and high-angle cinematography. Such repetitions can be found throughout cinema because they provide one potent means by which movies, and all other art forms, order their elements. What distinguishes *Taxi Driver* is not the existence of such patterns but rather their unusual density, variety, and, in some cases, their idiosyncratic deviation from Hollywood's stylistic norms.

Taxi Driver contains numerous repetitions incidental to the film's narrative substance (including slogans, buttons, and signs; an emphasis on names;

and the sounds of beating and clicking); however, the film's densest, most various and stylistically eccentric repetitions are visual. Throughout the movie, for instance, we see similar-looking shots of water, liquid, bubbles, fog, smoke, and haze (for examples, see Figures 6.4–6.5 and 6.14–6.16). Mirrors and windows serve other visual patterns (e.g., Figures 6.8–6.14), as do shots of empty hallways (e.g., Figure 6.6) and the colors red, green, and yellow (of, for instance, traffic lights [e.g., Figure 6.17], "don't walk" signs, taxicabs [e.g., Figure 6.4], and blood [e.g., Figure 6.22]).

The film's unusual cinematography contains repeated devices that do not strictly obey classical Hollywood norms. Three types of stylized shots figure prominently:

1. Slow-motion shots, especially shots of Travis's obsessions: Betsy, black men, prostitutes, liquid, and the candidate, Palantine;

2. Shots from directly or almost directly overhead (Figures 6.7, 6.16), especially shots of hands on desks and tables (Figures 6.15, 6.18–6.21); and

3. Slow tracking shots from unusual angles.

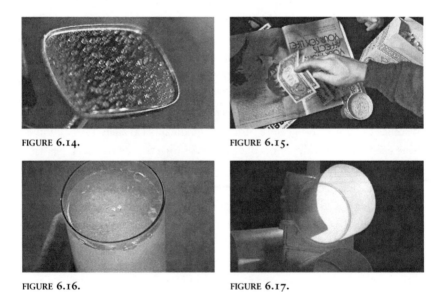

FIGURE 6.14.

FIGURE 6.15.

FIGURE 6.16.

FIGURE 6.17.

FIGURES 6.14–6.17. A few of *Taxi Driver*'s many images of water, liquid, bubbles, haze, and glass.

Other Hollywood films use such devices from time to time, but *Taxi Driver* does so in an unusually concentrated way. Moreover, often the narrative does not offer any justification for their presence in a scene. For instance, slow-motion shots of Travis's obsessions do not always represent Travis's optical point-of-view; indeed, in some cases, the film does not even depict Travis within the space in which the shots appear. Similarly, often the overhead shots do not represent character point-of-view (e.g., Figures 6.7, 6.19), or they draw attention to objects irrelevant to narrative causality (e.g., Figure 6.16). And, even when depicted objects in the three types of shots pertain to the main narrative, the unusual cinematography devices draw conspicuous attention to the film's visual style, distracting viewers from the story and violating Hollywood admonitions against unmotivated stylistic flourishes.[12]

In order to understand the ways in which *Taxi Driver*'s narration integrates dense, various, and eccentric stylistic patterns, we should examine their presence in a scene. The climactic shootout near the end of the film displays a dense network of the visual patterns that operate throughout the entire movie. The sequence depicts Travis killing three men: Iris's pimp,

FIGURE 6.18.

FIGURE 6.19.

FIGURE 6.20.

FIGURE 6.21.

FIGURES 6.18–6.21. *Taxi Driver*: high-angle shots of hands on desks and tables.

Sport; the manager of the seedy hotel in which Iris entertains her customers; and a gangster in the room with Iris. Throughout, the scene incorporates images, ideas, and cinematography devices that reverberate with one another and with moments from other parts of the movie. For instance, the colors red, green, and yellow permeate the scene. As Travis drives up to Sport's doorstep, we see not only Travis's bright yellow cab with its bright yellow lights but also red, green, and yellow flags draped across the street. The red blood of the hotel owner as it splatters against the wall of Iris's room, like the couch pillows, clashes with the room's red couch. Images of sparkling lights also reflect throughout the scene: the headlights and flashing roof lights of Travis's cab as he drives to the hotel, the lights on the street where he parks, the spark of Sport's cigarette when he throws it on Travis's jacket, the sparks that fly from firing guns, the sparkle of the candles in Iris's room as she hears Travis's gunshots, the bare lightbulbs in the hallways of the building, and, after the police arrive, the twirling colored lights of police cars outside.

Many ideas and images in the scene recall ideas and images from other parts of the movie. When Travis sits down on a doorstep after shooting Sport in the stomach, we see the image of a hazy television set in the background behind him, a moment that echoes three earlier scenes in which Travis sits down in front of a hazy television. Toward the end of the sequence, after police have entered the scene, Travis looks at them, makes his bloody fingers into the shape of a gun, and feigns shooting himself in the head (Figure 6.22): The image resembles three prior shots in the film in which characters pretend to shoot someone with their fingers. The blood that drips from Travis's fingers (Figure 6.22) reflects the numerous images of liquid throughout the movie, especially rain on Travis's windshield and side mirrors (Figure 6.14). When Travis shoots off the fingers of the hotel owner, the moment recalls the discussion between Betsy and Tom about the man at the newsstand who is missing several fingers and who, Tom suggests, might have had his fingers shot off by the mob. And the shot of Sport's ring, an image of an eye, mirrors the numerous shots of and references to eyes throughout the movie.

Scorsese also packs into the scene the three distinct cinematography devices that he intersperses throughout other parts of the movie:

> 1. Slow-motion shots of Travis as he moves upstairs, of Iris as she hears gunshots, and of the gangster as he steps out of the room to shoot Travis in the arm. None of the slow-motion shots represent the optical point-of-view of a character, which would have helped justify the device.

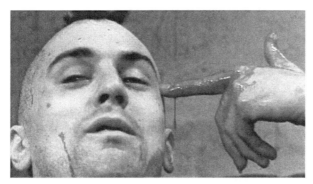

FIGURE 6.22. *Taxi Driver*: a shot of blood dripping from Travis's finger, one of four shots in the film in which characters pretend to shoot someone with their fingers.

2. Shots from directly overhead as the gangster steps out of Iris's room and as the camera surveys the carnage after the shooting (e.g., Figure 6.7).

3. Long, slow tracking shots from unusual angles. After the shootings, Scorsese includes a series of nine slow-moving tracking shots, linked by dissolves: The camera traces, in reverse, the progress of Travis's vigilante killings, tracking from the room in which Travis murdered the gangster and hotel manager (Figure 6.7), to the blood-splattered hallway, to Sport's ring and lifeless body, and then outside, where Travis sat before entering the building and where police, reporters, and a crowd of onlookers now observe the crime scene.

Such unusual expressions of style, although integrated with the film's narration, draw attention to their own peculiarity and repetitive presence.

But to what end? I have identified the presence of incongruous and unifying patterns in *Taxi Driver*, but we do not yet understand their effect on the spectator or how they contribute to the film's unusual narration. The next section addresses the function of *Taxi Driver*'s stylistic patterns and examines the ways in which they deviate from, and integrate with, Hollywood narrational norms.

FUNCTIONS OF STYLISTIC PATTERNING IN *TAXI DRIVER*

The formalist concepts of function and motivation can help us understand the ways in which stylistic patterning operates in *Taxi Driver*. For the Russian Formalists, every effective device within a work of art serves an aesthetic *function*, which is the device's purpose in the artwork or the device's effect on a perceiver.[13] A perceiver justifies the presence of a device by ascribing to it a *motivation*, which is the perceiver's understanding of the reason for the device's existence in the artwork. Functions are theoretically infinite, but Formalists and Neoformalists normally discuss a limited number of motivations.

Kristin Thompson—taking her cue from the Russian Formalists, as well as from Gérard Genette and David Bordwell—delineates what she considers the four types of motivations: compositional, realistic, transtextual, and artistic (*Breaking*, 15–20). *Compositional* motivation "justifies the inclusion of any device that is necessary for the construction of narrative causality, space, or time" (16). For example, *Taxi Driver* includes a scene in which Travis explains, through voice-over, that Betsy has agreed to go with him to a movie, a compositionally motivated moment that provides a cause for a subsequent scene in which we see them on a date. *Realistic* motivation uses "notions from the real world to justify the presence of a device," appealing to spectators' sense of what is plausible (16). Thus, as we hear Travis's voice-over about his upcoming date, we see a shot of his taxi picking up a passenger, a realistically motivated activity for a cab driver. The third type of motivation Thompson considers is *transtextual*, which involves an "appeal to the conventions of other artworks" (18).[14] Travis's voice-over is partly justified by similar voice-overs in other films, offering a transtextual motivation for an otherwise under-motivated device. In all three of these types of motivation, story information justifies the device's presence.

Artistic motivation is the rarest and most elusive of the four types and of primary concern here. Artistically motivated devices exist for their own sake. Bordwell calls "artistic motivation" a "residual category" because "the spectator has recourse to it only when the other sorts do not apply" (*Narration*, 36). Artistically motivated devices include, among other things, conspicuously artificial mise-en-scène elements, cinematographic flourishes, and the idiosyncratic and narratively incidental stylistic patterns that we have identified in *Taxi Driver*. Such patterns have no motivation except an artistic one, since they do not contribute to narrative causality, they do not appeal to conceptions of realism, and they do not follow the conventions of other artworks.

Hollywood has always favored compositional, realistic, and transtextual motivations because it relies so heavily on causality, realism, and standard practices. Classical Hollywood cinema disfavors artistic motivation since, according to Bordwell, Hollywood is obedient to "extrinsic norms" (an art form's standard practices) and does not encourage films to cultivate "idiosyncratic intrinsic norms" (an artwork's distinctive expressions of artistic individuality).[15] Still, some eccentric Hollywood filmmakers have developed their own artistically motivated stylistic systems that serve aesthetic functions beyond the range of their films' plots. I want to focus on three interrelated functions of *Taxi Driver*'s patterns of stylistic devices: ornamentation (what Thompson calls "excess"), stylistic structure, and harmony.

Ornamentation

Thompson uses the term "excess" to indicate when the presence of a device "retains a perceptual interest [for the spectator] beyond its function in the work" and deflects attention from the artwork's narrative or substantive purpose, as is the case, say, with ornamental patterns in Baroque architecture (*Breaking*, 259).[16] Although *Taxi Driver*'s stylistic patterns are sometimes too inconspicuous to command much perceptual attention, some of the film's stylistic ornamentation seems detached from story representation, eliciting a perceptual interest that briefly overpowers plot patterning. Examples would include some of the images of liquid and haze or the twenty-five-second shot of a hallway, which do not convey any essential narrative information. Other salient and stylized devices—such as slow-motion point-of-view shots of Travis's obsessions, the strange blocking of the policeman after Travis's shooting (Figure 6.7), and a lingering shot of his glass of Alka-Seltzer (Figure 6.16)—integrate more smoothly with plot patterns but nonetheless elicit focused interest in the film's stylistic devices, apart from their narrative functions.[17] In both cases, ornamental devices add a narratively superfluous and distracting stylistic system, diverting attention from the causal progress of *Taxi Driver*'s story. Although narratively incongruous, stylistic ornamentation enlivens the mise-en-scène by making it more vivid and by stimulating our perception of visual details. Unmotivated by genre convention (as would a dance number in a musical), realism, or plot patterning, such ornamentation causes *Taxi Driver* to veer away from classical narration, prompting spectators to attend to items that have nothing or little to do with the film's narrative matter.

Although the concept of ornamentation points us to the interest, and narrative incongruity, of peculiar devices within *Taxi Driver*'s stylistic patterning, the concept does not explain the aesthetic function of the patterning itself. To do so, we should separate the patterns into two types and look at their functions separately: *Salient* stylistic patterns offer the film "structure" (a means of organizing and linking elements of a work), whereas more *inconspicuous* patterns create "harmony" (the concord of such elements). Although one finds considerable overlap between salient and inconspicuous patterns and their functions, dividing them helps us define two separate effects on viewers.

Stylistic Structure

Taxi Driver's most salient patterns create a stylistic structure that rivals the film's narrative structure. The film's style—rather than cause-and-effect narration alone—serves as an additional organizing principle, structuring *Taxi Driver* according to a series of repeated unconventional stylistic devices. Bordwell calls this type of structure "parametric narration," in which a film develops "a narrow and strongly individual" group of stylistic devices and then repeats them regularly (*Narration*, 286). He is drawing on concepts from *Theory of Film Practice*, in which Noël Burch offers an encyclopedic catalogue of the types of "parameters" (by which Burch means stylistic devices) that filmmakers may use "to structure their work in an *abstract* way" (Burch, 63). Bordwell considers this use of parameters (which he identifies in several foreign films, such as those of Resnais, Tati, and Bresson) a form of "narration," in which the frequent and systematic use of a similar device across an entire film "establishes a distinctive intrinsic norm, often involving an unusually limited range of stylistic options" (288). Patterns of stylistic devices, according to Bordwell, cause the spectator to generate hypotheses and draw inferences about the "stylistic development of the film" (289).

Taxi Driver creates just those sorts of intrinsic norms through salient repetitions of unconventional stylistic parameters. Such parameters include the three distinct cinematography devices that frequently pepper the film's visuals; shots that center on causally irrelevant elements of the spatial environment (e.g. Figures 6.6, 6.14–6.17); and the abstract expressionism that permeates the film's cinematography and mise-en-scène. Such devices have no evident compositional or realistic motivation, nor do they have any stylistic basis in Hollywood convention. Adopting qualities of parametric narration, *Taxi Driver* develops an idiosyncratic and highly limited series of stylistic devices that become a system in their own right and that cue the spectator to recognize and anticipate pattern repetitions and variations.

Although present among some European and Asian films of the 1950s and 1960s, parametric narration appears rarely in Hollywood cinema, even in the films of stylistically unusual Hollywood filmmakers (such as Hitchcock) or film movements (such as *film noir*). In this way, *Taxi Driver* offers another illustrative example of the propensity of seventies filmmakers to adopt a "middle way" between classical Hollywood and foreign cinema. Indeed, Scorsese has frequently noted his indebtedness to both traditions,[18] which allow him, on the one hand, to exploit unrealized potentials within traditional Hollywood cinema (including, as we soon see, the tradition of stylized depictions of violence) and, on the other, to adopt some of the boldness and eccentricity of foreign cinema of the fifties and sixties, which, in the seventies, afforded an American filmmaker a wealth of stylistic techniques previously uncultivated in Hollywood.

Taxi Driver, however, obeys too many of classical cinema's codified devices—such as shot/reverse shot, master shots, classical framing, 180-degree rule, and narrative causality—to characterize its narration as predominantly parametric. According to Bordwell, parametric narration causes the film's plot to emerge "on the style's own terms" (*Narration*, 288); however, *Taxi Driver*, although it continually tests the boundaries of Hollywood classicism, mostly obeys classical norms. Relatively too limited to serve as the prime structuring pattern for the entire film, *Taxi Driver*'s visual devices offer intermittent stylistic structures behind or in between the film's more dominant classical structures. Although *Taxi Driver* is as stylistically eccentric a film as one is liable to see in Hollywood cinema, style is only one of the film's structuring patterns; the rest are classical.

Harmony

The more inconspicuous patterns in *Taxi Driver* are not salient enough either to serve as ornamentation or to form even a muted parametric structure. Examples of inconspicuous patterns include the colors red, green, and yellow; the sounds of beating and clicking (e.g., the sounds of Travis's taxi meter, a drummer on the street, or Bernard Hermann's clanking score); and the many other unobtrusive and insignificant repeating features that I have identified. Burch says, "even though there may be structures that are 'perceptible only to those who have created them,' they nonetheless play an important role in the final aesthetic result" (67). Such patterns, I suggest, offer the scenes in which they appear the same sense of harmony that barely noticeable rhymes offer a poem: They provide extra-meaningful systems of coherence that unify the artwork and encourage us to draw connections between the work's various parts.

Inconspicuous patterns offer a felicitous additional background harmony to Hollywood films that contain more obvious and dominant structuring devices in their foreground. One can see a rhyme-like element at work in the literal background of *North by Northwest* (1959), for example, when the image of a corn field (Figure 6.23), a strange-looking location for this film, nonetheless contains the same diagonal grid-like pattern we have seen, in various forms, since the opening credits (Figures 6.24 and 6.25).

One might also note the felicitous graphic relationship between the Ferris wheel on which Orson Welles and Joseph Cotten ride in *The Third Man* (1949) and the "cuckoo-clock speech" Welles delivers as they exit it. Although corn fields and cuckoo clocks emerge as incongruous revelations, the films have prepared for their arrival because the images they call up repeat elements that spectators have encountered previously. Unnoticed film scoring offers the same sort of harmonies, connecting scenes and characters in ways that work below the level of conscious observation. "Echoes and repetitions," Stephen Booth writes, "can make an artificial construct feel almost as inevitable . . . as an object in nature" (*Precious Nonsense*, 6).[19] No matter how incongruent a film's elements, echoes and repetitions contribute to our impression that, wherever we are in a film, our minds have been there before.

Taxi Driver's stylistic patterning establishes correlations among the film's incongruent parts, providing systems of coherence and correspondence outside of the film's narrative logic. The shootout scene, for instance, recalls a

FIGURE **6.23.**

FIGURE **6.24.**

FIGURE **6.25.**

FIGURES **6.23–6.25.** Three shots from *North by Northwest* that display a diagonal grid-like pattern, creating visual harmony among different segments of the movie.

moment even as disparate as Betsy and Tom's playful banter at Palantine headquarters, because, for one thing, both scenes contain some version of a man who has his fingers shot off. Of course, not all of an artwork's structural elements necessarily have aesthetic effects; some structures might be too inconspicuous or complex for perceivers to register. However, the inconspicuous stylistic patterns in *Taxi Driver*, while various and subtle, are still sufficiently redundant and readily enough perceived that, whether we register all of them or just some of them, the film prompts spectators to mentally flit through numerous incongruent moments in the movie as their eyes focus on one aspect of a shot or another. Echoes and repetitions help to harmonize portions of a movie that is in many ways an assortment of incongruous narrational devices, so that the elements that make up *Taxi Driver* are at the same time coming together and falling apart.

STYLIZATION IN SEVENTIES HOLLYWOOD

Several of the 1970s foremost directors imbued their work with artistically motivated devices far more eccentric than Hollywood was accustomed to. Consequently, we see filmmakers of the period elevating their films' styles almost to the level of prominence one might expect from foreign art-house directors, such as Antonioni, Bresson, Godard, Tati, and Ozu. Robert Altman's films of the period—such as *M*A*S*H* (1970), *McCabe & Mrs. Miller* (1971), *The Long Goodbye* (1973), *California Split* (1974), *Nashville* (1975), and *A Wedding* (1978)—often featured slowly drifting, roving, and zooming cameras; loose, gap-filled plots; ensemble casts whose stories variously diverged and integrated; abrupt scene transitions without causal connections; and improvised performances with overlapping dialogue and mumbled lines. Stanley Kubrick—in *2001: A Space Odyssey* (1968), *A Clockwork Orange* (1971), and *Barry Lyndon* (1975)—incorporated unusually long tracking shots and slow zooms, slowly delivered dialogue and extended segments without any dialogue at all, distorting wide-angle lenses, measured pacing, rigorously formal mise-en-scène, and audacious uses of orchestral music, such as the various classical and synthesized renditions of Beethoven and Rossini in *A Clockwork Orange*. Kubrick also combined what James Naremore calls "the aesthetics of the grotesque" (involving masked figures, caricatured faces and bodies, and a prurient fascination with bodily orifices) with a cool control of "photography, découpage, and performance" (*On Kubrick*, 25–40). Seventies experiments with stylistic eccentricity paved the way for films such as *Blue Velvet* (1986), *Raising Arizona* (1987), *Slacker*

(1991), *Reservoir Dogs* (1992), *Safe* (1995), *Welcome to the Dollhouse* (1996), *The Limey* (1999), *Magnolia* (1999), *Napoleon Dynamite* (2004), and *Time Code* (2006), which similarly flaunt the artistically motivated stylistic flourishes that have in many ways become the norm in contemporary indie cinema.

Woody Allen is one of the seventies' more intriguing stylists, and the progression of his films from the early seventies to the early eighties—from, say, *Bananas* (1971), to *Love and Death* (1975), to *Annie Hall* (1977), to *Manhattan* (1979), to *Stardust Memories* (1980)—demonstrates the developing idiosyncrasies of his style. For instance, during this period, Allen grew almost as fond of uninhabited space as Antonioni or Ozu. In *Annie Hall*, *Manhattan*, and *Stardust Memories*, Allen sometimes blocks his actors so that they move in and out of the frame, until, at some point, the frame has no characters in it at all. During the planetarium scene in *Manhattan*, large portions of the screen are black, the figures dwarfed by the mise-en-scène (Figure 6.26). Allen also makes it difficult sometimes for spectators to immediately connect the soundtrack with the image on the screen. For instance, during one seventy-seven-second shot in *Annie Hall* (the "Jew eat" scene, portrayed in one long take, another characteristic Allen device), it takes almost thirty seconds before we realize that the characters we hear talking are in fact in the shot: At the beginning of the shot—which starts as a static extreme long shot of a Manhattan street and eventually becomes a reverse-tracking medium-shot of the two actors—the characters take up such a tiny and inconspicuous portion of the frame (Figure 6.27) that perceivers could not possibly locate them until the actors have walked close enough to the camera to be noticed.

Similarly, Allen sometimes withholds reverse shots so that crucial spatial information, such as the identity of a character to whom another character is speaking, remains unclear for an unusually long time. Consider the scene in *Stardust Memories* in which Allen's character begins talking to the character played by Charlotte Rampling before we even know she's in the apartment with him. Or consider the moment in *Manhattan* in which Isaac (Allen) and Tracy (Mariel Hemingway) begin conversing with Yale (Michael Murphy) and Mary (Diane Keaton) at an art museum. The conversation begins before we see whom Isaac and Tracy are talking to, and we don't realize that Mary is even in the scene until, sometime into the conversation, she suddenly enters the frame. Allen's films offer no narrative excuses for such unconventional stylistic devices: The suppression of story information, for instance, is not transtextually motivated by genre, as in a mystery film. The stylistic devices seem motivated purely by the artistic idiosyncrasies of the filmmaker.

Many seventies filmmakers began to consciously pattern their filmmaking on the "auteurist" model established by foreign filmmakers, whose stylistic eccentricities had generally been frowned upon or flat-out prohibited in Hollywood filmmaking. The "auteur theory," articulated first in 1954 by Francois Truffaut as *"la politique des Auteurs"* in the French film journal *Cahiers du cinéma*, held that some celebrated directors—including Howard Hawks, Alfred Hitchcock, Jacques Tati, Robert Bresson, and Jean Renoir—like the authors (*auteurs*) of novels, imbued their films with a personal artistic vision. Truffaut and other filmmakers of the French New Wave partly justified their own stylistic idiosyncrasies by means of the theory, which has become associated primarily with European art cinema of the 1950s and 1960s.

The auteur theory made its way into American discourse in the 1960s, when journalists, film critics, and professors began to rely on the theory as

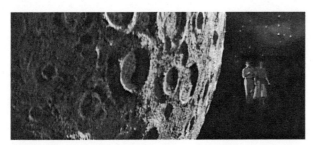

FIGURE 6.26. Characters dwarfed by the mise-en-scène in Woody Allen's *Manhattan*.

FIGURE 6.27. The beginning of a seventy-seven-second shot in *Annie Hall* in which the characters we hear are too small and inconspicuous to locate in the frame.

the foundation for film analyses. Foremost among these film commentators was Andrew Sarris, whose essay, "Notes on the Auteur Theory in 1962," and later book, *The American Cinema: Directors and Directions 1929–1968*, employed the theory to establish a pantheon of the fourteen greatest American film directors. In the seventies, the theory was espoused in film courses across the United States and still is. Many seventies filmmakers, including Scorsese, encountered the theory in film school. Influenced by *la politique des Auteurs* and the foreign films playing in American art houses, several of these filmmakers, uncommonly well versed in international cinema, developed stylistic eccentricities that served several artistic functions: The eccentricities added a hipness and cinema literacy to their films, they enabled the filmmakers to distinguish themselves from other filmmakers and to position their work within an international tradition, and they encouraged filmmakers to practice bold stylistic innovation and to establish themselves as more than film workers but as artists with a signature style.

At the same time, the studios, which traditionally discouraged stylistic eccentricity in their directors, saw directorial style as another form of product differentiation and a means of marketing a film. In the past, only a handful of celebrity directors, such as Alfred Hitchcock or Frank Capra, figured prominently in a film's promotion, but in the seventies the auteur theory had so pervaded the culture that promoting a film as an artistic expression of its director became a useful means of selling films that in other ways defied quick genre tagging. The posters and trailers for *A Clockwork Orange* read, "Stanley Kubrick's A Clockwork Orange," the director's name featured almost as boldly as the movie's title, and *Barry Lyndon*'s trailer emphasized Kubrick's role as the author of the film, citing reviews from film critics who praised the director's artistic achievement. United Artists marketed *Interiors* (1978) as a serious film by Woody Allen and *Manhattan* as his return to comic form; the tagline for *Manhattan* read, "Woody Allen's New Comedy Hit." The tagline for Altman's *Brewster McCloud* (1970) read, "'Something else' from the director of M*A*S*H." And the trailer for *Mean Streets* said the film "triumphantly heralds the arrival of Martin Scorsese." The director model of filmmaking, resisted for decades in the studio era, became a convenient means for promoting a film's artistry, for distinguishing its unique qualities, and for establishing its genre category (by director).

Taxi Driver emerged during a period when Hollywood had relaxed its limits on the idiosyncratic expressions of style, particularly for depictions of violence. Filmmakers of the 1930s, 40s, and 50s had already depicted violence with an unusual stylishness for Hollywood cinema. As Stephen Prince notes, studio-era filmmakers, largely in an effort to avoid PCA regulation and regional censorship, devised a "substitutional poetics, whereby unacceptable types of violence could be depicted not directly, but through various kinds of image substitution" (*Classical*, 205). Instead of depicting explicit violence, classical Hollywood films often used shadows (e.g., *Scarface* [1932], *G-Men* [1935], *Night and the City* [1950]), obscured action (*Captain Blood* [1935], *Objective Burma* [1945]), offscreen action (*Frankenstein* [1931], *Scarface*, [1932]), or images or sounds that stood in for the violent events (*Scarface*, *Doorway to Hell* [1930]).[20] Or the films centered on more neutral areas in the mise-en-scène, such as characters' faces (*Double Indemnity* [1944]) and nearby objects (*Brute Force* [1947], *The Set-Up* [1949], *Pickup on South Street* [1953]).[21] For Prince, the "poetics of violence" developed during the studio era helped not only to avoid regulatory action but also to "expand the creative possibilities of expression in American cinema" (205). The studio era's poetics of violence, he notes, has "left its visual legacy deeply embedded in American film," long after the period in which films were forced to curtail explicit depictions of violence in order to avoid regulatory action (251).

Filmmakers in the sixties and seventies drew on the tradition of stylized depictions of violence in Hollywood and—exploiting changing mores and the weakening and ultimate elimination of Code restrictions and regional film censorship—developed unrealized potentials in that tradition. With the liberalization of the Code in 1966 and its replacement by the Classification and Rating Administration (CARA) rating system in 1968, filmmakers took advantage of the new freedoms in Hollywood by presenting stylized violence with an explicitness previously forbidden in Hollywood. The rating system meant that filmmakers could show almost anything in their movies, provided they and their distributors were willing to have their films slapped with a restrictive rating, and by 1973 R-rated films began to outnumber every other rating category. Before *Taxi Driver*, Arthur Penn in *Bonnie and Clyde* (1967), Sam Peckinpah in *The Wild Bunch* (1969) and *Straw Dogs* (1971), Stanley Kubrick in *A Clockwork Orange* (1971), and Brian De Palma in *Sisters* (1973) and *Phantom of the Paradise* (1974) had already exploited some of the newly available aesthetic possibilities of cinema violence with slow-motion cinematography; shocking juxtapositions of violent images; balletic choreography of beatings, murders, and massacres; excessive bloodiness; and drawn-out and often graceful depictions of the moment of death. *Taxi Driver* drew on such devices—particularly the use of slow motion and excessive blood—in its depiction of the film's climactic massacre and, as we have seen, developed stylistic eccentricities of its own. Hence, the transtextual motivation afforded by previous crime films (along with horror and war films), the new freedoms afforded by an unregulated and uncensored cinema, and a relaxation of restrictions on artistically motivated devices helped enable the stylistic idiosyncrasies in *Taxi Driver* and other films of the seventies.

With *Taxi Driver*, we see the extent to which mainstream seventies cinema challenged narrational norms within Hollywood, both narratively and stylistically. Although Columbia Pictures gave Scorsese only a tiny production budget (the industry's customary strategy with films it's wary of), that a Hollywood studio financed the film at all, that the film achieved surprising success with critics and audiences (it earned $12.6 million in domestic rentals in its first run, almost ten times its negative cost), and that AMPAS recognized such an unusual film with four Oscar nominations, including one for Best Picture, and the Directors Guild with a nomination for Scorsese illustrate the degree to which audiences and the Hollywood film industry, albeit briefly, fostered narratively perverse filmmaking in the 1970s.

But we shouldn't exaggerate the film's subversiveness. Although eccentric, *Taxi Driver* stays largely within the framework of classical Hollywood. Other films of the period are truly subversive, abandoning classical cinema's narrational principles altogether. In the next chapter, through an examination of the work of one filmmaker, we look at radical narrative perversity let loose from classical narration.

CHAPTER 7 JOHN CASSAVETES'S RADICAL NARRATION

You're at a party. A man you don't recognize walks toward you and addresses you by name. You might say, "I've forgotten your name." You might say, "Have we met?" or "How do you know my name?" But more than likely you would not say, "You have me at a disadvantage." Few real people would say that. And no man, I presume, has ever said to his wife, "Darling, what's gotten into you? You're not yourself." And if a husband ever did say something so awkward, I doubt his wife would reply, "Yes I am, for the first time in my life." In a real conversation, these lines would sound bizarre, but we hear them a lot in movies, even well-written ones. When police show up at a bank robbery, do criminals say, "We got company"? And has a real police detective ever said to a reticent witness, "You and I are going downtown for a little chat"? At no point in my life has anyone used this idiom with me: "I hope so, Todd. I hope so." In fact, I hardly ever hear anyone use my name at all in conversation. I recently spoke with a good friend for an hour on the telephone and he did not use my name once. If he had, it would have sounded peculiar, yet in movies it happens all the time and sounds perfectly natural. Hollywood movie dialogue obeys its own customs. We accept it according to the terms of the cinema, not reality.

The virtue of stock movie lines—lines that frequently appear in movie dialogue but not in real speech—is their ability to advance narration in an efficient way. Stock lines have familiar, well-defined meanings, and they succinctly tell us what story information to expect next. A stock line, for instance, might indicate a turn in a scene ("I can't *take* it any more!"; "You're not going anywhere"; "It's so crazy it just might work"). Other lines indicate triumph, the final pronouncement in a contentious exchange. We know a winning line when we hear it ("I do care . . . more than you know"; "When you come back, I won't be here"). We recognize losing lines, too ("I am *not* crazy! You *must* believe me!"; "I can stop anytime I want"; "Do you think we lost 'em?"), lines given to characters in desperate trouble. Some lines indicate that a crisis will soon erupt ("It's quiet. *Too* quiet"; "He's either very stupid—or very smart"; "I have just one condition"; "One more job and then I'm out of this business for good"; "It's my only copy, so guard it with your life."). Because they have a musical rhythm and suggest closure, some stock lines enable a scene to end with a feeling of finality ("He's bound to slip up sometime, and, when he does, I'll be there"; "I got a feeling this is gonna be a lonnnnng night"). Lines have genres, just as movies have genres, and generic lines offer us the same comfort that genre in general offers: They tell us where we are and where we are going.

Part I. Perverse Movie Dialogue

Dialogue in Hollywood movies abides by conventions that do not pertain to regular conversation. I want to look briefly at four prominent conventions that will help explain why the dialogue in the movies of John Cassavetes is so perverse and peculiar.[1] Exhibiting the kind of non-linearity we expect from real speech, the dialogue in Cassavetes movies offers us an extreme example of the narrative perversity we see in so much seventies cinema. Digressive and fundamentally inefficient and uncommunicative, Cassavetes's dialogue radically violates the conventions that govern Hollywood movie dialogue. Not all Hollywood dialogue follows these conventions, but they pervade Hollywood cinema because they help keep classical narration on course.

1) *Separate characters' individual contributions to a dialogue in a Hollywood film unify into an overriding narrative purpose.* One can easily conceive of a camera or even a narrative as containing a single viewpoint; however, dialogue, by its nature, consists of contributions by figures with different perspectives and goals. It is therefore a peculiar characteristic of Hollywood movie dialogue that, although characters speak in ways that emphasize their conflicting objectives, together their dialogue contributes to a unified purpose within the narrative. Indeed, a character's own words will often "set up" the character to "lose" a scene. Although a character will appear to be striving to achieve his or her goals, the scene's dominant purpose overrides the character's individual contributions to the dialogue.

Consider as an example the following exchange from *Citizen Kane* (1941) between Kane and his stodgy financial manager, Mr. Thatcher, in which Thatcher tries to convince Kane to give up his interest in running a newspaper:

> THATCHER. Tell me, honestly, my boy, don't you think it's rather unwise to continue this philanthropic enterprise, this *Inquirer* that is costing you a million dollars a year?
>
> KANE. You're right, Mr. Thatcher. I did lose a million dollars last year. I expect to lose a million dollars *this* year. I expect to lose a million dollars *next* year. You know, Mr. Thatcher, at the rate of a million dollars a year, I'll have to close this place in—sixty years.[2]

Even the rhythms and repetitions in Kane's lines, which indicate his rhetorical authority and self-confidence, tell us he will win this exchange. And, although Thatcher's lines are about as confident as Kane's and although they indicate that he is trying to persuade Kane of his point of view, their starchy, smug tone exposes Thatcher, in accordance with the poetic justness of Hollywood movie dialogue, to Kane's witty and winning rejoinder.[3]

2) *Characters in Hollywood movies communicate effectively and efficiently through dialogue.* Conversations in movies tend to stay on subject, and movie characters usually listen to one another and convey what they mean. *Double Indemnity* (1944) contains an exchange that displays the kind of precisely tuned linguistic accord that we expect to hear between lovers in Hollywood movies. Phyllis Dietrichson meets with insurance salesman Walter Neff to discuss life insurance for her husband. We know where such conversations lead, as does Walter. Their flirtation closes with these lines:

> PHYLLIS. There's a speed limit in this state, Mr. Neff—forty-five miles an hour.
>
> WALTER. How fast was I going, officer?
>
> PHYLLIS. I'd say around ninety.
>
> WALTER. Suppose you get down off your motorcycle and give me a ticket?
>
> PHYLLIS. Suppose I let you off with a warning this time?
>
> WALTER. Suppose it doesn't take?
>
> PHYLLIS. Suppose I have to whack you over the knuckles?

> WALTER. Suppose I bust out crying and put my head on your shoulder?
> PHYLLIS. Suppose you try putting it on my husband's shoulder?
> WALTER. That tears it. Eight-thirty tomorrow evening, then?
> PHYLLIS. That's what I suggested.
> WALTER. Will you be here too?
> PHYLLIS. I guess so. I usually am.
> WALTER. Same chair, same perfume, same anklet?
> PHYLLIS. I wonder if I know what you mean.
> WALTER. I wonder if you wonder.

Phyllis and Walter communicate on many levels: They use the same tone (simultaneously seductive and antagonistic); they casually exchange sexually suggestive metaphors; and they even replay each others' phrases and syntax. Although both characters claim to have questions about the other's intentions ("I wonder if I know what you mean"), in fact, neither character misunderstands anything the other says. In Hollywood movies, rapport is the norm.

Classical Hollywood efficiency is achieved by packing dialogue with story information and eliminating the digressions that clutter real speech. Consider, as a gross but illustrative example, the following dialogue from an early scene in *Stagecoach* (1939) between Lt. Blanchard of the U.S. cavalry and stagecoach driver Curly. Their exchange lays out in shorthand the progressive locales of the entire film, as well as other pertinent story information:

> BLANCHARD. Captain Sickle has asked if you will deliver this dispatch in Lordsburg the moment you arrive. The telegraph line's been cut.
> CURLY. Sure.
> BLANCHARD. We're going with you as far as the noon station at Dry Fork. There'll be troop cavalry there and they'll take you on to Apache Wells. From Apache Wells you'll have another escort of soldiers into Lordsburg. But you must warn your passengers that they travel at their own risk.
> CURLY. At their own risk? Well, what's the trouble, Lieutenant?
> BLANCHARD. Geronimo.

Dense with exposition, this passage typifies movie dialogue's narrative efficiency. Through the dialogue, the audience quickly learns (or has reaffirmed) the three destinations of the stagecoach, that the telegraph is not working, that the coach must meet more than one escort, that the ride is risky, and that Geronimo is the source of the danger. About expositional dialogue of this sort, Sarah Kozloff says, "Generally, there is something forced about the amount of specific detail crammed into presumably incidental conversation" (40). One can almost hear in the dialogue the pressure of efficiency coming to bear on scriptwriter Dudley Nichols, who seems determined to pack as much exposition into as tight a space as possible and get on with something more interesting.

3) *Whereas real people tend to adjust what they are saying as they speak, movie characters tend to speak flawlessly.* Most movie characters use the language precisely, rarely amending their statements mid-sentence. To offer examples of this convention would be an exercise in obviousness; I can better illustrate it through some instructive exceptions. David Mamet often scripts lines whose syntax mutates as the lines progress, and the fact that his dialogue often sounds peculiar demonstrates the pervasiveness of the artificial norm. In the following line from *House of Games* (1987), for instance, each of the last three phrases belongs to a separate syntax: "You see, in my trade, this is called, what you did, you 'cracked-out-of-turn.'" A syntactically correct line would read, "This is called 'cracking-out-of-turn' in my trade," or "What you did was 'crack-out-of-turn,'" or simply, "You 'cracked-out-of-turn.'" The character who speaks the line appears to be constructing it phrase-by-phrase *as* he is speaking, until the sentence finally says all he wants it to say. Other lines from *House of Games* with shifting syntaxes include, "Man, you're living in the dream, your questions, 'cause there is a real world" and "Whether you mean it or not, and it's irrelevant to me, because you aren't going to do it." Mamet's splintered syntax makes his lines similar to real speech, but, partly because they violate a convention of movie dialogue, they can sound awkward and mannered.[4]

One could find numerous film conversations that violate the three previous conventions; however, such exceptions themselves illuminate a fourth convention of Hollywood movie dialogue.

4) *When a film violates movie dialogue convention, the transgression serves the causal progress of the narrative.* Movies, for instance, typically encourage spectators to view dialogue inefficiency or digression as compositionally motivated. Consider the rambling conversation between George and Mary from *It's a Wonderful Life* (1946) in which the absence of an overriding and unified narrative purpose to their dialogue, as they chat on Mary's couch, reveals their nervousness and mutual attraction. A communication failure among characters will, when it occurs, quickly become the focus of

the scene. Consider the scene in *Annie Hall* (1977) in which Alvy, trying to replicate the rapport he had with Annie, cooks lobster with his urbane date, a scene in which minor misunderstandings suggest that the speakers make a bad couple. A character's verbal flaws will likely contribute something significant to his or her characterization (The Dude in *The Big Lebowski* [1998]) or pose a problem the character must overcome (Billy Bibbit's stutter in *One Flew Over the Cuckoo's Nest* [1975]). When a Hollywood movie violates movie dialogue convention, the violation *means* something.

The four dialogue conventions point to a curious paradox about Hollywood movie dialogue: Such dialogue may strike us as real-sounding, but it is unlike real speech. Examining a real conversation will illustrate not only the differences between movie dialogue and real speech but also how odd real speech would sound if we found it in a movie. The following real-life exchange comes from a 1990 essay on conversation analysis. Two teenagers, Bonnie and Jim, are talking on the telephone:

> BONNIE. hhh 'n I was wondering if you'd let me borrow your gun.
>
> JIM. My gun? . . . *What* gun?
>
> BONNIE. Donchuh have a beebee gun? . . .
>
> JIM. Yeah. a*What* I meant was *which* gun?
>
> BONNIE. Tch! hh *Oh* uhm t hhh, well d'j'have a really long one? . . .
>
> JIM. Why would you like a really *long* one?
>
> BONNIE. Y'don' *have* a really long one.
>
> JIM. What?
>
> BONNIE. Y'—Donchuh have a l—really long one?
>
> JIM. Yeahhh A—all I wan' to know why you want a gun.
>
> BONNIE. Oh oh. OH. . . . Because I'm I'm doi—heheh hhh I am doing a pl—a thing hhh in drama. It's like kind of like you know what a pantomime is?
>
> JIM. Uhh hhh! Yeah. I know. . . . Yuh gonna be doin' it up on stage in front of the whole school?
>
> BONNIE. No. no. no. . . . Jis' in my drama class.
>
> JIM. Yeah I know. . . . I mean in your class when it ha hh like you do it at lunch?
>
> BONNIE. No uhm jis' do it during drama period. . . . Uhm and so I'm doing it off a record called "Annie Get your *Gun*" and it's called "Doin' What Comes Natchurly" an she's got a *gun*.

JIM. An you're Annie hh.

BONNIE. Yeah.

JIM. Ehheheh hh. You a good uh actress?

BONNIE. No heheheh?

JIM. Th'n how d'ju come out to be Annie?

BONNIE. No—I'm—it's jis' that everybody in the class has to do a different pantomime, you know?[5]

Were it to appear in a movie, this conversation would be highly unconventional. Indeed, it violates all four movie dialogue conventions. Let's begin with convention 1: *Separate characters' individual contributions to a dialogue unify into an overriding narrative purpose.* Whereas, in a movie, an exchange that begins "I was wondering if you'd let me borrow your gun" would likely lead somewhere narratively pointed, this conversation moves from idea to idea without direction. For instance, it slides from Bonnie's need to borrow Jim's gun to Jim's surprise (based on a misunderstanding) that Bonnie obtained the lead in a class performance. Each speaker's lines follow from those of the other speaker; however, because real conversations do not have narrative destinations, no unified and overriding purpose governs the progression of Bonnie and Jim's exchange.

Convention 2 says that *characters communicate effectively and efficiently through dialogue.* Incidental miscommunications (such as Jim's belief that Bonnie has a lead role), so rare in movie dialogue, frequently pepper real conversation. In fact, almost every one of Jim and Bonnie's statements either contains a misconception or is an effort to correct one. When Jim asks "What gun?" for instance, Bonnie thinks the question is rhetorical and that, with it, Jim is telling her that he does not own a gun (she replies, "Donchuh have a beebee gun?"); however, he is instead trying to establish which of his guns she wants to borrow ("What I meant was which gun?"). The rest of the dialogue continues the series of minor misunderstandings and corrections ("all I wan' to know why you want a gun." "No. no. . . ." "I mean in your class. . . ." "No uhm. . . ." "No—I'm- it's jis' that. . . .").

Convention 3 says, *whereas real people adjust what they are saying as they speak, movie characters tend to speak flawlessly.* Bonnie and Jim's conversation offers numerous examples of the way in which real people (like David Mamet's characters) continuously modify their sentences in the midst of speaking: "Y' Donchuh have a l—really long one?" "It's like kind of like you know what a pantomime is?" "I mean in your class when it ha hh like you do it at lunch?" Kozloff notes that, in movie dialogue, the "hesitations, repetitions, digressions, grunts, interruptions, and mutterings of everyday speech have either been pruned away, or, if not, deliberately included" (18). Whereas characters in movies seem to know, *before* they begin speaking, what they plan to say and how they plan to say it, real people typically construct their sentences *as* they speak, resulting in frequent mid-sentence adjustments in meaning and syntax.

None of the ways in which the conversation between Bonnie and Jim violates the conventions of movie dialogue *serves the causal progress of the narrative* (convention 4) because real conversations do not rely on causal narration or have the same pressures of unity, effective communication, efficiency, and flawless speech. We are generally more forgiving, therefore, of real speakers who violate the conventions than of movie characters who violate them. Indeed, in real conversation, oftentimes we don't even notice such speech patterns.

My larger point about the difference between movie dialogue and real speech is not strictly demonstrable, but I think it is persuasive: The conversation between Bonnie and Jim is a *real* conversation, yet, presented in scripted form, it seems stranger than the dialogue cited from movies. Indeed, all of the instances in which Bonnie and Jim's exchange violates the conventions of movie dialogue—the awkward syntaxes, minor misunderstandings, stammering, and the rambling and incidental insertions—stand out so strikingly, because we are not used to paying attention to them, that they make real speech look artificial. The effect is common: Real life often seems alien when represented in art.

John Cassavetes's Dialogue: Killing the Writer

The dialogue in John Cassavetes's movies sounds more like the conversation between Bonnie and Jim than it does conventional movie dialogue. Without an evident overriding purpose in his dialogue to govern his films' narration, his films appear to stay fixed on what seem like narrative detours. Rejecting the unity, effective communication, efficiency, and flawlessness that characterize Hollywood movie dialogue, Cassavetes's narratively perverse dialogue fixates on narrative dead ends, irrelevancies, and impediments to straightforwardness.

Cassavetes's dialogue comes so close to real speech that it often sounds as though the actors improvised their lines. Many film commentators think

Cassavetes's films are largely improvised, but they are not.[6] His first film, *Shadows* (1959), closes with the caption, "The film you have just seen was an improvisation." But even *Shadows* was not improvised in the usual sense of the word. The actors did not make up their lines in front of the camera. Cassavetes means that, developing the story in workshops, he and the actors did not use a written script. However, they worked on the dialogue in those scenes for months before shooting them. For all his later films, Cassavetes wrote complete scripts, and, although he and the actors sometimes changed lines in rehearsals, they rarely improvised dialogue on camera. Sometimes a crew member acted as a stenographer, taking down what Cassavetes and the actors made up in rehearsals so that they could reproduce it during filming. Gena Rowlands—Cassavetes's wife, who acted in most of his films—said, "We *do* use improvisation, but not as widely as people think. We start with a very complete script. . . . Then [Cassavetes] will go and rewrite it—it's not just straight improvisation. I'm asked a lot about this, and it's true, when I look at the films and I *see* that they look improvised in a lot of different places where I know they weren't" (Crist, *Take 22*, 256).

Cassavetes sought what he called "the impression of improvisation" without relying much on improvisation in the shooting process (Carney, *Cassavetes*, 161). Why would a filmmaker seek such an effect? My first answer is simple: Dialogue that sounds improvised is similar to real speech. That answer is *too* simple (and we have already seen that real speech often sounds artificial in art), but, for the moment, let us explore it in relation to a conversation from Cassavetes's 1974 film *A Woman Under the Influence*, a film that, according to Cassavetes, had only two lines of improvised dialogue.[7]

Mabel (played by Rowlands), the wife of Nick Longhetti (Falk), has had a mental breakdown, and he has committed her to an institution. The next day Nick inadvertently causes a coworker, Eddie, to fall down the side of a hill at their worksite. Almost frenzied, Nick then takes his kids and another coworker, Vito (Angelo Grisanti), to the beach. The following exchange occurs as Vito and Nick walk along the beach with the kids:

> VITO. What a day, Nick. I haven't been to the beach without my wife in—twelve years. I used to live in the water when I was a kid. Fish, they called me. I was thin, see, lips all blue, shaking. I was always lookin' for girls. My kids, they're all grown up now. My brother, Marco, he's a college graduate, communist. Couldn't keep a job. Too many big ideas. Reads too much. I say, let the girls read. They love to read. You know what I mean?

NICK. Okay, let's enjoy ourselves. Okay?

VITO. Okay.

NICK. I want to talk to my kids too.

VITO. Talk to your kids? They never listen. Why should they listen? *I* never listened. Did *you* listen? I mean, did *you* listen?

NICK. All right, right here. Come on, up here, we'll plop down right here. Come on. Come on. Come on.

VITO. Hey Nick, I'm usually a lot of fun, right? But to see a guy like Eddie fall and break all his bones, holy shit, I mean what a fall.

NICK. All right, knock it off, will you? We're here to have a good time. We're having a good time. We came to play with the kids. So let's play with the kids. Otherwise, we go home.

This conversation, which constitutes almost the entire scene, follows Cassavetes's shooting script practically word for word (Cassavetes, 89–90). However, it sounds improvised because, violating Hollywood's conventions of movie dialogue, it is as inefficient and rambling as real speech.[8] Let us examine the dialogue in light of the conventions.

Separate characters' individual contributions to a dialogue unify into an overriding narrative purpose. Like the conversation between real teenagers Bonnie and Jim, this one slides from topic to topic without a unified purpose. Consider Vito's first monologue. His opening lines ("I used to live in the water when I was a kid") suggest that he will tell Nick something about his childhood. The speech starts to ramble when Vito says, "My kids, they're all grown up now," which has the word "kid" in it and therefore sounds as though it might relate to the story he has begun, but the line ends at a point irrelevant to anything that precedes or follows. "My brother, Marco" echoes "my kids" of the previous sentence in a way that again sounds pregnant, but only at first. "He's a college graduate" leads naturally to "reads too much," which in turn leads to "let the girls read," echoing Vito's earlier statement that he was "always lookin' for girls." Although each sentence resonates with sentences that precede (words repeat, ideas meld into one another), the lines do not add up to any coherent story. Lacking a clearly identifiable focus and progressing from one mental association to another, the speech mimics the rambling quality of thought.

Once Nick joins the conversation, the direction of the scene shifts as he anxiously tries to silence Vito and as Vito tries at once to accommodate Nick's anxiety and to keep the conversation moving forward. A more conventional movie conversation—such as Thatcher and Kane's discussion about *The Inquirer* or the sexual banter between Walter and Phyllis in *Double Indemnity*—would have each character's individual lines of dialogue serve a unified narrative purpose. Kane's winning rejoinder, "I'll have to close this place in— sixty years," and Walter's witty intimation, "I wonder if you wonder," make the dialogue sound as though the lines of each character had been jointly working toward those conclusions all along. By contrast, the beach scene from *A Woman Under the Influence* prevents any single narrative purpose from governing. No overall tone emerges because each character sets his own tone: Vito sounds laid back and philosophical, while Nick seems manic and uptight, as though Vito were in one kind of scene and Nick in another. Their opposing perspectives, goals, and attitudes never integrate into a unified direction for the scene.

Characters in Hollywood movies communicate effectively and efficiently through dialogue. Vito and Nick's conversation lacks any sort of rapport. Vito does not seem to understand that Nick wants him to stop talking. The misunderstanding is not surprising because Nick does not convey his point directly ("Okay, let's enjoy ourselves. Okay?" "I want to talk to my kids too."). Nick does not acknowledge anything that Vito says to him, responding only to Vito's excessive talking. Vito and Nick listen to one another just enough to continue conversation, repeating each others' words (for instance, when Nick says he wants to talk to his kids, Vito responds that kids don't listen) but not communicating.

Movie characters tend to speak flawlessly. Similar to David Mamet's characters, Cassavetes's characters periodically readjust and refocus their sentences as they speak. For instance, when Nick says, "We're here to have a good time. We're having a good time," the second line sounds like a revision of the first. Similarly, Vito's "But to see a guy like Eddie fall and break all his bones, holy shit, I mean what a fall" changes syntax mid-sentence, as though Vito were thinking of what he has to say as he says it, not before.

When a film violates movie dialogue convention, the transgression serves the causal progress of the narrative. The most peculiar aspect of this passage is that none of the violations of dialogue convention serves narrative causality. Nick and Vito's inability to communicate has nothing to do with the film's main story line and is, in any case, too subtle to give the scene focus. Moreover, their dialogue peculiarly draws attention to information (Vito's family and childhood, swimming, looking for girls, kids who don't listen to their parents, etc.) that bears no direct relation to events in the causal chain.

The only causally relevant narrative information in the dialogue is Vito's remark about Eddie's fall, but the discussion is buried among lines to which the scene gives equal weight. Besides, this scene is the last we hear of the injury, which becomes, finally, a narrative dead-end. Cassavetes said about the dialogue in *A Woman Under the Influence*, "I try to make things believable and natural and seem like they're happening. I do write differently. I write looser dialogue. The words are there, but they don't necessarily have to come to a conclusion. . . . It's just what you hear in life" (Carney, *Cassavetes*, 341). Cassavetes resisted efficiency, conclusiveness, or anything in his dialogue that would betray a clear-cut narrative purpose.

In short, the exchange between Nick and Vito lacks the chief quality that differentiates movie dialogue from real speech: a sense that someone wrote the lines with a narrative intention. The four dialogue conventions betray a *design* behind Hollywood movie dialogue. Cassavetes's dialogue, by violating convention, lacks the sense of an implied scriptwriter. Similar to the exchange between Bonnie and Jim, Nick and Vito's scene seems to have no creative hand controlling the characters, directing the dialogue toward a defined conclusion, and giving the scene an overriding and unified narrative purpose.

Cassavetes, however, avoids overt authorial control for a purpose his filmmaking does not advertise: He wants his scenes to belong not to his own screenplay and direction but to the performers, who, he believes, will discover nuances and dormant meanings in the script only if it does not betray an authorial intention and if the actors do not feel limited by his directing. Referring to Falk and Grisanti (not to their characters, but to the actors), Cassavetes said about the performances in the beach scene:

> [T]hey are walking and Peter has some lines and he says the lines and then they don't know what to do. Now I could tell them, but that would kill it. . . . *He* has to do it. *I* can't do it. . . . I see so many things that developed [in the scene] that wouldn't have if you . . . didn't allow room for [the actors'] interpretation. I wrote it and as soon as I wrote it I killed the writer. (Carney, *Cassavetes*, 337)

Because the actors themselves cannot divine Cassavetes's intention from his script, and because the director refuses to tell them what he wants from a scene, they deliver their lines with an improvisational uncertainty similar to what one hears in real speech.

Cassavetes was not the only seventies filmmaker to imbue his dialogue with an air of improvisation or to incorporate dialogue that emphasizes the everyday qualities of real speech. In fact, the 1970s saw a vogue of this type of dialogue in such movies as *Five Easy Pieces* (1970), *The Heartbreak Kid* (1972), *American Graffiti* (1973), *Badlands* (1973), *The Last Detail* (1973), *Dog Day Afternoon* (1975), and *Mikey and Nicky* (1976). Robert Altman regularly allowed his actors to improvise lines, and his characters' sometimes mumbled, overlapping dialogue underscores the technique. *All the President's Men* (1976) makes use of overlapping dialogue in almost every scene, as well as misspoken lines ("Do any of you guys speak English? Er. Do any of you guys speak Spanish?") and strangely irrelevant dialogue insertions ("My neighbor's wife's been kidnapped," "Coffee's cold," "I don't want a cookie."). Similar to Cassavetes, Martin Scorsese taped his actors' improvisations when shooting *Mean Streets* (1973) and then wrote scripted dialogue based on the tapes (Thompson and Christie, 43). Woody Allen's linguistic stumbling has become a signature, and, like Cassavetes, he uses verbal tics and rambling speeches to generate dramatic tension.

None of these filmmakers, however, allows dialogue digressions to dominate narration in the way that Cassavetes does. Eventually, narrative causality regains control of their scenes and an overt authorial intention emerges. Allen, for instance, eventually brings his rambling speeches to a definitive resolution, and one ultimately feels the presence of the scriptwriter governing narration. Alvy Singer's opening monologue from *Annie Hall* (1977) provides a good example of Allen's dialogue style:

> You know, lately the strangest things have been going through my mind, 'cause I turned forty, tsch, and I guess I'm going through a life crisis or something, I don't know. I, uh—and I'm not worried about aging. I'm not one o' those characters, you know. Although I'm balding slightly on top, that's about the worst you can say about me. I, uh, I think I'm gonna get better as I get older, you know? I think I'm gonna be the—the balding virile type, you know, as opposed to the say, the, uh, distinguished gray, for instance, you know? 'Less I'm neither o' those two. Unless I'm one o' those guys with saliva dribbling out of his mouth who wanders into a cafeteria with a shopping bag screaming about socialism.

Listening to this passage, one wonders how the ideas will ever come together. Like Cassavetes's lines, Allen's progress by association, sliding from topic to topic without an evident predetermined direction, the lines peppered with stammered digressions and mutterings. In fact, the monologue would sound a lot like one of Cassavetes's if not for its perfectly phrased comic finish. Unlike Cassavetes's dialogue, Allen's eventually exposes the narrative purpose that results from a well-constructed punch line.

The Sound of Improvisation: Blending Art and Real Life

I noted earlier that dialogue in movies that closely mimics real conversation sounds artificial, yet I gather that, although Cassavetes's dialogue sounds unconventional, it has an air of reality. To address this contradiction, we must return to the question I asked earlier: Why would a filmmaker seek an "impression of improvisation"?

If actors are improvising, then their rambling and stammering seem appropriate, a natural consequence of composing their speech as they are speaking. When watching improvisations, we are likely to overlook such verbal digressions in the same way we overlook them in real conversations. If an actor is delivering scripted lines, however, then the same verbal digressions, unless compositionally motivated, would likely appear contrived because there would seem to be no justification for them other than a scriptwriter's overzealous commitment to realism. Dialogue sounds contrived anytime we can see the scriptwriter sweating.

But there is a third option, the one that Cassavetes takes: ambiguity. If we can't tell the difference between script and improvisation—if we can't tell the difference between the verbal digressions of the actor and the verbal digressions of the character—then our ability to distinguish between actor and character becomes compromised. Cassavetes's dialogue, more than conventional, tightly scripted dialogue, prevents spectators from easily distinguishing his actors' improvisations from the improvisations of Cassavetes's characters, who, like the actors playing them, appear to be composing their lines as they are speaking. Ambiguity avoids the artificiality of excessively veridical dialogue.

The blurring of actor and role in Cassavetes's films has frustrated many reviewers. For instance, in a pan in *New York* magazine of the original version of *The Killing of a Chinese Bookie* (1976), an annoyed John Simon says:

> So, for example, when Cosmo tells about two girls in Memphis who cut off
> a gopher's tail, ate it, and died of botulism, we wonder—there being no

botulism outside of canned food—who is being inept: the character, the improvising actor, or the filmmaker. . . . And when a mobster claims that Marx was wrong, that opium is not the religion of the people, we cannot tell who is garbling Marx here, and to what purpose.[9] ("Technical Exercise," 66)

Since Simon cannot tell whether the actors are delivering Cassavetes's lines or improvising their own, and since he cannot divine the "purpose" of the speech in any case, he can't maintain the customary distinctions between a character and an actor impersonating a character, and so he throws up his arms in critical aggravation.

Other reviewers regularly remarked on their inability to distinguish between actor and role when watching Cassavetes's movies, sometimes admiringly, sometimes with the same annoyance evident in Simon's review. Richard Combs, writing for *Sight and Sound*, notes that *Opening Night* (1977) "never bothers to make too close a distinction between actress Myrtle Gordon's [the character played by Rowlands] working out of her problems with a distasteful role on stage and Gena Rowlands' own experimentation with the part of Myrtle" (193). Hollis Alpert, writing in praise of *Husbands* (1970) for the *Saturday Review*, asks about Ben Gazzara and the part he plays, "Is Harry Gazzara, or Gazzara Harry? The fusing seems complete" (26). Pauline Kael, panning the same movie, says that the characters in *Husbands* "act very much like Gazzara, Falk, and Cassavetes doing their buddy-buddy thing on the 'Dick Cavett Show'" ("Megalomaniacs," 49). Indeed, Kael's review sometimes neglects to distinguish between her criticisms of the filmmakers and those of the characters they play, a confusion of actor and role that the movie apparently encourages.

To illustrate the ways in which Cassavetes's dialogue prevents audiences from distinguishing between actors and their characters, I want to look at two monologues from *A Woman Under the Influence* in which it might be impossible to determine from watching the movie whether the actors or the characters are improvising.

In the following monologue, Mama Longhetti, Nick's mother (played by Cassavetes's own mother, Katherine Cassavetes), is speaking to a group of people Nick has invited to the house in honor of Mabel's return from the mental hospital. Angered by what she considers the stupidity of such a party, she makes the following announcement to the guests:

> Everybody please. Quiet in here, please. Now you know Nicky loves you all. *I* love you all. Now you should know better to come here on a day like this when Mabel's coming out of the hospital. I'm not blaming you, but I'm saying the girl'll be here any minute, and you must go home, immediately! Please.

Mama says a number of incongruous things in this quick speech. She thinks, understandably, that people might feel offended when she kicks them out of the house, so she prefaces her remarks with a line that already suggests "don't get me wrong," even before she has said anything about leaving: "Now you know Nicky loves you all." Right after she says the line, however, she seems to realize that it implies that only Nick—and not she—loves the guests. So she adds another line, "*I* love you all." But Mama also wants to register her disapproval of the party: "you should know better to come here on a day like this when Mabel's coming out of the hospital." Just as she does, however, she acknowledges that it is not the fault of the guests that they were invited to the party, adding, "I'm not blaming you." Again she has compensated for what she has already said, even though she has indeed just blamed them for coming. (A missing word—"you should know better [*than*] to come here"— furthermore makes oatmeal of her logic.) Similarly, she compensates for the aggressiveness implicit in the line, "you must go home, immediately!" with the more modest "please." Mama continually says things that do not sound right to her, and she makes up for them by trying to alter the implication of what she just said. The result is an impression that the character is making up her words as she speaks.

What I am saying about Mama Longhetti, however, could just as well be said of the actor, Katherine Cassavetes, since such seemingly extemporaneous adjustments are as indicative of actorial improvisation as they are of improvisations in real speech. John Cassavetes's dialogue tends to hover around those moments when the two forms of improvisation become impossible to distinguish.

One more short passage will conclude my point. Earlier in the picture, after Nick has stood her up, Mabel spends the night with a stranger, Garson Cross (played by O. G. Dunn). In the morning, upset and behaving irrationally, Mabel goes into the bathroom, and Garson yells at her through the bathroom door:

> I'm gonna have to leave in a minute now. Listen, if this Nick fellow's on your mind and you consider me some kind of a threat to him, or if you're trying to

punish him with me or me with him, forget it! I never met the man! And don't blame yourself for me if that's what you're doing.

As in Mama Longhetti's monologue, the tone and substance of this speech—which follows the shooting script verbatim—transform as it progresses. When Garson says, "Listen, if this Nick fellow's on your mind and you consider me some kind of threat to him," he seems about to say something like "then don't worry about me, I'll leave and never bother you again." But the first part of his sentence fails to predict where his sentence in fact goes. Garson starts to chastise Mabel for what he fears she might be contemplating: "or if you're trying to punish him with me or me with him, forget it!" The "forget it" and "I never met the man" follow logically from the second part of the sentence but do not make sense with the sentence's initial dependent clause. Garson has changed his mind mid-sentence about what he wants to say to Mabel. "And don't blame yourself for me if that's what you're doing" is another adjustment, making sure now that Mabel does not feel guilty. Garson adds to his sentences until they say everything he wants them to say, even if, in the end, he violates the meaning and syntax of the beginning of his monologue.

Because we cannot tell from watching the movie whether the characters or the actors are improvising, Cassavetes's actors sound as though they might be stumbling through their performances in a way that mirrors the characters' own extemporaneous struggles. Indeed, Cassavetes solicited imperfect performances from his actors for that very reason. Actor O. G. Dunn desperately questioned Cassavetes about Garson Cross, and Cassavetes archly refused to tell him about the part, or to tell any other cast members anything about their parts. The director often preferred to use non-professional actors precisely in order to avoid the assuredness of a professional performance. He valued the sense of indecision that results from the performance of a serious amateur. For instance, to play the role of Dr. Zepp in the movie, Cassavetes enlisted the producer's brother, Eddie Shaw, who had never acted. According to Cassavetes, "When [Shaw] came in he kept on saying, 'What do I do?' I thought, 'That's *wonderful*! That's a *great* kind of a doctor to have! That's the doctors *I've* known!" (Carney, *Cassavetes*, 332). Between the *real* indecision of Cassavetes's actors and the *apparent* improvisation of their lines, Cassavetes films manage to blend art and reality in an uncontrolled mixture of the actors' own identities and the identities of the roles they perform.

Cassavetes's peculiar style of dialogue generates a sense of narrative aimlessness, as though his films, seemingly undesigned and improvised, have no authorial hand guiding them along a linear path. Whereas other seventies filmmakers admit impediments to linear narration, Cassavetes makes such impediments his primary narrative focus, so that the narrative perversity we have seen intermittently in seventies cinema ends up dominating his films' narration. The remainder of this chapter attempts to demonstrate the extremity to which Cassavetes takes the perversity characteristic of seventies narration. Although not the most representative filmmaker of the period— for most of his filmmaking career, Cassavetes worked outside the Hollywood mainstream—his independent films represent the radical end point of seventies narrative design.

PART II. THE HAZARDS OF RADICALISM

Until fairly recently, most critics considered John Cassavetes a minor film-maker. His first film *Shadows* (1959) helped to blast open the independent filmmaking scene, and he influenced many of his contemporaries (Martin Scorsese, Peter Bogdanovich, and Elaine May are a few of the directors to have acknowledged a debt to Cassavetes). Yet, he had only a handful of admirers among critics and scholars during his lifetime, and, except for *Faces* (1968) and *A Woman Under the Influence* (1974), his films were never popular.[10] Although a lot of people find his films a chore to watch, he has nonetheless gathered a loyal following since his death in 1989, as well as some critical attention, including a handful of books about him. All of his films have been revived in theaters, and, except for *Too Late Blues* (1962), all have had video releases, including a lavish DVD box set from the prestigious Criterion Company.[11] Those who admire Cassavetes consider him an artistic genius, a maverick filmmaker who did things with movies that no one else has had the talent or audacity to do. A lot of critics called him self-indulgent.[12]

Cassavetes matured as an independent filmmaker at a time when the American film industry, because of product shortages in the mid-1970s, courted independent filmmakers with lucrative distribution, exhibition, and financing deals. According to David Cook, "the 100–125 films per year produced by the majors during this period did not even come *close* to satisfying market demand, and, as distributors, [studios] came to depend more and more on privately financed independent producers to supply exhibitors with a full year's supply of product" (351). The major studios, focused increasingly on a blockbuster strategy, cut back production as the decade progressed, dropping their output from approximately 160 films per year in the mid-1960s to approximately 80 films per year in the mid-1970s (14). In the 1970s, distributors lowered their distribution fees in order to attract independents to fill the gap in production, and, although independent films generated only 10–15 percent of domestic rental receipts, by 1976 independent film production in the United States reached about two-thirds of the total output of American films (19, 352).

Complex new tax laws, in place between 1971 and 1976, including a 7 percent federal income tax credit for investing in domestic film production, further encouraged independent production. The new laws also created tax shelters that enabled investors to write off losses and defer profits if they reinvested in new domestic productions (see Cook, 11–14). The laws subsidized much independent and studio filmmaking in the seventies and sometimes made financing a feature film a win-win deal for investors, even if the film lost money at the box office. For the investors (many of them subsidized by loans from banks that were attracted to the deals because of the tremendous tax benefits), the purpose of the film was not necessarily to make money but to manufacture losses through tax sheltering, allowing films to find backing during the period 1971–1976 that would never have received funding in other years.

As a result of these various industry and government incentives, independent productions blossomed, cementing the filmmaking careers of Cassavetes, Roger Corman, John Waters, and many other independent filmmakers and producers. Studio directors Woody Allen, Peter Bogdanovich, Brian De Palma, John Frankenheimer, Stanley Kubrick, George Lucas, John Milius, Sam Peckinpah, Arthur Penn, and Martin Scorsese all worked for independent production companies at some point during the 1970s. In 1969, Francis Ford Coppola and George Lucas founded the American Zoetrope production company, with seed money from Warner Bros., which produced Coppola's *The Rain People* (1969) and *The Conversation* (1974) and Lucas's *THX 1138* (1971). In 1970, Robert Altman formed Lion's Gate, which produced his *Brewster McCloud* (1970), *3 Women* (1977), *A Wedding* (1978), and *Quintet* (1979), and Roger Corman formed New World Pictures, which distributed more than one hundred mostly profitable low-budget films in the 1970s. Independent production companies and so-called "instant majors" (smaller companies involved in the production and distribution of feature films) competed with the majors with such films as *A Man Called Horse* (1970, Cinerama Center Films), *The Boys in the Band* (1970, Cinema Center

100 Productions), *Little Big Man* (1970, Cinema Center 100 Productions), *The Honeymoon Killers* (1970, Cinerama Releasing Corporation), *Carnal Knowledge* (1971, Avco Embassy Pictures), *Big Jake* (1971, Cinema Center Films), *Pink Flamingos* (1972, Dreamland), *Deep Throat* (1972, Damiano), *Sleuth* (1972, Palomar Pictures), *Papillon* (1973, Allied Artists Pictures), *Chariots of the Gods* (1973, Sunn Classic Pictures), *The Life and Times of Grizzly Adams* (1974, Sunn Classic Pictures), *The Texas Chainsaw Massacre* (1974, Bryanston Distributing Company), *The Taking of Pelham One Two Three* (1974, Palomar Pictures), *The Stepford Wives* (1975, Fadsin Cinema Associates and Palomar Pictures), and *In Search of Noah's Ark* (1976, Sunn Classic Pictures).

Noting the popularity of some independent films (for instance, *Big Jake* took in $7.5 million in domestic rentals; *Carnal Knowledge*, $12.1 million; and *Deep Throat*, $20 million), the studios began to focus some of their own production resources on the kinds of projects that typically came under the purview of independent production, often teaming with independents in co-production in order to hedge their financial risks. For instance, after the success of *Easy Rider* (1969) and other "youth-market" films produced by independents, Columbia negotiated a six-film co-production deal with *Easy Rider* producer BBS (the independent production company of Bert Schneider, Bob Rafelson, and Steve Blauner) in 1970 that led to *Five Easy Pieces* (1970), *Drive, He Said* (1971), *The Last Picture Show* (1971), and *The King of Marvin Gardens* (1972). By 1970, almost all of the major studios had youth-market films in development, including *Zabriskie Point* (1970, MGM), *The Strawberry Statement* (1970, MGM), *Getting Straight* (1970, Columbia), *R.P.M.* (1970, Stanley Kramer Productions and Columbia), *Taking Off* (1971, Universal Pictures), *Little Fauss and Big Halsy* (1970, Alfran Productions and Paramount Pictures), and, most successfully, Robert Altman's *M*A*S*H* (1970, 20th Century Fox) (Cook, 163). In the early and mid-1970s, major studios produced cult films such as *The Rocky Horror Picture Show* (1975, 20th Century Fox); low-budget "personal films" such as *The Conversation* (1974, Paramount Pictures and American Zoetrope) and *Taxi Driver* (1976, Columbia Pictures and Michael and Julia Phillips); and off-beat, dark comedies such as *Harold and Maude* (1971, Paramount Pictures) and *The Heartbreak Kid* (1972, 20th Century Fox and Palomar Pictures). As troubled as his career was, a filmmaker like Cassavetes probably could not have emerged at any other time in American cinema.

A lot of writing and documentaries about Cassavetes address his unusual working methods and collaborative mode of filmmaking.[13] One image of Cassavetes in these treatments is that of an artist facilitating the creativity of his actors, many of whom (such as Gena Rowlands, Ben Gazzara, Peter Falk, Seymour Cassel, and Val Avery) frequently returned to his sets because of the enormous freedom to explore their craft. Cassavetes encouraged the tendency to view his films as largely actorial collaborations. "I don't have any concepts," he said in an interview, "so when the picture's done, it's what the actors want to bring to it" (*Anything for John*). He said such things all the time. However, the image of Cassavetes as creative chairperson, presiding over the inventions of his performers, is certainly not complete because one can see that, as a group, his films bear distinct narrative and stylistic markings, whichever actors they feature. Cassavetes exercised extraordinary creative control over his independent productions—as writer, director, and often actor, cinematographer, editor, and distributor—sometimes re-cutting his films years after their release in order to better realize his artistic vision.[14]

We can best understand Cassavetes's radical aesthetic by studying his unusual narrative strategies, three of which dominate his films: 1) narration tends to generate incongruous perspectives on depicted events, 2) narration obscures information that would afford viewers a full understanding of those events, and 3) the films show a marked tendency toward narrative density and disorganization.

I want to focus on one scene from *A Woman Under the Influence*—I'll call it the "committal scene" because it ends with Mabel's committal to a mental institution—to which we will return throughout the remainder of this chapter. Readers might be familiar with the scene because it depicts one of the central moments from Cassavetes's most commercially successful independent movie. (He made *A Woman Under the Influence* for a little more than $1 million—including negative costs and distribution costs—of his own and Peter Falk's money, and it grossed $12 million in domestic and foreign rentals during its initial release, an extraordinary profit for a self-distributed independent feature.) The scene can serve as a jumping-off point for everything this chapter has left to say about Cassavetes's peculiar narrative strategies.

Cassavetes sets the scene in the Longhetti living room. After an incident with a neighbor, Nick impetuously slaps Mabel, who becomes mentally unstrung and descends into what doctors in the seventies would probably have called a "nervous breakdown." Nick calls the family doctor for help, but as soon as Dr. Zepp arrives Nick tries unsuccessfully to get him to leave. Zepp interrogates Mabel, while Nick's mother, Mama Longhetti, stands on the staircase, disapproving and angry at Mabel for causing her son grief. Threatened by everyone's scrutiny, Mabel stands apart.

What follows is my own transcript of the dialogue from a short portion of the scene, dialogue that provides a more thorough representation of the scene than a plot summary can offer. The citation is long, but, because of Cassavetes's aversion to narrative efficiency, one cannot excerpt his dialogue and still retain its wealth of complexities. I cut what I could.

MABEL. Nick, I get, I get the idea there's some kind of conspiracy going on here. I mean, you been looking at me so quiet-like, and uh— [*realizing something as she points to Zepp's medical bag*]. He's got something in that bag.

ZEPP. Don't be concerned about this bag, Mabel.

MABEL. Yeah, he's gonna try and imprison me with something in that bag. . . . [*angrily*] Am I right, Nick? . . .

MAMA. Doctor, doctor, aren't you gonna give her a shot?

MABEL. No! No!

MAMA. Mabel, we're trying to help you.

MABEL. Pahh. Is *that* what you're trying to do! . . .

NICK. [*to Mabel*] One, you're acting crazy, and uh, for what? There's no reason. The man's here on a call, a social call. *Nobody's* sick. Why're you so insecure, mm? Everybody loves you.

MABEL. Do *you* love me, Nick? Do you? [*Nick looks sympathetically at Mabel.*]

MAMA. [*bursting in*] This woman! This woman has to go!

NICK. [*pointing at Mabel*] I love you—that's right.

MAMA. Nick, think of the children!

NICK. *I* love you.

MAMA. Nick, this woman can't *stay* in this house anymore! [*to Mabel*] You *can't stay* here!

NICK. [*to Mama*] For chrissakes, calm down.

MAMA. Listen, doctor, doctor! My son tells me stories!

NICK. Just don't, just don't rag on Mabel.

MAMA. He tells me stories, of the *talk*, the small *talk*, the little *things*, the insecurity!

NICK. [*trying to drown out his mother*] bah, bah, bah, bah, bah . . .

ZEPP. Mabel.

MABEL. [*confronting Mama*] Go ahead, tell me what he says! . . .

MAMA. [*screaming*] He says you give him *nothing*! You're *empty* inside! Your *children* are naked! *They're hungry*! *That's* what he says! [*to Zepp*] Doctor—. [*screaming at Mabel*] Last night you brought a *man in the house*! [*Mabel looks shocked.*] My son is a good boy, doctor, he's a good boy, he never says anything! He doesn't *say* anything! This woman is crazy! She's crazy! . . .

NICK. [*to Mama*] Now, go upstairs.

ZEPP. [*Pushing Mama toward the stairs to keep her away from Mabel*] Margaret, she's a grown person.

MAMA. [*Resisting Zepp's pushes*] I won't go upstairs!

The scene ends when Dr. Zepp and Nick, unable to calm Mabel, commit her to an institution.

Incongruous Perspectives

I have many things to say about this unconventional scene. I want first to look at the ways in which the scene refuses to offer a unified perspective from which to judge the depicted events.

A Hollywood movie typically aligns narration with the perspective of one character or one set of characters. The Indian attack scene in John Ford's *Stagecoach* (1939), for instance, mostly restricts narration to the perspective of the white stagecoach passengers, who escape death through a last-minute rescue by the U.S. cavalry, whereas Ford's *Cheyenne Autumn* (1964) aligns spectators with the Indians threatened by the savagery of the U.S. army. Narrational alignment primes spectators to sympathize with one character or set of characters over others. But alignment is not sufficient for developing spectators' allegiance to a character. According to Murray Smith, in order to "become allied with a character, the spectator must evaluate the character as representing a morally desirable (or at least preferable) set of traits, in relation to other characters within the fiction. On the basis of this evaluation, the spectator adopts an attitude of sympathy . . . towards the character" (*Engaging Characters*, 188). Cassavetes movies refuse to align narration with one set of characters and often develop spectator sympathy for characters with conflicting goals. Since the narration is not weighted too heavily in favor of one perspective, each characters' viewpoint during a conflict seems at least momentarily sympathetic, even when the viewpoints are fundamentally incongruous.

It may seem strange to pick the committal scene to illustrate this point because the scene creates immense sympathy for Mabel, who appears bullied into insanity by the other characters. However, handled by almost any other filmmaker, the scene would have defined its attitude toward the events in much more definitive terms. The film does not depict Mabel's perspective alone or morally peg, with any definitiveness, the characters with whom she interacts. *A Woman Under the Influence* has no Nurse Ratcheds. If the film portrayed Dr. Zepp as negligent or malicious, for instance, it would seem to condemn his indifference to Mabel's suffering, but Zepp seems genuinely concerned about helping Mabel and keeping her out of the hospital. Although Nick, like Zepp, does more harm than good—even as he tries to comfort his wife, his brashness only upsets her more—when Mama Longhetti picks on her, Nick supports his wife, not his mother. Toward the end of the scene, he holds up Mabel and shouts in her ear, "I'll lay down on the railroad tracks for you! If I did make a mistake, which I did, I'm sorry! But what's the difference? I love you, now relax, come back to me!" Although even at that moment Nick behaves impetuously, the lines suggest that he is not the obdurate thug he sometimes appears to be. Even Mama Longhetti—who comes across here as vicious, the closest thing to a heavy in the movie—seems genuinely concerned about protecting her son and grandchildren; she is not pure evil. (When Mabel later returns from the hospital, it is Mama Longhetti who compassionately allows Mabel to see the children, against the objections of other characters.) Her knowledge of Mabel's infidelity also helps explain her anger, and, although Mabel looks shocked at the accusation, Mama Longhetti is right: Mabel did sleep with another man the previous evening.

We can see Cassavetes's aversion to providing a unified perspective by looking at his treatment of Mabel's mental illness. Upon its release, *A Woman Under the Influence* sparked public discussion about the validity of societal definitions of insanity. Some commentators argued that people like Mabel are labeled "crazy" by an environment that cannot withstand nonconformity (see, for instance, Pechter, 67). That conception of insanity, manifested most forcefully in the works of Thomas Szasz and R. D. Laing, had wide cultural currency in the sixties and seventies and found expression in such films as *One Flew Over the Cuckoo's Nest* (1975) and *Equus* (1977).

However, commentators attributed to Cassavetes a point of view his film resists.[15] The movie—unlike, say, *Harvey* (1950) or *Don Juan de Marco*

(1995)—does not romanticize mental illness. Nor does it—like Szasz and Laing—portray insanity as the delusion of the people society calls "normal." Indeed, *A Woman* frequently portrays Mabel as incompetent, delusional, and dangerously irrational. When she awakens with Garson Cross in her bed, for instance, she adamantly calls him "Nick," apparently unable to cope with having slept with him. After he leaves, Mabel, in a panic, forgets that she has left her children with her mother and frantically darts around the house looking for them; the scene makes her look like an incompetent parent. Mabel, furthermore, withdraws whenever reality becomes intolerable, such as her dance on the furniture during the committal scene and her attempt to fight everyone back by putting her fingers in the shape of a cross. Mabel's environment does appear unhealthy and intolerant; indeed, the very people who try to help her, because of their own incompetence and dysfunction, only make her condition worse. Nonetheless, Zepp, Nick, and Mama Longhetti make a valid point: Mabel has psychological problems, and that fact prevents any single ideological perspective from dominating the scene. "I absolutely refuse to judge the characters in my films," Cassavetes has said. "I refrain from leading people by their noses by imposing a stereotyped moral vision in my work" (Carney, "Cassavetes," 24).

Unlike Cassavetes, many of today's independent filmmakers, for all their creative talent, make largely sardonic films, such as *Flirting with Disaster* (1996, David O. Russell), *Happiness* (1998, Todd Solondz), *Your Friends & Neighbors* (1998, Neil LaBute), *Election* (1999, Alexander Payne), *American Movie* (1999, Chris Smith), *American Psycho* (2000, Mary Harron), *Requiem for a Dream* (2000, Darren Aronofsky), *Bully* (2001, Larry Clark), *Mysterious Skin* (2004, Gregg Araki), *Bubble* (2005, Steven Soderbergh), many Coen brothers' movies, and perhaps everything by Christopher Guest. Such films expose the depravity or ridiculousness of their characters, characters that seem designed so that we might feel superior to them. Cassavetes sought to *understand* his characters, not judge them. "I'm sure we could have had a much more successful film," Cassavetes said in an interview, "if *A Woman Under the Influence* had depicted Mabel's life as being rougher, more brutal; if it made statements so that people could definitely take sides. But along the way I'd have to look at myself and say 'Yes, we were successful in creating another horror in the world'" (Carney, "Cassavetes," 29). We can see in this quotation not only Cassavetes's attitude toward commercial success but also a glimpse of his aesthetic: Cassavetes wants us to appreciate the perspectives of *all* of his characters, not just the characters we like.

Narrative Obscurity

Because cinema predicates a spectator who, unobserved, watches the activities of other people, scholars often talk about film-going as a form of voyeurism; however, movies do not typically *feel* voyeuristic. Voyeurism implies transgression, whereas movies normally feel as though they are designed with spectators in mind. Classical Hollywood cinema angles actors' bodies toward the camera, it keeps spectators spatially and temporally oriented, it front-loads expositional information, it quickly fills causal gaps in the narrative, and it tends to give viewers the most advantageous optical perspective on the scene (see Bordwell, *Narration*, 160–161). Such devices ensure that Hollywood films tailor narration to meet spectators' most immediate informational needs.[16]

Cassavetes films, however, feel more truly voyeuristic because the narration often obscures information that would afford spectators a complete and coherent understanding of the story. I can illustrate my point most straightforwardly by examining his films' tendency to exclude information that would fill causal gaps in his narratives. Cassavetes said that viewers of *A Woman Under the Influence* repeatedly asked him how Nick's mother knew of Mabel's infidelity. As far as viewers knew, even Nick never found out about her tryst with Garson Cross; Mama Longhetti's knowledge of it is baffling. (Cassavetes's shooting script says that Nick smelled another man on Mabel [77], but Cassavetes left that explanation out of the movie and said that it did not seem important that the audience should see Nick tell his mother [Carney, *Cassavetes*, 371–372].) Sometimes Cassavetes's films—unlike classical Hollywood films, which disclose story information in an order convenient to spectators' need to know it—supply information only after we need it. For instance, at one point in *Husbands* (1970), Gus jokes with his friends about putting his dirty fingers in people's mouths. The joke makes no sense until, in a subsequent scene, we discover that he is a dentist. For the first half of *Love Streams* (1984), we do not know that the two principle characters are siblings. We find out in such an offhand manner that it feels as though we must have missed an earlier line of dialogue that explained their relationship. Rowlands said about one cryptic moment in *Gloria* (1980):

> There was originally a line in the taxi, where I said, "Now get in there, we're going to my sister's apartment." Then John cut that line. And I said, "But then they're not going to know whose apartment that is." He said, "Who cares? It's an *apartment*—an apartment of a friend, or a sister." That's very

much in John's way of thinking. He doesn't believe in everything being laid out, especially if it's not some essential quality. Just to help the audience know where they are, that's not something that John considers enormously important. (Crist, *Take 22*, 251)

Watching a Cassavetes movie is like reading a letter from someone we do not know to someone else we do not know; his films sometimes seem as though they are not intended for us.

Cassavetes's unconventional staging, cinematography, and editing suggest that he concertedly thwarted spectator understanding. Conventional Hollywood movies devise camera position and editing in order to clearly communicate story information: Classical filmmakers normally position characters and props so that the camera, placed in an ideal position for narrative intelligibility, can record information pertinent to understanding the scene (see Bordwell, "Classical Hollywood," 22). Live theater calls a similar activity "cheating toward the audience" (when actors turn three-quarters toward the seats) since blocking is artificially manipulated for spectator visibility. Seemingly averse to communicativeness, Cassavetes refuses to cheat. Consider the scene in *Faces* (1968) in which four housewives watch a young man, Chet, as he dances for them. The scene refuses to answer the question posed by the shots of the embarrassed and excited women: What are they looking at? We see the women laugh and make faces, yet we have little idea what they are responding to since most of the time we cannot see Chet. Even a filmmaker who wanted to center our attention on the housewives, as Cassavetes evidently does, would generally provide an eye-line match so as to fill the spatial gap created by the women's gazes and reactions. Cassavetes, seemingly unconcerned about creating a complete map of the action in the space, flouts the mode of editing that dominates Hollywood cinema in which one shot poses a spatial question and the subsequent shot answers it (see Bordwell, Staiger, and Thompson, 59).

Cassavetes's scenes seem not to be designed for the camera and often seem not to be designed at all. Like real people caught on film, his characters appear to behave freely in a world that we momentarily witness. Consider the scene from *The Killing of a Chinese Bookie* in which our protagonist, Cosmo Vitelli, argues with the mother of his girlfriend. Unlike conventional movies, in which the cinematography "foresees" the action of the scene, here camera movement and editing appear to "follow behind" the actions of the characters: The camera operator seems to have no foreknowledge of the characters' actions and shifts back and forth between them as though it were trying to guess who will speak and when. When Cosmo, at one point, leaps out of his chair, the camera doesn't anticipate the movement and fails to catch most of it. Oftentimes, Cassavetes films appear merely to *record* the scenes they depict, not create them.

Cassavetes's unusual filmmaking process bears out the foregoing observations. Very often, the crew did not know what would happen in a scene and the operator would have to figure out the scene as it occurred. Indeed, Cassavetes had frequent arguments with his operators, who generally wanted to block scenes beforehand and supply marks on the floor to indicate where the actors should stand, whereas Cassavetes wanted the operator to follow the actors. He said about filming *A Woman*: "The important thing is for the operator to shoot whatever action is most interesting at the moment. I'm not going to stand over the camera operator's shoulder and say, 'Swing over to that. Do you have a good frame there?' It's more like documentary work . . . . And thinking that you have to have the actors hit marks is a fallacy. It's a nonsense rule that's been passed down" (Carney, *Cassavetes*, 344–345).

Cassavetes's indifference to the informational needs of spectators gives the action in his films an apparent existence beyond the limits of the movie. One watches from a limited vantage point, like peeking through a window on a world that does not provide complete knowledge of its events. The cryptic references; the failure to fill causal gaps in the narrative; and staging, cinematography, and editing that refuse to create full spatial maps make his films seem fundamentally fragmented and incomplete. Rather than presenting a complete story in a total space, as in a classical Hollywood film, they depict only a cross section of events and spaces and let spectators infer the rest.

Narrative Density and Disorganization

Although, to my mind, so much happens in a Cassavetes movie that I often find it difficult to keep up, spectators often complain that nothing happens in them at all. Cassavetes himself acknowledged this reaction:

> The lights dim, the movie begins, and they say, "All right, let's get going." They watch for a few minutes and say it again. They watch a few minutes more and say it one more time. But what they don't realize is that the film has been going all along—going like crazy—but somewhere they don't understand, somewhere, maybe, they don't want to go. (Cited in Carney, *John Cassavetes*, 2)

The spectators that Cassavetes describes are, I suspect, responding to the very qualities that cause others (like Cassavetes himself) to feel as though his films are "going like crazy": the films' narrative density and disorganization. I do not mean "dense" in the figurative sense of containing complex ideas difficult to penetrate. Rather, they are dense in the literal sense: crowded with things.

Typically, classical Hollywood movies restrict themselves to one primary narrative activity at any given moment in order to avoid cluttering scenes and distributing narrative emphasis too broadly. Such single-mindedness serves the needs of narrative linearity since the activity depicted at each moment instigates the activity depicted in the next moment and so on. Cassavetes takes the opposite approach: His scenes typically depict several events jointly.

In order to demonstrate A Woman's narrative density, I want to describe the action in one seventy-five-second shot from the committal scene. The shot, which concludes the passage of dialogue that I cited earlier, begins when Nick says to Mabel, "I love you—that's right" and ends shortly after Mama says "I won't go upstairs!" More narrative activity happens during these seventy-five seconds than in entire scenes in mainstream cinema.

The shot draws attention mostly to Mama Longhetti—putting her in the foreground and usually keeping her in focus—who tries at once to persuade her son to leave his wife, to express her anger toward Mabel, and to resist Zepp's efforts to shut her up. What follows is a description of most of the important story information conveyed during those seventy-five seconds, although I have doubtlessly left out some particulars.

When Nick tells Mabel that he loves her, he seems to be making up for his mother's verbal abuse of his wife, as well as for the fact that, earlier in the scene, he tried to distance himself from her ("I don't know who you are"). His attitude, however, only upsets Mama Longhetti, who tries both to convince her son that Mabel should leave the Longhetti home ("Nick, think of the children!") and to vent her anger at Mabel ("You can't stay here!"). Nick, in turn, tries to drown out Mama ("bah, bah, bah"), thereby allying himself with Mabel against his mother. However, he also seems to want to prevent Mabel from hearing what he has revealed to his mother; indeed, Mama's lines show that Nick is close enough to his mother to have confided in her about his problems with Mabel. Mabel yells at Mama, "Go ahead, tell me what he says!" trying, it seems, at once to find out what Nick has told Mama as well as to confront her mother-in-law. But the more antagonistic Mabel becomes and the more Nick balks at his mother's ranting, the more vitriol Mama expresses toward Mabel ("He says you give him *nothing*! You're *empty* inside!").

All the while, Dr. Zepp grows visibly bothered by the exchange. Although Mama, at various points in the shot, appeals to the doctor for support ("My son is a good boy, doctor"), Zepp mostly tries to shut her up and eventually to shoo her out of the room. Mama, in turn, resists Zepp's efforts both verbally ("I won't go upstairs!") and by pushing him away from her. Zepp also tries to distract Mabel from her mother-in-law's abuse. When he says to Mama, "Margaret, she's a grown person," the line seems intended as much to show Mabel that he respects her as it is to convince Mama to treat Mabel more respectfully.

I see three narrative climaxes (or turning points) in the sequence, a lot for seventy-five seconds of screen time but no more than we might find in several other seventy-five-second sequences in the scene: 1) Nick finally tells Mabel that he loves her, after refusing to say so previously in the scene, and thereafter in the shot he defends Mabel against his mother; 2) Mama and Mabel's argument reaches a climax when she reveals that she knows Mabel brought a man home the previous night, and Mabel suddenly backs off in shock; and 3) Mama and Zepp's argument climaxes when she refuses to leave the room. The narration has packed these climaxes—each of which concerns a different pairing of the three characters in the scene—so closely together that the scene requires viewers either to consider the climaxes' repercussions simultaneously or else immediately shift attention away from each climax and quickly attend to the next. Indeed, the argument between Mama and Mabel occurs at the same time as the argument between Mama and Zepp, and both occur during the shot's first climax, as Nick switches his energies to supporting Mabel by challenging his mother.

Cinematography and mise-en-scène, meanwhile, draw attention to several narrative activities in the scene at once. Although Mama mostly remains at the center of the frame during the shot, and her ranting keeps her central to the narrative, the blocking has her facing away from the camera much of the time, thereby dividing spectator attention between her and the other characters as they move in and out of the frame and in and out of focus. For instance, when Mama yells, "Last night you brought a *man in the house!*" she turns away from us, and the camera reframes and refocuses on Mabel (Figure 7.1). Although the camera immediately re-centers on Mama when she turns to Zepp, we can still see Mabel—now in the background and out of focus—looking shocked and confused, and perhaps looking to Nick for an explanation of Mama's accusation of infidelity, the one-night stand that, it suddenly seems, Mabel has forgotten about (Figure 7.2). Hence, even though Mama's address to Zepp re-centers the attention of the scene on her, the framing encourages us to linger on Mabel's reaction, simultaneously sending narrative attention, albeit only for a moment, in two disparate directions.

All of the elements I have described occur in just the one shot (admittedly a long take), and, although I selected the seventy-five-second sequence partly for its density, I could have chosen any number of others. Cassavetes can pack so much narrative information into such a small timeframe because, rather than constructing a linear series of events linked by cause-and-effect,

FIGURE 7.1. The shot briefly centers on Mabel, as Mama accuses her of infidelity.

FIGURE 7.2. The shot quickly re-centers on Mama when she turns to plead with Dr. Zepp; Mabel looks shocked and confused in the background.

FIGURES 7.1–7.2. A single shot from *A Woman Under the Influence* draws spectator attention to more than one narrative activity at once.

he stages his characters' actions simultaneously. Cassavetes foregoes the efficiency and forward momentum that attends classical narration and replaces those qualities with narrative density and disorganization.

Radical Narrative Perversity

A story summary of Cassavetes's *The Killing of a Chinese Bookie* makes the film sound exciting and suspenseful: Strip-club owner and Korean War veteran Cosmo Vitelli pays off his long-standing loan to a group of gangsters and then celebrates with a night of gambling that lands him in debt to them for $23,000. Bullied by the gangsters into eliminating his debt, Cosmo reluctantly sneaks into the camp of a bookie and manages to kill him, along with some guards. But the bookie is really a rival gang boss, whom the gangsters never expected Cosmo to kill. They were setting Cosmo up to get killed himself in order to acquire his club. Now the gangsters must murder Cosmo. Chased inside an abandoned warehouse, Cosmo kills one of the gangsters and outsmarts another. But he's been shot, and, by the time he makes it back to his club, his death is imminent.

That's the story of the movie, as far as I understand it (the film leaves key story information obscure, so I'm speculating about some of it). But that's not the movie. Not nearly as thrilling or suspenseful as its story, *Chinese Bookie* seems more interested in everything that goes on *around* the story. Richard Combs, reviewing the re-edited 1978 version of the film for *Sight and Sound*, astutely notes this quality: "The gangland killing which the hero of *The Killing of a Chinese Bookie* is forced to carry out serves to identify the narrative, but it never really gains the expected purchase on either the characters or the atmosphere, which dreamily find more idiosyncratic routes out of the *film noir* situation" (193). Combs recognizes the film's inclination to swerve away from straightforward narration, and the movie's narrational devices support his observation. As Cosmo argues with one of the mobsters at a poker parlor, for instance, the camera centers not on Cosmo and the mobster but on Cosmo's girlfriend, who looks only slightly interested in the dispute; most of the time, we can't even see Cosmo during the argument because another gambler blocks the camera's view of him (Figure 7.3).

The chase in the abandoned warehouse is perhaps the least suspenseful chase scene ever filmed. Rather than portraying Cosmo's efforts to stay alive, Cassavetes squanders a perfect opportunity for Hollywood-style suspense and excitement by keeping the camera almost entirely on the gangster as he searches the warehouse fruitlessly, moving through empty corridors and

FIGURE 7.3. A shot from Cassavetes's *The Killing of a Chinese Bookie* obscures the primary action and centers on peripheral narrative information.

opening doors behind which Cosmo does not hide. The scene might have generated some suspense had it shown Cosmo eluding pursuit, escaping the warehouse, setting traps, or confronting the gangster. Instead, Cassavetes supplies a few visually obscure shots of Cosmo as he stands in the dark, waiting for his pursuer to give up and leave. The final major sequence of the film is Cosmo's speech to his performers on the virtues of being "comfortable," an engaging speech that, though it offers insight into our protagonist and his feelings toward his performers, is rhetorically incoherent and practically irrelevant to the main narrative. Rather than focusing on a cause-and-effect narrative chain, *Chinese Bookie* fixates on subtle revelations of character and on Cosmo's nuanced interactions with the gangsters and his employees that occur along the way to the film's key narrative destinations.

Cassavetes clutters his films with so many narrative perversities that they become not impediments to narration but rather the film's primary narrational activity. As we have seen, many of the seventies most prominent filmmakers—including Coppola, Friedkin, Altman, Kubrick, Allen, and Scorsese—strategically incorporate narrative perversities into their largely classical films in order to create potent, although limited, aesthetic effects. In Cassavetes's films, narrative perversity is not an intermittent practice but the dominant narrational structure, pervading his films and relating the various stylistic, narrative, and thematic devices to one another.[17]

We see in Cassavetes's films the radical extension—and some of the commercial hazards—of the perverse narrative strategies that distinguish American cinema of the 1970s. Like *The Godfather, Part II, Annie Hall,*

Taxi Driver, and *Nashville*, his films integrate narrative and stylistic devices counterproductive to causal linearity and forward momentum. Such devices distract spectators from plot patterning and scuttle the films' potential to generate suspense and excitement. Like *Get Carter*, *Carrie*, and *Manhattan*, his films resist the resolution necessitated by the Hollywood paradigm, leaving key story information obscure or unresolved and refusing to settle incongruous ideas provoked by his films' narration. Cassavetes films furthermore prompt spectator responses more uncertain and discomforting than those characteristic of more typical Hollywood cinema. As in *Chinatown* and *The Conversation*, story information can come across as obscure, incomplete, or incongruous, and his films show striking indifference to spectator curiosity and informational needs. As in *Patton* and *The Exorcist*, conceptual incongruities prompt spectators to evaluate his stories and characters in antithetical ways. And by encouraging spectators to sympathize with incongruous perspectives (even, as in *The French Connection*, *Badlands*, and *A Clockwork Orange*, those of contemptible characters), the films cue spectator responses that fluctuate unpredictably, incongruously and uncomfortably. His films resemble these others, but their perversity is far more pervasive and extreme, an extremity that has caused some reviewers to criticize the films as chaotic.

Such extremity always plagued Cassavetes, who forewent commercial success (who seemed, in fact, determined to avoid it) by rejecting classical Hollywood's narrative efficiency and linearity, instead making narrative perversity—which, in mainstream films of the 1970s, only complicates the process of narration—his films' dominant narrational strategy. Cassavetes has also missed the kind of critical attention given to other influential American filmmakers of the period, at least in part because his films lack the virtuoso displays of technique that we see in Martin Scorsese, Woody Allen, and Stanley Kubrick, or the confident political statements in the films of Arthur Penn, Robert Altman, and Sidney Lumet, or the sensationalism of Sam Peckinpah, Brian De Palma, and William Friedkin.

Cassavetes has nonetheless gathered a devoted audience, a consequence of the very extremity that once made his movies so obscure and unpopular. Severed from classical Hollywood's time-tested strategies for keeping narratives on course, his films fixate on obstructions to narrative linearity and causal progress. The payoff is a body of work that stimulates spectators to resolve incongruous perspectives, to creatively fill in narrative information that might be vital to understanding story causality, and to sort through and arrange story information that the films insist on presenting in an uncommonly dense and disorganized way. As long as Cassavetes's spectators are willing to devote the commitment and exertion such mental activity demands—and his typically poor reviews and box office indicate that few spectators are—the films succeed in exercising our cognitive agility as we dodge our way through the narrational equivalent of an obstacle course, a playing field of incongruous events, characters, and perspectives.

CONCLUSION

From the viewpoint of the Hollywood film industry, every artistic decision should serve at least one of two commercial functions: add quality or minimize risk. During the 1970s, these two goals merged to create an atmosphere of experimentation in which narrative perversity could flourish in Hollywood. This atmosphere resulted from an unusual set of historical conditions: audience exhaustion with traditional cinema and the strange popularity of art cinema, the relaxation of Hollywood's restrictions on lurid material and idiosyncratic expressions of directorial style, a new and excited generation of cine-literate filmmakers and filmgoers, product shortages and tax shelters that encouraged small-scale and independent film production, and, perhaps most crucially, the industry's financial insecurity and its inclination to hedge the risks of blockbuster filmmaking by investing in eager young filmmakers willing to work with comparatively miniscule budgets. "We want one big picture a year," Frank Yablans, president of Paramount Pictures, said at the time. "The rest are budgeted to minimize risk, and hopefully, they will make money too" (Pye and Myles, 89). These mostly young, low-budget filmmakers, like their B-unit predecessors in the studio era, employed narrative strategies that big-budget cinema quickly adopted as well. Narrative perversity added quality to film production by inspiring innovation and artistic achievement, and it minimized risk by serving (often inexpensively) a large sector in the moviegoing population underserved by more traditional entertainment. Such a convergence of historical conditions had never happened before in Hollywood, and we haven't seen anything like it since.

The 1970s marks the turning point between the narrative strategies of the studio era and the "New Hollywood." During the period 1970 to 1977, the studios released dozens of mainstream films that displayed narrative perversities rarely seen in popular American cinema. The seventies, however, did not mark a radical break with Hollywood's narrative tradition, merely a skillful intensification of elements already present in classical narration, creating something of a Golden Age of narrative perversity in Hollywood cinema. By modifying traditional strategies and adapting and tempering art-cinema narrational devices, films such as *The Godfather*, *The Godfather, Part II*, *The French Connection*, *The Exorcist*, and *Taxi Driver* looked refreshing upon their release, and in some ways still do.

Although narrative modes shifted in the late 1970s, the influence of the seventies continues. We see it exhibited in some of the most artistically risky and exciting movies to come out of the United States in the past thirty years, not as much among top-grossing films, as was the case in the 1970s, but in less mainstream movies—many of them by directors who gained renown in the 1970s—geared toward more narrowly defined audiences: *Raging Bull* (1980), *The Elephant Man* (1980), *Tempest* (1982), *Tender Mercies* (1983), *The Hunger* (1983), *The King of Comedy* (1983), *Choose Me* (1984), *Blood Simple* (1984), *Brazil* (1985), *House of Games* (1987), *Do the Right Thing* (1989), *Crimes and Misdemeanors* (1989), *sex, lies, and videotape* (1989), *Reservoir Dogs* (1992), *Kids* (1995), *The Apostle* (1997), *Magnolia* (1999), *The Talented Mr. Ripley* (1999), *Gosford Park* (2001), *Match Point* (2005), *There Will Be Blood* (2007), *Rachel Getting Married* (2008). When *Magnolia* presents story events that defy logic and probability (for instance, all nine of the main characters singing the same song at the same moment in different settings, a policeman's gun dropping a few feet from him hours after he lost it, frogs falling from the sky), the film has strained spectators' willingness to resolve incongruous story information. But if the film succeeds, if it hasn't put so much pressure on story logic and probability that resolution is too onerous or impossible, then it has enabled in spectators something like mental magic: the ability to take something that logic and probability say should not be so and, through thinking, make it so.

We can also see the legacy of seventies narrative perversity in a small brood of mainstream Hollywood movies with blockbuster grosses, such as *Goodfellas* (1990), *Silence of the Lambs* (1991), *Cape Fear* (1991), *Thelma and Louise* (1991), *Unforgiven* (1992), *Pulp Fiction* (1994), *Black Hawk Down* (2001), *The Others* (2001), *Inside Man* (2006), and *The Dark Knight*

(2008). A film such as *Unforgiven*, for instance, could only appear during or after the 1970s. In fact, David Webb Peoples wrote the film's original shooting script in 1976, inspired, he said, by having just seen *Taxi Driver* (*All on Accounta*). And, like *Taxi Driver*, the film employs the three key narrative modes that characterize seventies cinema generally.

> 1. *It frustrates straightforward narration and avoids fulfilling narrative promises in conventionally satisfying ways.* William Munny's killing of Davey Bunting, for instance, seems designed to avoid the thrills normally associated with vengeful violence in Hollywood movies, and the film's climactic gunfight comes across more as a bloodbath than a heroic showdown.[1]
>
> 2. *It exploits and modifies conventional genre devices in order to create subtle, unsettling, and unresolved narrative incongruities.* Numerous moments in the film—the cutting of Delilah, the torture and murder of Ned, Munny's confident arrival at Skinny's saloon, and shots of Little Bill surreptitiously reaching for his gun while our protagonist remains oblivious to his own danger—cue spectators to anticipate a straightforward narration of conventional Western scenarios, scenarios the film ends up defying in subtle and unsettling ways.
>
> 3. *It creates troubling conceptual incongruities by generating ideas and emotions counterproductive to the film's essential concepts and overt narrative purpose.* At the end, Munny achieves his (partly just) goal when he transforms into the man the film has commended him for *not* being all along; the ending surrounds our protagonist with the kind of imagery and music normally reserved for monsters in horror movies; and the epilogue's serene score and flowery prose run contrary to, and convey no empathy for, the feeling of the film's dark, horrific climax.

Clint Eastwood, who purchased the script in 1983, did not direct the film until the 1990s, but *Unforgiven* is seventies filmmaking of the highest order.

Such films, like the mainstream seventies films analyzed in this book, use the Hollywood paradigm as a point of departure, mining it for ideological incongruities, logical and characterological inconsistencies, and other unconventional and unsettling narrative perversities that seventies cinema made more common. Although seventies modes of narration became less pervasive after 1977, seventies filmmakers, by pushing against the limits of classical narration, discovered narrative options previously unexplored in Hollywood, options that quickly became part of Hollywood's regular repertoire of narrative strategies.

It may sound inconclusive that a period that many regard as a renaissance for Hollywood is founded on modifications of, rather than a break with, filmmaking traditions. It would be more historically and intellectually convenient to find a firm distinction between the films that some regard as the height of Hollywood achievement and those they consider artistically ordinary. The scholarly tendency to locate the artistic worth of films of this period in their left-leaning ideologies results in part from a desire for clear-cut distinctions since such ideologies may rightly mark a qualitative break from Hollywood's more politically conservative bent before and after the seventies. This study takes the less convenient, but I think more interesting and accurate, position that details, rather than grand designs, make the difference between the films people consider great and those they consider merely good. Remember that Ginger Rogers could do the very steps that Fred Astaire could do, and, when they dance together to "Isn't This a Lovely Day?" in *Top Hat* (1935), there she goes, dancing the same steps just as perfectly as Astaire; she doesn't make one mistake. Yet, I think most people would say that Astaire's dancing looks better. The difference between great dancing like Astaire's and good dancing like Rogers's ultimately amounts to a large number of subtle and skillful movements, not anything particularly innovative or conceptually distinct. By subtly and skillfully heightening incongruities already present in Hollywood cinema, seventies filmmakers created some of the American film industry's most celebrated, admired, and financially successful films and permanently expanded the narrative possibilities in mainstream filmmaking.

Some readers may still find it strange to think of incoherence in a film as an aesthetic virtue since people often describe bad movies as incoherent. Indeed, many great movies have something in common with bad movies: They are often disorganized, disjointed, or inconsistent. Their lapses in unity and story logic, however, generally fall just beyond the range of spectators' conscious detection. Bad movies often strike us as being full of holes. Great movies are also full of holes, sometimes gaping ones, but they do not appear to be so. Often a great classical movie enables its spectators to glide effortlessly over its holes—to casually resolve in their minds what the movie, narrative pattern and probability, or reason itself refuse to resolve—and stimulates complex and imaginative cognitive activities unavailable to spectators of either unswervingly harmonious movies or non-classical cinema experiments.

Such cognitive activities—solving a problem that cannot be solved through precise logic, inferring a connection between incongruous story information, finding a resolution or relationship predicated more on imagination than on close scrutiny or crisp reasoning—liberate the mind from day-to-day good sense. Humor researcher John Morreall discusses the pleasure of resolving incongruities:

> Part of the delight we feel in this use of our imagination is the feeling of liberation it brings. Instead of following well-worn mental paths of attention and thought, we switch to new paths, notice things we didn't notice before, and countenance possibilities, and even absurdities, as easily as actualities. (*Taking Laughter*, 91)

For Morreall, the value of resolving incongruous information rests in our "drive to seek variety in our cognitive input," a drive, he points out, found in all mammals with sophisticated nervous systems ("Funny Ha-Ha," 201). Because spectators grow acclimated to Hollywood plot patterning, its effect fades and can grow tiresome. Narrative incongruities prevent stories from becoming too orderly and predictable, adding detours to an otherwise straightforward story and reducing the numbing effects of genre, conceptual coherence, and causal linearity. Narrative incongruities enable us to make improbable connections, exercising our creativity, problem-solving abilities, and mental agility. And in threatening a film with incoherence, narrative incongruities complicate what would otherwise have been a straightforward exposition of a story and excite spectators to perform—casually, gracefully, and often obliviously—acts of creative mental distortion.

Intensifying their narrative incongruities almost to the point at which resolution would be impossible, seventies cinema often cues spectators to connect narrative elements that seem determined to remain separate and resolve ideas and story information that the films insist on presenting incongruously. The greater the incongruity, several studies of humor suggest, the greater the pleasure,[2] so long as spectators can somehow *find the fit* between incongruous elements, even a fit that defies probability or relies on specious reasoning or free association. The fictional context gives license to mental processes that situations with higher stakes normally inhibit.

Film commentators such as V. F. Perkins taught us that great movies rely on proportion, thematic unity, and a harmonious marriage of artistic devices.

I hope that readers of this book conclude that, for many great movies, the opposite is true. Many great artworks seem on the point of some narrative, conceptual, or stylistic collapse, yet still they retain our trust in their underlying reliability. That principle holds true for the mainstream seventies films analyzed here. Their uneasy marriage to classical narration leads them to flirt with perverse narrative strategies that threaten Hollywood cinema's harmony and stability. Contrary to what many film commentators believe, disunity does not indicate bad filmmaking. Disunity oftentimes indicates good filmmaking—filmmaking that is unpredictable and varied, filmmaking that takes us to destinations that we could not foresee but that nonetheless feel, once we make an improbable connection or resolve an incongruity, as inevitably the right place. The fact that we enjoy a group of Hollywood films so disunified, even when they arouse our uncertainty and discomfort, reveals not only the versatility of Hollywood narration but also our capacity for aesthetic pleasure.

BEST FILMS OF THE 1970S
Best Picture Awards, Critics
Lists and Other Rankings, and
Box Office Grosses

BEST PICTURE AWARDS

NEW YORK FILM CRITICS CIRCLE AWARD WINNERS FOR BEST PICTURE (1970–1979)

Five Easy Pieces (1970)
A Clockwork Orange (1971)
Viskningar och rop (1972)
La Nuit américaine (1973)
Amarcord (1974)
Nashville (1975)
All the President's Men (1976)
Annie Hall (1977)
The Deer Hunter (1978)
Kramer vs. Kramer (1979)

ACADEMY OF MOTION PICTURE ARTS AND SCIENCES OSCAR AWARD WINNERS FOR BEST PICTURE (1970–1979)

Patton (1970)
The French Connection (1971)
The Godfather (1972)
The Sting (1973)
The Godfather, Part II (1974)
One Flew Over the Cuckoo's Nest (1975)
Rocky (1976)
Annie Hall (1977)
The Deer Hunter (1978)
Kramer vs. Kramer (1979)

LOS ANGELES FILM CRITICS ASSOCIATION AWARD WINNERS
FOR BEST PICTURE (1975–1979)

> *Dog Day Afternoon* (1975)
> *Network* (1976)
> *Star Wars* (1977)
> *Coming Home* (1978)
> *Kramer vs. Kramer* (1979)

U.S. NATIONAL SOCIETY OF FILM CRITICS AWARD WINNERS
FOR BEST PICTURE (1970–1979)

> *M*A*S*H* (1970)
> *Claire's Knee* (1971)
> *The Discreet Charm Of The Bourgeoisie* (1972)
> *Day For Night* (1973)
> *Scenes from a Marriage* (1974)
> *Nashville* (1975)
> *All The President's Men* (1976)
> *Annie Hall* (1977)
> *Get Out Your Handkerchiefs* (1978)
> *Breaking Away* (1979)

CRITICS LISTS AND OTHER RANKINGS

AMERICAN FILM NOW (1968–1977)

In 1978, James Monaco asked twenty leading critics to list the ten best American films made between 1968 and 1977. The group consisted of Peter Biskind, Vincent Canby, Richard Corliss, Peter Cowie, Jan Dawson, Stephen Farber, Michael Goodwin, Molly Haskell, Diane Jacobs, Richard T. Jameson, Stanley Kauffmann, Greil Marcus, Janet Maslin, Gene Moskowitz, Frank Rich, Clayton Riley, Andrew Sarris, Richard Schickel, David Thomson and Francois Truffaut. The following tally contains the English-language films named on at least five critics' lists. The source is James Monaco, *American Film Now* (New York: New American Library, 1984), 447.

> (12 votes) *The Godfather, Part II* (1974)
> (12) *Nashville* (1975)
> (10) *The Godfather* (1972)
> (9) *Petulia* (1968)
> (9) *Annie Hall* (1977)
> (7) *Mean Streets* (1973)
> (6) *2001: A Space Odyssey* (1968)
> (6) *The Wild Bunch* (1969)
> (5) *American Graffiti* (1973)

(5) *Badlands* (1973)

(5) *Taxi Driver* (1976)

(5) *McCabe & Mrs. Miller* (1971)

(5) *Chinatown* (1974)

(5) *Barry Lyndon* (1975)

INTERNET MOVIE DATABASE (IMDB) TOP-RATED ENGLISH-LANGUAGE FILMS 1970–1979
The Internet Movie Database Web site asks users to rate movies. The site has tallied
the ratings of regular users to produce a list of the top fifty theatrical release films
from the 1970s (as well as from other decades). Their ratings indicate what one very
large group of movie fans (152,079 users helped to rank *The Godfather* number 1,
for instance) considers the best films of the decade. The tally below, accurate as of
October 6, 2009, includes only the list's English-language theatrical release films
from the 1970s and excludes films with fewer than ten thousand votes. Source: http://
uk.imdb.com/chart/1970s.

TABLE A.1

RANK	RATING	TITLE (YEAR OF RELEASE)	VOTERS
1	9.1	*The Godfather* (1972)	367,280
2	9.0	*The Godfather: Part II* (1974)	215,011
3	8.8	*One Flew Over the Cuckoo's Nest* (1975)	186,986
4	8.8	*Star Wars* (1977)	291,927
5	8.6	*Apocalypse Now* (1979)	155,497
6	8.6	*Taxi Driver* (1976)	136,267
7	8.5	*Alien* (1979)	159,210
8	8.5	*A Clockwork Orange* (1971)	171,650
9	8.5	*Chinatown* (1974)	69,565
10	8.4	*Monty Python and the Holy Grail* (1975)	141,168
11	8.3	*The Sting* (1973)	58,727
12	8.3	*Jaws* (1975)	123,233
13	8.2	*Annie Hall* (1977)	57,924
14	8.2	*The Deer Hunter* (1978)	78,164
15	8.2	*Sleuth* (1972)	15,102
16	8.2	*Life of Brian* (1979)	83,519
17	8.1	*Dog Day Afternoon* (1975)	52,045
18	8.1	*The Conversation* (1974)	28,778
19	8.1	*Network* (1976)	28,847
20	8.1	*Manhattan* (1979)	34,014
21	8.0	*The Last Picture Show* (1971)	13,351
22	8.0	*The Exorcist* (1973)	90,676
23	8.0	*Patton* (1970)	35,477
24	8.0	*Harold and Maude* (1971)	25,860
25	8.0	*Barry Lyndon* (1975)	34,897
26	8.0	*Rocky* (1976)	82,256
27	8.0	*All the President's Men* (1976)	29,700

continues on following page

continued from previous page: TABLE **A.1**

28	8.0	*Papillon* (1973)	25,537
29	8.0	*The Man Who Would Be King* (1975)	17,153
30	8.0	*Dawn of the Dead* (1978)	37,980
31	8.0	*Young Frankenstein* (1974)	53,514
32	8.0	*Days of Heaven* (1978)	10,537
33	7.9	*Being There* (1979)	22,634
34	7.9	*Halloween* (1978)	57,464
35	7.9	*Badlands* (1973)	14,350
36	7.9	*The French Connection* (1971)	30,302
37	7.9	*Deliverance* (1972)	32,976
38	7.9	*The Day of the Jackal* (1973)	12,366

AMERICAN FILM INSTITUTE (AFI)

In 1998, AFI released a list of its "blue-ribbon" panel's choice of the 100 Greatest American Movies. Reported criteria: feature-length American fiction film, critical recognition, major award winner, popularity over time, historical significance, cultural impact. The following list contains the AFI's eighteen films from the 1970s, which had more films represented than any other decade.

TABLE **A.2**

RANK	TITLE (YEAR OF RELEASE)
3	*The Godfather* (1972)
15	*Star Wars* (1977)
19	*Chinatown* (1974)
20	*One Flew Over the Cuckoo's Nest* (1975)
28	*Apocalypse Now* (1979)
31	*Annie Hall* (1977)
32	*The Godfather, Part II* (1974)
46	*A Clockwork Orange* (1971)
47	*Taxi Driver* (1976)
48	*Jaws* (1975)
56	*M*A*S*H* (1970)
64	*Close Encounters of the Third Kind* (1977)
66	*Network* (1976)
70	*The French Connection* (1971)
77	*American Graffiti* (1973)
78	*Rocky* (1976)
79	*The Deer Hunter* (1978)
89	*Patton* (1970)

NATIONAL FILM REGISTRY OF THE U.S. LIBRARY OF CONGRESS

As of 2008, the following American movies from the 1970s had been admitted to the National Film Registry, which selects twenty-five films annually. To be eligible for the Registry, a film must be American, at least ten years old, and "culturally, historically, or aesthetically significant."

Alien (1979)

All That Jazz (1979)

American Graffiti (1973)

Annie Hall (1977)

Antonia: Portrait of the Woman (1974)

Apocalypse Now (1979)

Badlands (1973)

The Black Stallion (1979)

Blazing Saddles (1974)

The Buffalo Creek Flood: An Act of Man (1975)

Cabaret (1972)

Chinatown (1974)

Chulas Fronteras (1976)

Close Encounters of the Third Kind (1977)

The Conversation (1974)

Days of Heaven (1978)

The Deer Hunter (1978)

Deliverance (1972)

Enter the Dragon (1973)

Eraserhead (1978)

Film Portrait (1970)

Five Easy Pieces (1970)

Frank Film (1973)

Free Radicals (1979)

The French Connection (1971)

Fuji (1974)

The Godfather (1972)

The Godfather, Part II (1974)

Halloween (1978)

Harlan County, U.S.A. (1976)

Harold and Maude (1971)

Hospital (1970)

The Hospital (1971)

Jaws (1975)

Killer of Sheep (1977)

King: A Filmed Record . . . Montgomery To Memphis (1970)

The Last Picture Show (1971)

M*A*S*H (1970)

Manhattan (1979)

Mean Streets (1973)

Multiple Sidosis (1970)

Nashville (1975)

National Lampoon's Animal House (1978)

Network (1976)

No Lies (1973)

Nostalgia (1971)

One Flew Over the Cuckoo's Nest (1975)

The Outlaw Josey Wales (1976)

Patton (1970)

Peege (1972)

Powers of Ten (1978)

Reminiscences of a Journey to Lithuania (1971)

Rocky (1976)

The Rocky Horror Picture Show (1975)

Serene Velocity (1970)

Shaft (1971)

Star Wars (1977)

The Sting (1973)

Taxi Driver (1976)

To Fly (1976)

A Woman Under the Influence (1974)

Woodstock (1970)

Young Frankenstein (1974)

BOX OFFICE GROSSES

TOP TEN RENTAL FILMS 1970–1979 IN THE YEAR OF RELEASE

The following table lists the ten films with the highest domestic rentals for each year between 1970 and 1979. Information was gathered (with minor corrections) from David Cook, *Lost Illusions: American Cinema in the Shadow of Watergate and Vietnam, 1970–1979* (New York: Charles Scribner's Sons, 2000) 497–502; rental figures come from *Variety* and *The Hollywood Reporter*.

TABLE A.3 Rentals in Millions

1970		1971	
Love Story	$48.7	Fiddler on the Roof	$38.2
Airport	$45.2	Billy Jack	$32.5
M*A*S*H	$36.7	The French Connection	$26.3
Patton	$28.1	Summer of '42	$20.5
Woodstock	$16.4	Deep Throat	$20.0
Ryan's Daughter	$14.6	Diamonds are Forever	$19.8
Tora! Tora! Tora!	$14.5	Dirty Harry	$18.1
The Aristocats	$11.5	A Clockwork Orange	$17.5
Joe	$9.5	Little Big Man	$17.0
Catch-22	$9.3	The Last Picture Show	$14.1

continues on following page

continued from previous page: TABLE A.3

1972	
The Godfather	$86.3
The Poseidon Adventure	$42.1
What's Up, Doc?	$28.5
Deliverance	$22.6
Jeremiah Johnson	$21.9
Cabaret	$20.2
The Getaway	$18.4
Lady Sings the Blues	$11.0
Sounder	$9.5
Pete 'n' Tillie	$8.7

1973	
The Exorcist	$88.5
The Sting	$78.2
American Graffiti	$55.3
The Way We Were	$25.8
Papillon	$22.5
Magnum Force	$20.1
Robin Hood	$17.2
Last Tango in Paris	$16.7
Paper Moon	$16.6
Live and Let Die	$16.0

1974	
The Towering Inferno	$48.8
Blazing Saddles	$47.8
Earthquake	$35.9
The Trial of Billy Jack	$31.1
Benji	$30.8
The Godfather, Part II	$30.7
Young Frankenstein	$30.1
Airport 1975	$25.3
The Longest Yard	$23.0
That's Entertainment!	$19.1

1975	
Jaws	$129.5
One Flew Over the Cuckoo's Nest	$60.0
Shampoo	$24.5
Dog Day Afternoon	$22.5
Return of the Pink Panther	$22.1
Grizzly Adams	$21.9
Three Days of the Condor	$21.5
Funny Lady	$19.3
The Other Side of the Mountain	$18.0
Tommy	$17.8

1976	
Rocky	$56.5
A Star is Born	$37.1
King Kong	$36.9
All the President's Men	$31.0
Silver Streak	$30.0
The Omen	$28.5
The Bad News Bears	$24.3
The Enforcer	$24.1
Midway	$21.6
Silent Movie	$21.2

1977	
Star Wars	$193.8
Close Encounters of the Third Kind	$82.8
Saturday Night Fever	$74.1
Smokey and the Bandit	$59.0
The Goodbye Girl	$41.9
Oh, God!	$31.5
The Deep	$31.2
The Spy Who Loved Me	$24.3
In Search of Noah's Ark	$23.8
Semi-Tough	$22.9

1978	
Grease	$96.3
Superman	$82.8
National Lampoon's Animal House	$70.9
Every Which Way But Loose	$51.9
Jaws 2	$50.4
Heaven Can Wait	$49.4
Hooper	$34.9
California Suite	$29.2
The Deer Hunter	$28.0
Foul Play	$27.5

1979	
Kramer vs. Kramer	$59.9
Star Trek: The Motion Picture	$56.0
The Jerk	$43.0
Rocky II	$42.1
Alien	$40.3
Apocalypse Now	$37.9
"10"	$37.4
The Amityville Horror	$35.4
Moonraker	$34.0
The Muppet Movie	$32.8

STUDY OF FILM INCOHERENCE

I enlisted a sample of eight film experts (individuals with an earned PhD in film or a related field working in film studies at institutions throughout the United States), unfamiliar with my hypotheses about seventies cinema, to rate a group of sixty films according to whether each film was "less coherent" than or "as coherent" as most Hollywood films in its genre. The group was composed of the highest domestic box office-grossing films of the first two years of the 1960s, 1970s, and 1980s. (For brevity, I picked only the first two years of the decade. Appendix A contains a list of the top ten grossers for every year of the 1970s.) Box office revenue was gathered from statistics in *Variety*. Raters were instructed to code a film as "less coherent" if it had at least one of the following traits to an uncommon degree, when compared to most Hollywood films in its genre:

- a main character whose traits are not consistent
- genre conventions that are used in nontraditional ways
- unresolved scenes or plotlines
- ideological ambiguities
- logical incoherencies
- factual contradictions
- narratively irrelevant scenes or elements
- narrative or stylistic devices that interfere with linear narration
- the film does not fulfill narrative expectations in conventionally satisfying ways

Raters were also given samples to guide their ratings.

SUMMARY DATA

The following tables display the top ten domestic box office-grossing films of the first two years of the 1960s, 1970s, and 1980s, respectively. Numbers in the left-hand column indicate box office rank, and a black dot in the right-hand column indicates that at least half of the film experts enlisted for the study coded the film as "less co-herent" than most films in its genre.

TABLE B.1 Top-Grossing Films of 1960

RANKING	TITLE	"LESS COHERENT"
1	Spartacus	
2	Psycho	•
3	Swiss Family Robinson	
4	Exodus	
5	The World of Suzie Wong	
6	The Alamo	
7	Operation Petticoat	
8	Suddenly Last Summer	•
9	The Apartment	
10	From the Terrace	

TABLE B.2 Top-Grossing Films of 1961

RANKING	TITLE	"LESS COHERENT"
1	West Side Story	
2	The Guns of Navarone	
3	Lover Come Back	
4	The Absent-Minded Professor	
5	El Cid	
6	The Parent Trap	
7	King of Kings	
8	Blue Hawaii	
9	101 Dalmatians	
10	Splendor in the Grass	

Total 1960 and 1961 = 2 "less coherent" films

TABLE B.3 Top-Grossing Films of 1970

RANKING	TITLE	"LESS COHERENT"
1	Love Story	
2	Airport	
3	M*A*S*H	•
4	Patton	
5	Woodstock	•
6	Ryan's Daughter	
7	Tora! Tora! Tora!	
8	The Aristocats	
9	Joe	
10	Catch-22	•

TABLE **B.4** Top-Grossing Films of 1971

RANKING	TITLE	"LESS COHERENT"
1	Fiddler on the Roof	
2	Billy Jack	
3	The French Connection	•
4	Summer of '42	
5	Deep Throat	•
6	Diamonds are Forever	
7	Dirty Harry	
8	A Clockwork Orange	•
9	Little Big Man	•
10	The Last Picture Show	

Total 1970 and 1971 = 7 "less coherent" films

TABLE **B.5** Top-Grossing Films of 1980

RANKING	TITLE	"LESS COHERENT"
1	9 to 5	
2	Stir Crazy	
3	Airplane!	
4	Any Which Way You Can	
5	Private Benjamin	
6	Popeye	•
7	Urban Cowboy	
8	The Shining	•
9	Caddyshack	
10	Friday the 13th	

TABLE **B.6** Top-Grossing Films of 1981

RANKING	TITLE	"LESS COHERENT"
1	Raiders of the Lost Ark	
2	Superman 2	
3	Stripes	
4	The Cannonball Run	
5	Clash of the Titans	
6	Tarzan, The Ape Man	
7	Excalibur	
8	Fort Apache, The Bronx	
9	The French Lieutenant's Woman	•
10	Escape From New York	

Total 1980 and 1981 = 3 "less coherent" films

Analysis

Of the top-grossing seventies films, 35 percent were coded by the experts as "less coherent" than most films in their genres, and 65 percent were coded as "as coherent." By contrast, of the sixties and eighties films, only 12.5 percent were coded "less coherent" than most films in their genres and the remaining 87.5 percent displayed, as far as the expert coders were concerned, standard-issue Hollywood coherence. Hence, the experts coded the seventies films as "less coherent" almost three times as often as they did films from the sixties and eighties.

STUDY OF THE DEGREE
OF RESOLUTION OF FILM
ENDINGS

I enlisted a sample of sixteen film experts (individuals with an earned PhD or MFA in film or a related field working in film studies at institutions throughout the United States), unfamiliar with this book's hypothesis, to rate 390 movies according to whether the films' endings were "highly resolved," "mostly resolved," "mostly unresolved," or "highly unresolved." The movies were the top ten-grossing American films for each year between 1954 and 1992, according to statistics gathered from *Variety*. The raters were instructed that, for the purposes of the study, a *resolved* ending was one in which all of the major plotlines had been tied up and they experienced a feeling of closure at the film's conclusion, whereas an *unresolved* ending violated both of these two principles. Raters were given examples to guide their ratings. Each coder's ratings were forced to have a mean of zero and a standard deviation of one in order to eliminate biases in the way individual coders might use the rating scale. As a result, for the overall data set, the mean is zero and the standard deviation is one.

Analysis
As indicated in Graph 2.1 in Chapter Two, the top ten domestic grossers released during the years 1957, 1966, 1968–1975, 1977, and 1979–1981 had endings coded as less resolved than average. Other years' top ten grossers were regarded as having endings more resolved than average.

STUDY OF BEST PICTURE
LISTS AND INCOHERENCE

For this study, the same eight film experts indicated in
Appendix B coded the highest-rated American films
from the period 1970–1977 (indicated by a variety of independent critical, industry,
and film fan ratings) according to whether each film was "less coherent" than or "as
coherent" as most Hollywood films in its genre. A "less coherent" film was defined
using the same criteria indicated in Appendix B.

For a systematic assessment of film fan opinion, I relied on the ratings of the
participating users of the popular Internet Movie Database (IMDB), limiting the
sample to films that at least twenty-five hundred IMDB users had rated. Table D.1
shows IMDB's twenty-five highest-rated American films from the period 1970–1977.
Black dots in the far right column indicate films that the film experts coded as "less
coherent" than most films in the genre.

TABLE D.1 Internet Movie Database Participating Users Highest-Rated American
Films 1970–1977

IMDB RANK	IMDB RATING	TITLE (YEAR OF RELEASE)	"LESS COHERENT"
1	9.1	*The Godfather* (1972)	
2	8.9	*The Godfather, Part II* (1974)	•
3	8.8	*Star Wars* (1977)	
	8.8	*One Flew Over the Cuckoo's Nest* (1975)	
5	8.5	*Taxi Driver* (1976)	•
6	8.4	*Chinatown* (1974)	•
	8.4	*A Clockwork Orange* (1971)	•
8	8.3	*The Sting* (1973)	
9	8.2	*Jaws* (1975)	
	8.2	*Annie Hall* (1977)	•
11	8.1	*Patton* (1970)	
	8.1	*The Conversation* (1974)	•

continues on following page

continued from previous page: TABLE D.1

	8.1	*Sleuth* (1972)	
14	8.0	*Barry Lyndon* (1975)	•
	8.0	*The Exorcist* (1973)	•
	8.0	*Dog Day Afternoon* (1975)	•
	8.0	*Young Frankenstein* (1974)	
	8.0	*The Last Picture Show* (1971)	
	8.0	*The Man Who Would Be King* (1975)	
20	7.9	*Badlands* (1973)	•
	7.9	*Harold and Maude* (1971)	•
	7.9	*Network* (1976)	•
	7.9	*All the President's Men* (1976)	
24	7.8	*Rocky* (1976)	
	7.8	*The French Connection* (1971)	•
	7.8	*Cabaret* (1972)	•
	7.8	*Deliverance* (1972)	•
	7.8	*Little Big Man* (1970)	•
	7.8	*Paper Moon* (1973)	
	7.8	*Papillon* (1973)	
	7.8	*M*A*S*H* (1970)	•
		Total "less coherent" films	**17**

The following table of twenty-five films compiles the "Best Picture" lists for the period 1970–1977 of the New York Film Critics Circle (NY Critics), the Los Angeles Film Critics Association (LA Critics, which started its Best Picture awards in 1975), a 1978 survey of twenty leading international film critics conducted by James Monaco for his book *American Film Now* (AFN), the Academy of Motion Picture Arts and Sciences (AMPAS, which gives out the Oscars), and the American Film Institute (AFI, which in 1998 published a list of the "100 Greatest American Movies" according to its fifteen hundred-member blue ribbon panel). A black dot in the "Less Coherent" column indicates a film that film experts coded as "less coherent" than most films in the genre.

TABLE D.2 "Best Picture" lists, 1970–1977: Academy of Motion Picture Arts and Sciences, American Film Institute, New York Film Critics Circle, Los Angeles Film Critics Association, and *American Film Now*'s Twenty Leading International Film Critics

	"LESS COHERENT"	AMPAS	AFI	NY CRITICS	LA CRITICS	AFN
All the President's Men (1976)				•		
American Graffiti (1973)			•			•
Annie Hall (1977)	•	•	•	•		•
Badlands (1973)	•					•
Barry Lyndon (1975)	•					•
Chinatown (1974)	•		•			•

continues on following page

continued from previous page: TABLE D.2

A Clockwork Orange (1971)	•		•	•		
Close Encounters of the Third Kind (1977)	•		•			
Dog Day Afternoon (1975)	•				•	
Five Easy Pieces (1970)	•			•		
The French Connection (1971)	•	•	•			
The Godfather (1972)		•	•			•
The Godfather, Part II (1974)	•	•	•			•
Jaws (1975)			•			
M*A*S*H (1970)	•		•			
McCabe & Mrs. Miller (1971)	•					•
Mean Streets (1973)	•					•
Nashville (1975)	•			•		•
Network (1976)	•		•		•	
One Flew Over the Cuckoo's Nest (1975)		•	•			
Patton (1970)		•	•			
Rocky (1976)		•	•			
Star Wars (1977)					•	
The Sting (1973)		•				
Taxi Driver (1976)	•					•
Totals	**16**	**8**	**14**	**5**	**3**	**11**

NOTES

PART I

Chapter One

1. Robin Wood regards the seventies as a failed political critique, and James Bernardoni says that "the New Hollywood cinema [of the 1970s], considered as an aesthetic phenomenon, . . . has merely passed into a maturity whose disappointing characteristics were already evident in its infancy" (4). For a more positive treatment of the decade, see Pye and Myles.

2. Most box office figures in this book come from *Variety*, the film industry trade publication. *Variety*'s figures, although generally exaggerated in the 1970s because distributors and exhibitors themselves reported box office earnings, are in most cases the most reliable available.

3. See Appendix A for various critical, box office, fan, and industry rankings of films of the 1970s.

4. For a discussion of art-cinema exhibition in the United States, see the chapter, "Ethnic Theatres and Art Cinemas," in Gomery, *Shared Pleasures*, 171–196. To see seventies filmmakers discuss the influence of foreign art cinema on their work, see the documentary, *A Decade Under the Influence*.

5. See the chapter, "Art-Cinema Narration," in Bordwell, *Narration*, 205–233.

6. For discussions of the impact of art cinema on seventies cinema, see, for example, King, 36–48; Man, 7; and Cook, 160.

7. See the discussion of *Joe* in Cagin and Dray (213) and in Lev (24) and Palmer's chapter on *Go Tell the Spartans*.

8. Bordwell has argued that cinema, contrary to popular belief, does not necessarily reflect common societal attitudes; see his *Poetics*, 31.

9. This book maintains narratology's useful distinction between story and plot, or what the Russian Formalists called *fabula* and *syuzhet*. An imaginary construct of the perceiver, the story (or *fabula*) contains all the narrative information of the artwork in chronological order. By contrast, the plot (*syuzhet*) is the means by which

the work of art arranges and renders story information to the perceiver. Whereas the story is always chronological, the plot needn't be, such as in *Citizen Kane* or *Memento*, in which the stories are rendered out of chronological order. In short, the plot cues perceivers to construct the story.

10. See Chatman, 27.

11. See, for example, Stravinsky, Taylor, Chatman, Buckland, and Bordwell, *Poetics*.

12. Bordwell distinguishes between what he calls "analytical poetics" and "historical poetics." Analytical poetics seeks to answer the question: "What are the principles according to which films are constructed and through which they achieve particular effects?" By contrast, historical poetics asks, "How and why have these principles arisen and changed in particular empirical circumstances?" *Poetics*, 23.

13. Most of the essays collected in Stokes and Maltby also explore the individuality (rather than the commonality) of audience responses to films.

14. Among the scholarly works that examine the ways in which films guide spectators toward complex, shared film experiences, I would include *The Classical Hollywood Cinema*, of which Staiger is coauthor with Bordwell and Thompson.

15. As my discussion of *The French Connection* in Chapter Four demonstrates, sometimes our sense of our own deviation from the norm is itself a "normative" response. Normative responses, moreover, are not, as Staiger says, the ideal responses of an "ideal spectator" (39) or those anticipated by the filmmakers, but rather the responses that a large group of spectators *in fact* have to a given film. For instance, the makers of *The Rocky Horror Picture Show* (1975) did not predict the film's potential for interactive activities that regularly occur at screenings, activities that by now we should consider normative. Indeed, many of the responses Staiger describes as "perverse" in her book are themselves, according to her own description, normative for the demographic she's considering (gay spectators, for instance). If many spectators respond to a film in a similarly perverse way, then their responses are not perverse at all; anticipated or not, the responses are normative.

16. Joseph Anderson suggests that filmmakers imagine themselves as the viewers of their own films in order to "test the outcome" of their films on the minds of spectators: "This might be considered a fairly risky procedure, because each human mind is a little different. . . . But the filmmakers-turned-viewers are not proceeding completely recklessly and irresponsibly, because the 'hardware' of the mind and most of the 'software' is standard and universal" (13).

17. David Bordwell and Noël Carroll have written extensively about cognitivist approaches to film study. See, in particular, Bordwell's *Narration* and "A Case for Cognitivism" and Bordwell and Carroll. Wolfgang Iser is a phenomenologist examining the ways in which readers process literary texts.

Chapter Two

1. A comprehensive analysis of classical Hollywood narrative conventions can be found in the chapter, "Classical Narration: The Hollywood Example," in Bordwell, *Narration*, 156–204.

2. Wood's essay reappeared in his book, *Hollywood from Vietnam to Reagan*. In it, he says, "I am concerned with films that don't wish to be, or to appear, incoherent but are so nonetheless, works in which the drive toward the ordering of experience has been visibly defeated" (47).

3. Wood, for instance, calls *Taxi Driver* (1976), *Looking for Mr. Goodbar* (1977), and *Cruising* (1980) "works that do not know what they want to say" (47).

4. Carroll alludes to this blindness when he says, "Perkins has supplied us with no reason to believe that the absence of the type of coherence he enjoys might not be the measure of cinematic goodness for certain kinds of narrative films," *Philosophical Problems*, 236.

5. The two other leading theories of humor are Superiority Theory, whose advocates have included Plato, Aristotle, and Thomas Hobbes, and Tension-Relief Theory, advocated by Herbert Spencer, Sigmund Freud, and others.

6. For reviews of empirical research on Incongruity Theory, see Chapman and Foot.

7. See, for example, Ivanko and Pexman; Lippman and Tragesser; Cundall; and Alden, Mukherjee, and Hoyer.

8. For a discussion of joke appreciation as a process of solving problems, see Suls, 42.

9. About Brando's hand gesture during the scene, James Naremore writes, "All of Brando's energy seems collected in that hand" (*Acting*, 210).

10. For a discussion of story causality, see Chatman, 45–48, 53–56.

11. See "The Art Cinema as a Mode of Film Practice," in Bordwell, *Poetics*, 151–169.

12. For a discussion of the use of songs in *Nashville* and other Hollywood films since the 1960s, see Berliner and Furia.

13. Richard Neupert suggests that ideological closure helps "determine plausible or 'appropriate' endings" in Hollywood cinema (73).

14. See, for example, Nerhardt; Gerber and Routh; and Deckers and Kizer.

15. The quotation is Kael's slight revision of a passage from her brief 1971 review of *Get Carter* in the *New Yorker*.

16. Appendix B presents more complete information on the design and results of the study.

17. Appendix C contains more details of the study.

18. I converted the ordinal data to numerical data in order to equalize each respondent's use of the coding instrument. The conversion enables me to present descriptive statistics representing respondents' collective opinions and to eliminate biases in the way individual coders might have used the rating scale. Each coder's ratings were forced to have a mean of zero and a standard deviation of one; as a result, for the overall data set, the mean is zero and the standard deviation is one. I am grateful to Dale Cohen, Professor of Psychology at the University of North Carolina Wilmington, who helped me design the study and interpret the results.

19. It would be interesting to determine why 1976 is an anomalous year in the study; however, we can speculate. In 1976, blockbusters (such as *Rocky*, *King*

Kong, and *Midway*) dominated Hollywood's top ten box office earners even more so than before and drove less resolved films first into lower box office rankings and, by the 1980s, out of most mainstream cinema altogether. The year 1976 saw the release of several films that, I suspect, coders might have considered more unresolved than average but that did not earn enough box office revenue to make the top ten, including *Carrie*, *Taxi Driver*, *Bound for Glory*, *The Killing of a Chinese Bookie*, *The Man Who Fell to Earth*, *Mikey and Nicky*, *The Missouri Breaks*, and *Network*. A study that includes films beyond the top ten grossers of each year would test this hypothesis.

20. If we consider the four years before and after the period, the graph suggests that the irresolution characteristic of movies released between 1970 and 1977 began to manifest as early as 1966 and continued as late as 1981. Indeed, only one year (1957) outside of that sixteen-year period displayed a greater than average degree of irresolution.

21. IMDB ratings are accurate as of February 9, 2006.

22. In 1978, James Monaco asked twenty leading film critics to list the ten best American films made between 1968 and 1977. He surveyed the following critics: Peter Biskind, Vincent Canby, Richard Corliss, Peter Cowie, Jan Dawson, Stephen Farber, Michael Goodwin, Molly Haskell, Diane Jacobs, Richard T. Jameson, Stanley Kauffmann, Greil Marcus, Janet Maslin, Gene Moskowitz, Frank Rich, Clayton Riley, Andrew Sarris, Richard Schickel, David Thomson, and Francois Truffaut. Appendix A of my book indicates the films that topped Monaco's list. The complete list and the top ten lists of each critic may be found in his *American Film Now*, 447–451.

23. AMPAS gives out the Oscars.

24. In 1998, AFI published a list of the "100 Greatest American Movies" according to its 1,500-member blue ribbon panel.

25. The lists of films can be found in Appendix A, and Appendix D provides details of the study.

26. For a discussion of European art cinema as a mode of practice, see the chapter "Art-Cinema Narration" in Bordwell, *Narration*, 205–233.

PART II
Chapter Three

1. For a compendium of film sequels and remakes, see Nowlan and Nowlan.

2. For scholarly treatments of various horror film series, see, for example, Budra; Clover; and Dika.

3. Felber begins her essay on sequels by saying, "The idea that 'sequels are always disappointing' suggests that both a reader's failure to repeat an original reading experience and the inferiority of a work produced merely to capitalize on a previous success are inevitable" (119). As do many of the essayists in the collection, Felber seeks to complicate the universality of this premise by examining some illustrative exceptions.

4. McLarty says that Hollywood sequels "are often promoted as 'new and improved,' suggesting that the sequel will deliver more than the first" (204–205).

5. Citing Pauline Kael as evidence, Jon Lewis says that *Part II* "was a great success with the critics" (*Whom God*, 17); however, Kael wrote one of the few altogether positive reviews the sequel received from a major critic.

6. Some critics might have seen an early cut of the movie, now unavailable, that was apparently somewhat more confusing than the final cut released to the public. However, critical opinion on the film's disorganization was virtually unanimous, regardless of the version reviewed.

7. The Golden Globe Awards represent the opinions of the Hollywood Foreign Press, an association of about eighty foreign journalists who cover American film. That year *Chinatown* swept the awards, including awards for best picture (drama), best director, and best actor. The New York Film Critics Circle is an association of critics who vote yearly on achievements in motion pictures. *Amarcord* won their best picture award that year, and Federico Fellini won the best director award.

8. The National Board of Review began as the National Board of Censorship in 1909, a volunteer citizens committee that previewed and evaluated films' content, temporarily averting governmental attempts to censor Hollywood. After the name change, it began, among other things, awarding prizes to motion pictures. It conducts what is considered the oldest of the "best picture" polls.

9. I collected the 1974 "Best Film of the Year" lists of twenty-five nationally known critics. In my survey, *The Conversation* appeared in the lists of 64 percent of critics (sixteen total votes), whereas only 40 percent (ten critics) considered *The Godfather, Part II* one of the best movies of 1974, and none of the twenty-five critics considered it the best movie of the year. Both of Coppola's films were surpassed by

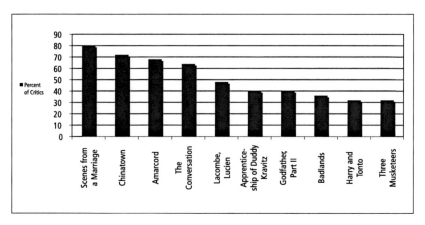

GRAPH 3.1. "Top Ten" for 1974: Compilation of Twenty-Five Critics' Lists

Amarcord (68 percent), *Chinatown* (72 percent), and *Scenes from a Marriage* (80 percent). The critics were Joy Gould Boyum, Vincent Canby, Pat Collins, Kathleen Carroll, Jay Cocks, Judith Crist, Jim D'Anna, Bernard Drew, David Elliott, Joseph Gelmis, Michael Goodwin, Molly Haskell, Howard Kissel, Stephen Klain, Stuart Klein, Martin Levine, the National Board of Review, Rex Reed, Charles Phillips Reilly, Andrew Sarris, Walter Spencer, Frances Taylor, Archer Winsten, Bill Wolf, and Paul D. Zimmerman. All of the critics had compiled their lists by the end of January 1975. Graph 3.1 summarizes the top ten films named by the critics in my survey. The vertical axis indicates the percentage of critics who included the films listed in the horizontal axis in their lists of the top ten films of 1974.

10. Some of the other notable "good reviews" came from Judith Crist, "All in the Family"; Murf., "The Godfather, Part II"; and Frank Rich. Most of the critics, however, did not consider the sequel superior at the time, and, even among favorable reviews, "though flawed" is an often repeated phrase.

11. In her 1974 review of the movie, "The Corleone Saga Sags," Haskell wrote, "Without [*The Godfather*'s violence], the characters are not only not mythic—they are not even very interesting. . . . The use of Italian dialogue, with English sub-titles, can't quite conceal its inanity" (88).

12. Appendix A lists the critics Monaco surveyed. The top ten lists of each critic may be found in his *American Film Now*, 447–451.

13. Early in 1975, Monaco had surveyed ten leading critics to determine their opinions of the best films of 1974. At that point, only three of the critics he surveyed included *Part II* on their lists, and no critic considered the sequel the best picture of even that one year. Moreover, although in early 1975 most of Monaco's critics ranked *The Conversation* higher than Coppola's *Godfather* sequel, in Monaco's 1978 survey *The Conversation* received only three votes, tied with three other movies for fifteenth place.

14. By the time Paramount released *The Godfather, Part III* in 1990, the tendency to group the first two movies had become standard practice among critics. A few critics of *Godfather III* gestured toward differentiating the first two *Godfathers*. In the *National Review*, John Simon said, "There is nothing here that wasn't done as well or better in Parts I and II (especially II)" ("The Godfather, Part III," 65). David Denby of *New York Magazine* does more than other critics to distinguish the virtues of the first two films in his review of the third, but he does not consider *Part II* inferior: "Though perhaps not as exciting or as emotionally involving as the first film, *Godfather II* was a work of aggressive high intelligence, a bitter and sardonic view of the corruption of America" (57). For Denby, *The Godfather* was exciting, *Part II* intelligent.

15. Chown notes that scenes in *Part II* are "juxtaposed with our memory of the first *Godfather* film," and he also describes the degeneration of Michael and the Corleones (106).

16. The end of *The Godfather* depicts the murders of the heads of the other families during the baptism of Connie's baby. At the end of *Part II*, Fredo says "Hail Marys" just before he is shot. The sequel also contrasts Vito's murder of Don Fanucci

with a religious procession through the streets of Little Italy, and Vito's brother Paolo is murdered during the funeral procession of their father.

17. De Niro said about playing the character Brando played, "I was given certain things, and so I had to stick to those. . . . I had to play it in my way but connect it to him physically as much as I could" ("Dialogue on Film," 44).

18. Though scholars often suggest that Coppola is more of a harsh realist than the romantic Puzo, the director makes his Vito a good deal more scrupulous than the Vito from Puzo's novel. The movie draws the flashbacks from what Vincent Canby calls "the bits and pieces of Mr. Puzo's novel that didn't fit into the first [*Godfather*]" ("Hard to Define," 58), but the films leave out the ways in which Vito gained power by bullying his customers into buying from him, by violently destroying his competition, and by having Luca Brasi hack off the limbs of a rival family's gunmen.

19. Although the scene strongly recalls *The Godfather*, one element differentiates it from that movie, beyond the fact that these events take place before the beginning of *The Godfather*: We remain remote from the characters, never quite entering their world. I can best illustrate this idea by focusing on a single detail—the cinematography as Tessio brings a birthday cake to the table. We glimpse the cake as the characters open the cake box, and we see them admire the cake, but, if this were a scene from *The Godfather*, we would see a shot of the cake from their perspective. Instead, *we* look at *them* while *they* look at the *cake*. The flashback feels like a flashback (rather than, say, an early unused scene) in part because the cinematography keeps us spatially removed from the optical perspectives of the characters.

20. I do not intend to invoke the controversy between "illusion" and "imagination" theories of film spectatorship but merely to point to the paradox of "double identity" that underpins all fiction. Readers hoping to wrangle with that controversy can begin with Smith, "Film Spectatorship."

21. In Murray Smith's typology, *The Godfather, Part II* exhibits a "graduated moral structure," characterized by "a spectrum of moral gradations rather than a binary opposition of values" (*Engaging Characters*, 207).

Chapter Four

1. Cook says that a "new historical film consciousness [in the 1970s] enabled . . . a new category of self-reflexive films that fetishized the practices of 'lost Hollywood'— either through parody or memorialization" (284).

2. For more on the musical's concealment and exposure of its artifice, see Feuer, especially 126–130.

3. For a more thorough discussion of the use of songs in seventies and post-seventies cinema, see Berliner and Furia.

4. Dick Powell, famous as the high-voiced star of Warner Brothers musicals, played Marlowe in *Murder My Sweet* (1944). When RKO cast Powell in the role, it was almost as much against type as casting Gould in Altman's movie. However, when Powell played Marlowe, he was attempting to break out of his typecasting and redefine his image, playing the tough guy few people thought he had in him. When

Gould played Marlowe, Altman was attempting not to redefine Gould's image but to redefine Marlowe, and Elliot Gould played the same old Elliot Gould.

5. For a more thorough description of caper movie conventions, see "Variations on a Major Genre: The Big Caper Film" in Kaminsky, 100–129.

6. See Thompson's chapter, "Realism in the Cinema: *Bicycle Thieves*," in which she argues that "neorealist films like *Bicycle Thieves* appeal to notions of the randomness of reality when they fail to provide other motivation for incidental or coincidental events" (*Breaking*, 208).

7. Wood says about *Taxi Driver*, "We can see the film in relation to both the Western and the horror film. With the former, Travis is the gunfighter-hero whose traditional function has always been to clean up the town; with the latter, he is the psychopath-monster produced by an indefensible society" (53).

8. The advertising on the video box was devised for the video release, but the original 1971 ad campaign also stressed the film's action, not the detectives' failure: One of the tag lines on the original poster read, "The time is just right for an out and out thriller like this." The main tag line for the poster—"Doyle is bad news but a good cop"—acknowledges Doyle's brutality, even as it tries to contain it. The poster shot itself has a similar effect: It shows the climactic shot of the film's centerpiece chase sequence, when Doyle shoots his criminal suspect (see Figure 4.5). Some viewers of the poster, however, might have trouble with the fact that Doyle is shooting his unarmed suspect in the back.

9. Reed analyzes the pleasure of repeatedly returning to the same film scenarios.

10. Pauline Kael refers to the scene in her pan of *The French Connection*: "At first, we're confused as to who the victims are, and we stare at them thinking they must be characters in the movie. It takes a few seconds to realize that they bear no relation whatsoever to the plot" ("Urban Gothic," 114).

11. Kael, for instance, writes that Doyle has "a complete catalogue of race prejudices. . . . The movie turns old clichés into new clichés by depriving the central figure of *any* attractive qualities" ("Urban Gothic," 114). Schickel, writing for *Life* magazine, says that Doyle "pursues pushers with a dedication that seems admirable at first, then comic, finally dangerous, maniacal" ("A Real Look," 13). Knight's review also acknowledges an ambivalence toward Doyle, who, he says, "packs a drive and intensity that make one at once grateful and troubled that he is on our side of the law" (70).

12. The real-life "Popeye" Egan, incidentally, did not kill the real-life federal agent, Frank Waters. "I used to beat up on him once a week just for exercise, but I never shot him." Cited in Segaloff, 119.

Chapter Five

1. Naremore, *More Than Night*, 99–100, 118. See, in particular, Naremore's discussion of traces of the censor in *Crossfire* (1947) and other *noir* films (96–135). His discussion of censorship's effects on film follows that of Christian Metz in *The Imaginary Signifier*.

2. Thomas Doherty, for instance, says, "More unbridled, salacious, subversive, and just plain bizarre than what came afterwards, [pre-Code films from 1930–1934] look like Hollywood cinema but the moral terrain is so off-kilter they seem imported from a parallel universe" (2).

3. The Hays Office was certifying films with an MPAA seal of approval during the years 1930–1934, but the office did not yet have the authority that it gained in 1934 when the major studios (and most of the independents) committed to distribute only films that earned a PCA seal. Consequently, filmmakers during the period 1930–1934 often ignored Hays Office requests.

4. The gangster Tony Camonte, for instance, dies both in *Scarface*'s (1932) original ending (in which police shoot him down on the sidewalk) and in the ending that followed the recommendation of the Hays Office (in which Camonte dies on the gallows), both of which were exhibited.

5. One provision of the Code says explicitly, "In lands and ages of less developed civilization and moral principles, revenge may sometimes be presented." Prince says, "the PCA was relatively more permissive and less worried about shootings or killings" in Westerns and war films (*Classical*, 33).

6. Film scholars and Cagney himself have suggested that *Angels with Dirty Faces* contains an ambiguous ending because the mental breakdown of Cagney's character, when he is led to the electric chair, may not be a pretense. Naremore says, "Cagney has said in his autobiography that he played the scene for its ambiguity and that for a long time afterward children would come up and ask him if Rocky was really a coward" (*Acting*, 172).

7. *Detour* (1945) develops and sustains some compelling ideological paradoxes by portraying its protagonist as barely responsible for his own crimes. Because Al Roberts has so little control over his doomed circumstances, the character's failures have more to do with the paranoia and imprudence of his behavior than with its illegality. Consequently, his arrest in the final seconds of the film, an ending forced upon the filmmakers by the PCA, feels generically appropriate but morally unwarranted.

8. *The Asphalt Jungle* (1950) intensifies the crime genre's conflicted attitude toward criminals and police about as thoroughly as any Hollywood film from the studio era, an attitude emblematized by the paradoxical logic of a line delivered by the film's lead criminal, Doc Riedenschneider (Sam Jaffe): "Experience has taught me never to trust a policeman. Just when you think he's all right, he turns legit."

9. Naremore points to the "vaguely repellent" portrayal of private detective Mike Hammer in *Kiss Me Deadly* (1955) (*More Than Night*, 153).

10. For an instance of one filmgoer's stunned reaction to seventies narrative perversity, see the quotation from Leslie Halliwell in Chapter One.

11. According to Tudor, only eighteen horror movies were distributed in Britain in 1970, whereas there were thirty-eight new horror films in 1971, forty-one in 1973, and forty-one in 1974. (He somehow neglected to report the statistics for 1972.) These figures point to, Tudor says, an "unprecedented expansion" in horror film distribution (25, 56).

12. Paul examines *The Exorcist*'s somewhat contradictory status at the time of its release: "*The Exorcist* does have an air of seriousness about it and a deliberateness of pacing that is more like an art film than standard horror, so that it does effectively conflate horror with more ambitious filmmaking" (290).

13. Warner Bros. released *The Exorcist* with a strategy known as "four walling," in which the distributor can dominate regional markets by renting theaters for a flat rate and taking in all of the box office proceeds. In 1976, the Justice Department instituted a ten-year ban on four walling as a violation of the consent decrees (Cook, 40).

14. A similar fate befell the hordes of possession and devil movies that tried to capitalize on *The Exorcist*'s success. In 1975, filmgoers could see *Devil Within Her*, *Abby*, *La endemoniada*, *The Devil's Rain*, and *Magdalena—Possessed by the Devil*; in 1976, *Burnt Offerings* and *Audrey Rose*; and in 1977, *Cathy's Curse*, *House of Exorcism*, *Naked Exorcism*, and *The Sexorcist*. *Exorcist II: The Heretic*, also 1977, returned to the same world as that of its predecessor, yet it was a commercial and critical flop.

15. Warner Brothers' 2000 re-release, titled *The Exorcist: The Version You've Never Seen*, had a negative cost of less than $1 million and a $15 million marketing budget. With a $67 million total gross, the re-release grossed more than four times its cost. Aside from *Star Wars* (which had a phenomenally successful re-release in 1997) and some Disney cartoon features, few films have fared that well in re-release; see Diorio.

16. William Friedkin's director's commentary comes from the DVD, *The Exorcist: The Version You've Never Seen (Special Edition)*.

17. Horror is often bound to a set of rules, some of them extrinsic to the individual film (e.g., crosses in vampire movies or silver bullets in werewolf movies) and others intrinsic (the vaccine found in Dr. Neville's blood in *The Omega Man* [1971] or the life cycle of the monster in *Alien* [1979]). The rules add limits to the fantastic logic that governs many films in the genre.

18. Richard Neupert distinguishes between two separate strategies that films use to indicate resolution: 1) *story resolution*, or the completeness of the major story actions, and 2) *discursive closure*, Neupert's term for the system of narrative devices (such as music, voice-over narration, and framing devices) that films use to indicate closure; Neupert calls them "closure devices" (170).

19. Blatty was not the only commentator to try to shove a happy ending onto the movie; many others have argued similarly. Something about the film's ending evidently elicits a desire to explain it in positive terms. However, the fact that critics feel they must explain the positive meaning of the ending suggests that the movie itself resists their interpretations; see, for instance, Derry, 106. Friedkin shot a more uplifting denouement than the one that appears in the original movie, but ultimately thought it gratuitously upbeat and cut it out. He also systematically deleted all of the scenes that gave meaning to the events, such as one in which Merrin tells Karras that, as Blatty describes the scene, "the purpose of the possession was to make everyone surrounding [Regan] despair of

their own humanity and decide that even if there really was a God, that he couldn't love anyone as bestial as we are." Blatty felt this scene and others like it were the film's moral center and approved a version that included them, a version twenty minutes longer than the two-hour cut released to the public in 1973. Without Blatty's approval, Friedkin deleted those scenes, rather than pause for what he called a "theological commercial" (Clagett, 123). The 2000 re-release of the film, subtitled *The Version You've Never Seen*, includes the scenes Friedkin deleted from the 1973 version.

PART III
Chapter Six

1. About the "crucifixion scene" at the end of *Boxcar Bertha*, Scorsese said, "I liked the way we shot it, the angles we used, and in particular the way you saw the nails coming through the wood" (Thompson and Christie, 36).

2. For more information on technological advances in cinematography in the 1970s, see cinematographer John A. Alonzo's interview in Schaefer and Salvato (24 and 41) and the chapter, "Technological Innovation and Aesthetic Response," in Cook, 355–396.

3. "The thing, more or less new I guess, for which I was most grateful on the technological front, was the wonderful set of Zeiss Super Speeds with which we shot [*Taxi Driver* and *Raging Bull*]. They were amazingly accurately calibrated so that 2.8 was really 2.8 and 1.9 really 1.9. Most lenses are nowhere near so true." Michael Chapman, email to author, 6 November 2001.

4. According to Cook, the Arriflex was a relatively new, tractable, and lightweight (15 pounds unloaded) camera that debuted in the United States in *Across 110th Street* (1972) (371).

5. For a discussion of the visual unities and incongruities in Scorsese's *Raging Bull*, see Berliner, "Visual Absurdity."

6. All told, De Niro has so far starred in nine of Scorsese's feature films, and Schrader has written or contributed to the scripts of four.

7. Michener says that Scorsese is "a fantasist who supercharges the clichés of *Taxi Driver* into the surreal figments of a nightmare that is at once comic, romantic and terrifying" (4). Patterson and Farber refer to the film's "baroque visuals" (26). Kael discusses Scorsese's "expressionist use of the city" ("Underground Man," 82). And, according to Rosenbaum, the film turned "New York into an expressionist moonscape" (2).

8. Art critics use the term "abstract expressionism" to describe a nonfigurative style of art that emphasizes colors and abstract shapes, as in the works of Jackson Pollock, Mark Rothko, and Willem de Kooning.

9. Patterson and Farber also recognized the mix: "Par for a Scorsese film is the jamming of styles: Fritz Lang expressionism, Bresson's distanced realism, and Corman's low-budget horrifics" (27).

10. For a discussion of realism as an effect created by the use of conventional devices, see "A Formal Look at Realism" in Thompson, *Breaking*, 197–217.

11. Kolker says, "Scorsese's work contains such a severe *anti*-realistic element that the world he creates often becomes expressionistic, a closed space that reflects a particular, often stressed, state of mind" (165).

12. For Gombrich, the flourish is "the expression of the joyful exuberance of the craftsman who displayed both his skill and his inventiveness" (*Sense of Order*, 239).

13. See, for example, Tzvetan Todorov, "Some Approaches to Russian Formalism" in Bann and Bowlt, 11.

14. *Transtextual motivation* was not explicitly discussed by Russian Formalist Boris Tomashevsky who, in his analysis of artistic motivation, "Thematics," laid out only three types (Lemon and Reis, 61–98). Bordwell adopted the term *transtextual* from Gérard Genette.

15. See Bordwell, *Narration*, 164. For more on classical Hollywood's obedience to extrinsic norms, see his chapter, "Classical Narration: The Hollywood Example," 156–166.

16. Thompson originally developed the idea of excess in her book, *Eisenstein's Ivan the Terrible.*

17. Thompson calls such devices "tame excess" (*Breaking*, 259–260).

18. See, for example, Thompson and Christie, as well as Scorsese's documentaries on American cinema, *A Personal Journey with Martin Scorsese Through American Movies*, and Italian Cinema, *Il mio viaggio in Italia.*

19. For more on substantively irrelevant repetitions in works of literature, see Booth's "Close Reading without Readings."

20. Prince calls this device, "metonymic displacement" (*Classical*, 220).

21. Prince calls this device, "spatial displacement" (*Classical*, 208).

Chapter Seven

1. When I refer to Cassavetes's movies, I mean his independent ones, over which he had complete control, not the movies he made early in his career for the studios— *Too Late Blues* (1962) and *A Child Is Waiting* (1963)—nor *Big Trouble* (1986), which he directed for money. *Gloria* (1980) falls somewhere between a Cassavetes movie and the other type. "I wrote the story to sell, strictly to sell," Cassavetes said in an interview. "It was no great shakes" (Stevenson, 48). But Columbia wouldn't buy the script to *Gloria* unless Cassavetes also agreed to direct it, which he did, after reworking the script and turning the film into something he was willing to have his name on.

2. Quotations from movies are my own transcriptions, unless designated otherwise.

3. Kozloff refers to lines like Kane's as "toppers," retorts that "attempt to close off a conversational topic by their finality or nastiness" (75).

4. All three lines are spoken in the film as Mamet wrote them in his shooting script. Cf. Mamet, 67, 10, and 13.

5. From Emanuel A. Schegloff, "On the Organization of Sequences as a Source of 'Coherence' in Talk-in-Interaction," in Dorval 56–58. In addition to shortening the

quotation for convenience, I have altered it in minor ways for clarity, since it appears originally in a technical transcription notation.

6. John Simon, for instance, in his pan of *A Woman Under the Influence*, says, "Cassavetes claims that his films are thoroughly scripted . . . but I prefer to think that he is fibbing" (54). Many other reviews, both positive and negative, assume the film was improvised. See Kauffmann's review of *A Woman Under the Influence*, for example. Kozloff, referring to Cassavetes's "informal" style of dialogue, wrongly assumes that the dialogue in Cassavetes's *Faces* (1968) relies on improvisation (23).

7. The two improvised lines are Peter Falk's "bah, bah, bah" in the committal scene and Rowlands's driving instructions to her mother (Carney, *Cassavetes*, 341).

8. Cassavetes would frequently base lines from his scripts on real conversations he had had or overheard. He said in an interview, "I see Gena around the house and with the kids and I tape record what I see. . . . I'm not a *writer* at all! I just record what I hear. . . . I have a good ear for prattle" (Carney, *Cassavetes*, 311).

9. The scene Simon refers to appears only in the 1976 version of the film, not in Cassavetes's re-edited 1978 release.

10. If anything, Cassavetes fled commercial success. He first achieved prominence as an actor, appearing in the television detective series *Johnny Staccato* and in such films as *Crime in the Streets* (1956) and *Edge of the City* (1957). He used his earnings to finance his first film, the independently produced *Shadows* (1959). Afterward, he was on his way to becoming an established studio filmmaker. He made two films for Paramount—*Too Late Blues* (1962) and *A Child Is Waiting* (1963)—and was signed to make more. But, he said, "[In 1964] I looked back at my accomplishments and I could find only two that I considered worthwhile, *Shadows* and *Edge of the City*. All the rest of my time had been spent playing games—painful and stupid, falsely satisfying and economically rewarding" (cited in Carney, *American Dreaming*, 63). After *A Child Is Waiting*, he began to work independently again.

11. Noting the revival of Cassavetes movies in theaters, David Sterritt, writing for the *Christian Science Monitor* in 1994, says, "Five years after his death, Cassavetes is now beginning to reap the respect he earned during his quarter-century filmmaking career" (18). Essayist Phillip Lopate says, "John Cassavetes's reputation as a director has undergone a remarkable transformation since his death in 1989. An embattled maverick, once viewed as an amateurish hobbyist who brokered self-indulgent improvisations by his actor-friends, he has come to be seen, especially abroad, as one of the three or four major American filmmakers of the last thirty years" (161).

12. See, for instance, Cook, 130; Robert E. Lauder, "Genius," 427; and Hatch, 254.

13. For discussions of Cassavetes's working methods, see Carney, *Cassavetes*; Viera; and Margulies.

14. For two illustrative examples of Cassavetes's inclination to re-cut his films, see Carney's discussion of the re-editing of *Shadows* (79–84) and of *The Killing of a Chinese Bookie* (434–435) in *Cassavetes*.

15. See, for instance, Kauffmann, *A Woman* (20), and Kael, "Dames" (172).

16. Gerrig and Prentice argue that films generally treat spectators as "side participants," a term that refers to individuals present at a conversation who do not contribute as either speakers or addressees. When side participants are present, speakers construct comments in ways that keep them properly informed, filling in information that side participants need in order to understand what is being said. Similarly, while films rarely address the spectator directly, they nonetheless behave as though spectators are present.

17. Drawing on Russian formalist criticism, Kristin Thompson explains the function of an artwork's "dominant" in *Breaking the Glass Armor* (43–44).

Conclusion

1. Plantinga notes that, in the scene of Davey Bunting's death, "spectators' sympathies now become entirely conflicted" because "our allegiance shifts to the doomed cowboy" and also that the final gunfight "splits our allegiance in subtle ways" among Munny, Little Bill, and the deputies, complicating spectators' responses to Munny's actions (76).

2. See, for instance, Nerhardt; Gerber and Routh; Deckers and Kizer; and Deckers and Salais.

BIBLIOGRAPHY

Aigner, Hal, and Michael Goodwin. "The Bearded Immigrant from Tinsel Town." *City* (June 1974): 36.

Alden, Dana L., Ashesh Mukherjee, and Wayne D. Hoyer. "The Effects of Incongruity, Surprise and Positive Moderators on Perceived Humor in Television Advertising." *Journal of Advertising* 29, no. 2 (Summer 2000): 1–15.

All on Accounta Pullin' a Trigger. Directed by Jerry Hogrewe. Pond Films, LLC. Distributed by Warner Home Video, 2002.

Allen, Woody. *Four Films of Woody Allen: Annie Hall, Interiors, Manhattan, Stardust Memories*. New York: Random House, 1982.

Alpert, Hollis. "The Triumph of the Actor." Rev. of *Husbands*. *Saturday Review* 53 (12 December 1970): 26.

Altman, Rick. "A Semantic/Syntactic Approach to Film Genre." In *Film Genre Reader*, ed. Barry Keith Grant. Austin: University of Texas Press, 1986, 26–40.

Anderson, Joseph. *The Reality of Illusion: An Ecological Approach to Cognitive Film Theory*. Carbondale: Southern Illinois University Press, 1998.

Anything for John. Directed by Doug Headline and Dominique Cazenave. Made for French TV and shown in the United States on the Independent Film Channel. Distributed by AB Distribution International. Canal-Shadows Films Productions, 1999.

Atlas, Jacob, and Ann Guerin. "Robert Altman, Julie Christie and Warren Beatty Make the Western Real." *Show* (August 1971): 20.

Balio, Tino. "The Art Film Market in the New Hollywood." In *Hollywood & Europe: Economics, Culture, National Identity 1945–95*, ed. Geoffrey Nowell-Smith and Steven Ricci. London: British Film Institute, 1998, 63–73.

Bann, Stephen, and John E. Bowlt, eds. *Russian Formalism: A Collection of Articles and Texts in Translation*. New York: Harper & Row, 1973.

Bartholomew. "'Taxi Driver' Tough, Engrossing, Powerful—a Hit." Rev. of *Taxi Driver*. *Film Bulletin* 445 (February 1976): 35.

Baudry, Jean-Louis. "Ideological Effects of the Basic Cinematographic Apparatus." In *Film Theory and Criticism*, 5th ed., ed. Leo Braudy and Marshall Cohen. New York: Oxford University Press, 1999, 345–355.

Bazin, Andre. *What is Cinema?* Vol. 2, trans. Hugh Gray. Berkeley: University of California Press, 1971.

Beattie, James. *Essays*, 3rd ed. London: 1779.

Belton, John. *American Cinema/American Culture*. New York: McGraw-Hill, Inc., 1994.

Berliner, Todd. "Hollywood Movie Dialogue and the 'Real Realism' of John Cassavetes." *Film Quarterly* 52, no. 3 (Spring 1999): 2–16.

———. "Visual Absurdity in *Raging Bull*." In *Martin Scorsese's* Raging Bull: *A Cambridge Film Handbook*, ed. Kevin Hayes. Cambridge, U.K.: Cambridge University Press, 2005, 41–68.

Berliner, Todd, and Philip Furia. "The Sounds of Silence: Songs in Hollywood Films Since the 1960s." *Style* 36, no. 1 (Spring 2002): 19–35.

Bernardoni, James. *The New Hollywood: What the Movies Did with the New Freedoms of the Seventies*. Jefferson, N.C.: McFarland, 1991.

Biskind, Peter. *Easy Riders, Raging Bulls: How the Sex-Drugs-and-Rock 'N' Roll Generation Saved Hollywood*. New York: Simon & Schuster, 1998.

———. *The Godfather Companion*. New York: HarperCollins, 1990.

Blatty, William Peter. *William Peter Blatty on* The Exorcist *from Novel to Film*. New York: Bantam Books, 1974.

Bookbinder, Robert. *The Films of the Seventies*. Secaucus, N.J.: Citadel Press, 1982.

Booth, Stephen. "Close Reading without Readings." In *Shakespeare Reread: The Texts in New Contexts*, ed. Russ McDonald. Ithaca: Cornell University Press, 1994, 42–55.

———. *Precious Nonsense: The Gettysburg Address, Ben Jonson's Epitaphs on His Children, and Twelfth Night*. Berkeley: University of California Press, 1998.

Bordwell, David. "A Case for Cognitivism." *Iris* 9 (Spring 1989): 11–40.

———. "Classical Hollywood Cinema: Narrational Principles and Procedures." In *Narrative, Apparatus, Ideology*, ed. Philip Rosen. New York: Columbia University Press, 1986, 17–34.

———. *Making Meaning: Inference and Rhetoric in the Interpretation of Cinema*. Cambridge, Mass.: Harvard University Press, 1989.

———. *Narration in the Fiction Film*. Madison: University of Wisconsin Press, 1985.

———. *Poetics of Cinema*. New York: Routledge, 2008.

———. *The Way Hollywood Tells It: Story and Style in Modern Movies*. Berkeley: University of California Press, 2006.

Bordwell, David, and Noël Carroll, eds. *Post-Theory: Reconstructing Film Studies*. Madison: University of Wisconsin Press, 1996.

Bordwell, David, Janet Staiger, and Kristin Thompson. *The Classical Hollywood Cinema: Film Style & Mode of Production to 1960*. New York: Routledge, 1988.

Braudy, Leo. *The World in a Frame*. Garden City: Anchor Books, 1977.

Buckland, Warren. *Directed by Steven Spielberg: Poetics of the Contemporary Hollywood Blockbuster.* New York: Continuum Press, 2006.

Budra, Paul. "Recurrent Monsters: Why Freddy, Michael, and Jason Keep Coming Back." In *Part Two: Reflections on the Sequel,* ed. Paul Budra and Betty A. Schellenberg. Toronto, Ontario: University of Toronto Press, 1998, 189–199.

Budra, Paul, and Betty A. Schellenberg, eds. *Part Two: Reflections on the Sequel.* Toronto, Ontario: University of Toronto Press, 1998.

Burch, Noël. *Theory of Film Practice,* trans. Helen R. Lane. New York: Praeger, 1973.

Cagin, Seth, and Philip Dray. *Hollywood Films of the Seventies: Sex, Drugs, Violence, Rock 'n' roll & Politics.* New York: Harper & Row, 1984.

Canby, Vincent. Rev. of *The Exorcist. New York Times,* 27 December 1973.

———. "'The Godfather, Part II': One Godfather Too Many." Rev. of *The Godfather, Part II. New York Times,* 22 December 1974.

———. "'Godfather, Part II' is Hard to Define." Rev. of *Godfather, Part II. New York Times,* 13 December 1974.

Carney, Ray. *American Dreaming: The Films of John Cassavetes and the American Experience.* Berkeley: University of California Press, 1985.

———. "Cassavetes on Cassavetes." *Visions Magazine* 7 (Summer 1992): 22–29.

———, ed. *Cassavetes on Cassavetes.* London: Faber and Faber, 2001.

———. *The Films of John Cassavetes: Pragmatism, Modernism, and the Movies.* Photographs by Sam Shaw and Larry Shaw. Cambridge U.K.: Cambridge University Press, 1994.

———. *John Cassavetes: The Adventure of Insecurity, A Pocket Guide to the Films.* Walpole, Mass.: Company C Publishing, 2000.

Carroll, Noël. *Interpreting the Moving Image.* New York: Cambridge University Press, 1998.

———. *Philosophical Problems of Classical Film Theory.* Princeton: Princeton University Press, 1988.

———. *The Philosophy of Horror, or, Paradoxes of the Heart.* New York: Routledge, 1990.

Cassavetes, John. *A Woman Under the Influence,* screenplay. Faces Music, Inc., 1972.

Castle, Terry. *Masquerade and Civilization: The Carnivalesque in Eighteenth-Century English Literature and Fiction.* Stanford: Stanford University Press, 1986.

Cawelti, John. "*Chinatown* and Generic Transformation in Recent American Films." In *Film Genre Reader,* ed. Barry Keith Grant. Austin: University of Texas Press, 1986, 183–201.

Chapman, Antony J., and Hugh C. Foot, eds. *Humour and Laughter: Theory, Research and Applications.* New Brunswick, N.J.: Transaction Publishers, 2007.

Chatman, Seymour. *Story and Discourse: Narrative Structure in Fiction and Film.* Ithaca: Cornell University Press, 1978.

Chion, Michel. *Audio-Vision: Sound on Screen,* ed. and trans. Claudia Gorbman. New York: Columbia University Press, 1994.

Chown, Jeffrey. *Hollywood Auteur: Francis Coppola*. New York: Praeger, 1988.

Clagett, Thomas D. *William Friedkin: Films of Aberration, Obsession, and Reality*. Jefferson, N.C.: McFarland, 1990.

Clarens, Carlos. *Crime Movies: An Illustrated History*. New York: W. W. Norton, 1980.

Clover, Carol J. *Men, Women, and Chain Saws: Gender in the Modern Horror Film*. Princeton, N.J.: Princeton University Press, 1992.

Coleman, John. "Family Snaps." Rev. of *The Godfather, Part II*. *New Statesman* (16 May 1975): 669.

Combs, Richard. Rev. of *Opening Night*. *Sight and Sound* 47, no. 3 (Summer 1978): 192–193.

Cook, David A. *Lost Illusions: American Cinema in the Shadow of Watergate and Vietnam, 1970–1979*. New York: Charles Scribner's Sons, 2000.

Coppola, Francis Ford, and Mario Puzo. *The Godfather, Part II*, shooting script, second draft. 24 September 1973.

Cowie, Peter. *Coppola*. New York: Scribner, 1990.

Crist, Judith. "All in the Family." Rev. of *The Godfather, Part II*. *New York Magazine* (23 December 1974): 70–71.

———. *Take 22: Moviemakers on Moviemaking*, co-ed. Shirley Sealy. New York: Viking, 1984.

Cull, Nick. "*The Exorcist*." *History Today* 50, no. 5 (May 2000): 46–51.

Cundall, Michael K., Jr. "Humor and the Limits of Incongruity." *Creativity Research Journal* 19, nos. 2–3 (2007): 203–211.

A Decade Under the Influence. Directed by Ted Demme and Richard LaGravenese. Constant Communication, Written in Stone, IFC Films, 2003.

Deckers, Lambert, and Philip Kizer. "Humor and the Incongruity Hypothesis." *Journal of Psychology: Interdisciplinary and Applied* 90, no. 2 (July 1975): 215–218.

Deckers, Lambert, and Debra Salais. "Humor as a Negatively Accelerated Function of the Degree of Incongruity." *Motivation and Emotion* 7, no. 4 (December 1983): 357–363.

Deckers, Lambert, and Robert Thayer Buttram. "Humor as a Response to Incongruities within or between Schemata." *Humor* 3, no. 1 (1990): 53–64.

Dempsey, Michael. "*The Exorcist*," *Film Quarterly* 27 (Fall 1974): 61–62.

Denby, David. "The Grandfather." Rev. of *The Godfather, Part III*. *New York* 7 (January 1991): 57.

Derry, Charles. *Dark Dreams: A Psychological History of the Modern Horror Film*. South Brunswick, N.J.: A. S. Barnes and Co., 1977.

"Dialogue on Film: Robert De Niro." *American Film* 6.5 (March 1981): 39–48.

Dika, Vera. *Games of Terror: Halloween, Friday the 13th, and the Films of the Stalker Cycle*. London: Associated University Press, 1990.

Diorio, Carl. "'Exorcist' Turning Heads Once Again," *Variety*, 6 December 2000.

Doherty, Thomas. *Pre-Code Hollywood: Sex, Immorality, and Insurrection in American Cinema 1930–1934*. New York: Columbia University Press, 1999.

Dorval, Bruce, ed. *Conversational Organization and Its Development*. Norwood, N.J.: Ablex, 1990.

Ebert, Roger. Rev. of *Cat People*. http://rogerebert.suntimes.com/apps/pbcs.dll/article ?AID=/20060312/REVIEWS08/603120301 (accessed 29 May 2008).

Elsaesser, Thomas, Alexander Horwath, and Noel King, eds. *The Last Great American Picture Show: New Hollywood Cinema in the 1970s*. Amsterdam: Amsterdam University Press, 2004.

Epps, Garrett. "Does Popeye Doyle Teach Us to Be Fascist?" *New York Times*, 21 May 1972.

The Exorcist: The Version You've Never Seen (Special Edition). Directed by William Friedkin. DVD. Warner Brothers, 2000.

Felber, Lynette. "Trollope's Phineas Diptych as Sequel and Sequence Novel." In *Part Two: Reflections on the Sequel*, ed. Paul Budra and Betty A. Schellenberg. Toronto, Ontario: University of Toronto Press, 1998, 118–130.

Feuer, Jane. *The Hollywood Musical*, 2nd ed. Bloomington: Indiana University Press, 1993.

"The Film School Generation." *American Cinema*. Video co-production of the New York Center for Visual History, KCET/Los Angeles, and the BBC. South Burlington, Vt.: Annenberg/CPB Collection, 1994.

Freud, Sigmund. *Jokes and their Relation to the Unconscious*, trans. J. Strachey. New York: W. W. Norton, 1960. Originally published 1905.

Gans, Herbert J. "*The Exorcist*: A Devilish Attack on Women." *Social Policy* 5 (May–June 1974): 71–73.

Gehring, Wes D., ed. *Handbook of American Film Genres*. New York: Greenwood Press, 1988.

Gelmis, Joseph. *The Film Director as Superstar*. Garden City, N.Y.: Doubleday and Co., Inc., 1970.

Gerber, W. S., and D. K. Routh. "Humor Response as Related to Violation of Expectancies and to Stimulus Intensity in a Weight-Judgment Task." *Perceptual and Motor Skills* 41 (1975): 673–674.

Gerrig, Richard J., and Deborah A Prentice. "Notes on Audience Response." In *Post-Theory: Reconstructing Film Studies*, ed. David Bordwell and Noël Carroll. Madison: University of Wisconsin Press, 1996, 388–403.

Glynn, Edward. "On Exorcising 'The Exorcist.'" *America* 130 (2 February 1974): 65.

Gombrich, E. H. *Art and Illusion: A Study in the Psychology of Pictorial Representation*. Princeton, N.J.: Princeton University Press, 1969.

———. *The Sense of Order: A Study in the Psychology of Decorative Art*. Ithaca, N.Y.: Cornell University Press, 1979.

Gomery, Douglas. "Motion Picture Exhibition in 1970s America." In *Lost Illusions: American Cinema in the Shadow of Watergate and Vietnam, 1970–1979*, by David Cook. New York: Charles Scribner's Sons, 2000, 397–416.

———. *Shared Pleasures: A History of Movie Presentation in the United States*. Madison: University of Wisconsin Press, 1992.

Goodwin, Michael and Naomi Wise. *On the Edge: The Life and Times of Francis Coppola*. New York: William Morrow and Company, 1989.

Gow, Gordon. Rev. of *Taxi Driver*. *Films and Filming* 22 (September 1976): 31–32.

Grant, Barry Keith, ed. *Film Genre Reader*. Austin: University of Texas Press, 1986.

———. ed. *Planks of Reason: Essays on the Horror Film*. Metuchen, N.J.: Scarecrow Press, 1984.

Halliwell, Leslie. *Halliwell's Film Guide*. New York: Charles Scribner's Sons, 1983.

Haskell, Molly. "*The Godfather Part II*: The Corleone Saga Sags." Rev. of *The Godfather, Part II*. *Village Voice* 23 (December 1974): 88–89.

Hatch, Robert. Rev. of *Taxi Driver* and *The Killing of a Chinese Bookie*. *Nation*, no. 222 (28 February 1976): 253–254.

Hess, John. "*Godfather II*: A Deal Coppola Couldn't Refuse." In *Movies and Methods, Volume I*, ed. Bill Nichols. Berkeley: University of California Press, 1976, 81–90.

Hirschberg, Lynn. "The Two Hollywoods: The Directors, Woody Allen and Martin Scorsese," *New York Times Magazine*, 16 November 1997, Section 6: 91–96.

Hobbes, Thomas. *The English Works of Thomas Hobbes of Malmesbury, Volume IV*, ed. William Molesworth. London: John Bohn, 1839.

Hoppe, Ronald A. "Artificial Humor and Uncertainty." *Perceptual and Motor Skills* 42 (1976): 1051–1056.

"I'm Almost Not Crazy . . ." John Cassavetes: The Man and His Work. Written and directed by Michael Ventura. Golan-Globus Production, 1984.

Iser, Wolfgang. *The Implied Reader; Patterns of Communication in Prose Fiction from Bunyan to Beckett*. Baltimore: Johns Hopkins University Press, 1974.

Ivanko, Stacey L., and Penny M. Pexman. "Context Incongruity and Irony Processing." *Discourse Processes* 35, no. 3: 241–279.

Jacobs, Diane. *Hollywood Renaissance*. South Brunswick, N.J.: A. S. Barnes, 1977.

Jones, J. M. "Cognitive Factors in the Appreciation of Humor: A Theoretical and Experimental Analysis." Doctoral dissertation, Yale University, 1970.

Kael, Pauline. "Back to the Ouija Board." Rev. of *The Exorcist*. *New Yorker* (7 January 1974): 59–62.

———. "Dames." Rev. of *A Woman Under the Influence*. *New Yorker* (9 December 1974): 172.

———. "Fathers and Sons." Rev. of *The Godfather, Part II*. *New Yorker* (23 December 1974): 63–66.

———. *5001 Nights at the Movies*. New York: Henry Holt, 1991.

———. Rev. of *Get Carter*. *New Yorker* (27 March 1971): 22.

———. "Megalomaniacs." Rev. of *Husbands*. *New Yorker* (2 January 1971): 49.

———. "On the Future of the Movies." *New Yorker* (5 August 1974).

———. "Underground Man." Rev. of *Taxi Driver*. *New Yorker* (9 February 1976): 82–85.

———. "Urban Gothic." Rev. of *The French Connection*. *New Yorker* (30 October 1971): 114.

Kaminsky, Stuart M. *American Film Genres: Approaches to a Critical Theory of Popular Film*. New York: Dell Publishing, 1974.

Kant, Immanuel. *Critique of Judgment*, trans. Werner S. Pluhar. Indianapolis: Hackett, 1987.

Kauffmann, Stanley. Rev. of *The Godfather Part II*. *New Republic* (18 January 1975): 22.

———. Rev. of *A Woman Under the Influence* and *Murder on the Orient Express*. *New Republic* (28 December 1974): 20, 34.

Kelly, Mary Pat. *Martin Scorsese: A Journey*. New York: Thunder's Mouth Press, 1991.

Kermode, Mark. *The Exorcist*, BFI Modern Classics. London: British Film Institute, 1997.

Keyser, Les. *Martin Scorsese*. New York: Twayne Publishers, 1995.

King, Geoff. *New Hollywood Cinema: An Introduction*. New York: Columbia University Press, 2002.

Klein, Michael. "*Nashville* and the American Dream." *Jump Cut* (October/December 1975): 4–7.

Knight, Arthur. "Crime in the Cities." Rev. of *The French Connection*. *Saturday Review* 54 (6 November 1971): 70.

Kolker, Robert Phillip. *A Cinema of Loneliness: Penn, Kubrick, Scorsese, Altman*, 2nd ed. New York and Oxford: Oxford University Press, 1988.

Kozloff, Sarah. *Overhearing Film Dialogue*. Berkeley: University of California Press, 2000.

Lauder, Robert E. "The Genius of John Cassavetes." *America* 134, no. 19 (15 May 1976): 427–428.

———. "Hell on Wheels." Rev. of *Taxi Driver*. *Christian Century* 93 (12 May 1976): 467–469.

Lemon, Lee T., and Marion J. Reis, ed. and trans. *Russian Formalist Criticism: Four Essays*. Lincoln: University of Nebraska Press, 1965.

Lev, Peter. *American Films of the 70s: Conflicting Visions*. Austin: University of Texas Press, 2000.

Lewis, Jon, ed. *The New American Cinema*. Durham: Duke University Press, 1998.

———. *Whom God Wishes to Destroy . . . : Francis Coppola and the New Hollywood*. Durham: Duke University Press, 1995.

Lippman, Louis G., and Sarah Tragesser. "Constructing Something Funny: Levels of Associative Connection in Tom Swifties." *Journal of General Psychology* 132, no. 3 (2005): 231–242.

Lopate, Phillip. *Totally, Tenderly, Tragically: Essays and Criticism from a Lifelong Love Affair with the Movies*. New York: Doubleday Dell Publishing Group, 1998.

Madsen, Axel. *The New Hollywood: American Movies in the '70s*. New York: Thomas Y. Crowell Company, 1975.

Maltby, Richard. *Hollywood Cinema: An Introduction*. Cambridge, Mass.: Blackwell Publishers Inc., 1995.

———. "'Nobody Knows Everything': Post-Classical Historiographies and the Consolidated Entertainment." In *Contemporary Hollywood Cinema*, ed. Steve Neal and Murray Smith. London: Routledge, 1998, 21–44.

Mamet, David. *House of Games: The Complete Screenplay*. New York: Grove Weidenfeld, 1985.

Man, Glenn. *Radical Visions: American Film Renaissance, 1967–1976*. Westport, Conn.: Greenwood Press, 1994.

Margulies, Ivone. "John Cassavetes: Amateur Director." In *The New American Cinema*, ed. Jon Lewis. Durham: Duke University Press, 1998, 275–306.

Mast, Gerald. *A Short History of the Movies*, 2nd ed. Indianapolis: Bobbs-Merrill Company, 1978.

———. *A Short History of the Movies*, 3rd ed. Indianapolis: Bobbs-Merrill Company, 1981.

———. *A Short History of the Movies*, 4th ed. New York: Macmillan Publishing Company, 1986.

McCormick, Ruth. "In Defense of *Nashville*." *Cineaste* 7, no. 1 (Fall 1975): 25.

McDonald, Russ. *Shakespeare Reread: The Texts in New Contexts*. Ithaca: Cornell University Press, 1994.

McGhee, Paul E. "Children's Appreciation of Humor: A Test of the Cognitive Congruency Principle." *Child Development* 47 (1976): 420–426.

McGhee, Paul E., and Jeffrey H. Goldstein, eds. *Handbook of Humor Research, Vol. 1, Basic Issues*. New York: Springer-Verlag, 1983.

McLarty, Lianne. "'I'll be back': Hollywood, Sequelization, and History." In *Part Two: Reflections on the Sequel*, ed. Paul Budra and Betty A. Schellenberg. Toronto, Ontario: University of Toronto Press, 1998, 200–218.

Metz, Christian. *Film Language: A Semiotics of the Cinema*. New York: Oxford University Press, 1978.

———. *The Imaginary Signifier*, trans. Celia Britton, Annwyl Williams, Ben Brewster, and Alfred Guzzetti. Bloomington: Indiana University Press, 1982.

Michener, Charles. Rev. of *Taxi Driver*. *Film Comment* (March-April 1976): 4–5.

Miller, Stephen Paul. *The Seventies Now: Culture as Surveillance*. Durham: Duke University Press, 1999.

Il mio viaggio in Italia. Directed by Martin Scorsese and produced by Giorgio Armani. Miramax Films, 1999.

Monaco, James. *American Film Now*. New York: New American Library, 1984.

Morreall, John. "Funny Ha-Ha, Funny Strange, and Other Reactions to Incongruity." In *The Philosophy of Laughter and Humor*, ed. John Morreall. Albany, N.Y.: State University of New York Press, 1987, 188–207.

———. *Taking Laughter Seriously*. Albany: State University of New York Press, 1983.

Murf. Rev. of *The Godfather, Part II*. *Variety* (11 December 1974): 16.

———. Rev. of *Taxi Driver*. *Variety* (4 February 1976): 3.

Murray, William. "Playboy Interview: Francis Ford Coppola." *Playboy* 22 (July 1975): 53.

Naremore, James. *Acting in the Cinema*. Berkeley: University of California Press, 1988.

———. *More Than Night: Film Noir in Its Contexts*. Berkeley: University of California Press, 1998.

—————. *On Kubrick*. London: British Film Institute, 2007.

Neale, Stephen. *Genre*. London: British Film Institute-Film Availability Services, 1980.

Neale, Steve, and Murray Smith, eds. *Contemporary Hollywood Cinema*. London: Routledge, 1998.

Nerhardt, Göran. "Humor and Inclinations of Humor: Emotional Reactions to Stimuli of Different Divergence from a Range of Expectancy." *Scandinavian Journal of Psychology* 11 (1970): 185–195.

Neupert, Richard. *The End: Narration and Closure in the Cinema*. Detroit: Wayne State University Press, 1995.

Nowell-Smith, Geoffrey, and Steven Ricci, eds. *Hollywood & Europe: Economics, Culture, National Identity 1945–95*. London: British Film Institute, 1998.

Nowlan, Robert A., and Gwendolyn Wright Nowlan. *Cinema Sequels and Remakes, 1903–1987*. Jefferson, N.C.: McFarland & Co., 1989.

Oring, Elliott. *Engaging Humor*. Urbana: University of Illinois Press, 2003.

Palmer, William J. *The Films of the Seventies: A Social History*. Metuchen, N.J.: Scarecrow Press, 1987.

Patterson, Patricia, and Manny Farber. "The Power & the Gory." Rev. of *Taxi Driver*. *Film Comment* (May/June 1976): 26–30.

Paul, William. *Laughing Screaming: Modern Hollywood Horror and Comedy*. New York: Columbia University Press, 1994.

Pechter, William S. Rev. of *A Woman Under the Influence*. *Commentary* 59, no. 5 (May 1975): 67.

Perkins, V. F. *Film as Film: Understanding and Judging Movies*. New York: Da Capo Press, 1993.

A Personal Journey with Martin Scorsese Through American Movies. Directed by Martin Scorsese and produced by Florence Dauman. Buena Vista Home Video, 1995.

Pinedo, Isabel Cristina. "Postmodern Elements of the Contemporary Horror Film." In *The Horror Film*, ed. Stephen Prince. New Brunswick, N.J.: Rutgers University Press, 2004, 85–117.

Plantinga, Carl. "Spectacles of Death: Clint Eastwood and Violence in *Unforgiven*." *Cinema Journal* 37, no. 2 (Winter 1998): 65–83.

Prince, Stephen. *Classical Film Violence: Designing and Regulating Brutality in Hollywood Cinema, 1930–1968*. New Brunswick, N.J.: Rutgers University Press, 2003.

—————, ed. *The Horror Film*. New Brunswick, N.J.: Rutgers University Press, 2004.

Pye, Michael, and Lynda Myles. *The Movie Brats: How the Film Generation Took Over Hollywood*. New York: Holt, Rinehart, and Winston, 1979.

Pym, John, ed. *Time Out Film Guide*. London: Penguin Books, 1997.

Reed, Joseph. *American Scenarios: The Uses of Film Genre*. Middletown, Conn.: Wesleyan University Press, 1989.

Rich, Frank. "Beyond the Corleones." Rev. of *The Godfather, Part II*. *New Times* (27 December 1974): 56–58.

Rosen, Philip, ed. *Narrative, Apparatus, Ideology.* New York: Columbia University Press, 1986.

Rosenbaum, Jonathan. Rev. of *Taxi Driver. Film Comment* (July–August 1976): 2–4.

Sarris, Andrew. *The American Cinema: Directors and Directions, 1929–1968.* New York: E. P. Dutton & Company, 1968.

———. "Notes on the Auteur Theory in 1962." *Film Culture,* no. 27 (Winter 1962–1963).

Schaefer, Dennis, and Larry Salvato. *Masters of Light: Conversations with Contemporary Cinematographers.* Berkeley: University of California Press, 1984.

Schaeffer, Neil. *The Art of Laughter.* New York: Columbia University Press, 1981.

Schatz, Thomas. "Boss Men." *Film Comment* 26, no. 1 (January–February 1990): 28–31.

———. *Hollywood Genres.* New York: Random House, 1981.

Schickel, Richard. "The Final Act of a Family Epic." Rev. of *The Godfather, Part II. Time* (16 December 1974): 70–73.

———. "A Real Look at a Tough Cop." Rev. of *The French Connection. Life* 71 (19 November 1971): 13.

Schopenhauer, Arthur. *The World as Will and Idea,* trans. R. B. Haldane and J. Kemp. London: Routledge & Kegan Paul, 1964.

Segaloff, Nat. *Hurricane Billy: The Stormy Life and Films of William Friedkin.* New York: William Morrow and Company, 1990.

Sharff, Stefan. *The Elements of Cinema: Toward a Theory of Cinesthetic Impact.* New York: Columbia University Press, 1982.

Shedlin, Michael. "Police Oscar: *The French Connection.*" *Film Quarterly* 25 (Summer 1972): 2–9.

Shultz, T. R. "A Cognitive-Developmental Analysis of Humour." In Antony J. Chapman and Hugh C. Foot, eds. *Humour and Laughter: Theory, Research and Applications,* 11–36. New Brunswick N.J.: Transaction Publishers, 2007, 11–36.

———. "The Role of Incongruity and Resolution in Children's Appreciation of Cartoon Humor." *Journal of Experimental Child Psychology* 13 (1972): 456–477.

Shultz, Thomas, and F. Horibe. "Development of the Appreciation of Verbal Jokes." *Developmental Psychology* 10 (1974): 13–20.

Sigoloff, Marc. *The Films of the Seventies: A Filmography of American, British and Canadian Films 1970–1979.* Jefferson, N.C.: McFarland, 1984.

Simon, John. Rev. of *The Godfather, Part III. National Review* (28 January 1991): 65.

———. "Technical Exercise, Exercise in Futility." Rev. of *The Killing of a Chinese Bookie. New York,* no. 9 (1 March 1976): 66.

———. Rev. of *A Woman Under the Influence. Esquire,* no. 83 (April 1975): 54, 58, 60.

Simon, William G., and Louise Spence. "Cowboy Wonderland, History and Myth: 'It Ain't All That Different than Real Life.'" *Journal of Film and Video* 47 (Spring–Fall 1995): 79.

S. K. Rev. of *Taxi Driver. Independent Film Journal* 77 (4 February 1976): 7.

Smith, Murray. *Engaging Characters: Fiction, Emotion, and the Cinema.* Oxford: Oxford University Press, 1995.

———. "Film Spectatorship and the Institution of Fiction." *Journal of Aesthetics and Art Criticism* 53: 2 (Spring 1995): 113–127.

———. "Gangsters, Cannibals, Aesthetes, or Apparently Perverse Allegiances." In *Passionate Views: Film, Cognition, and Emotion*, ed. Carl Plantinga and Greg M. Smith. Baltimore: Johns Hopkins University Press, 1999, 217–238.

Sontag, Susan. *Against Interpretation and other Essays*. New York: Dell Publishing, 1966.

"Special Issue: John Cassavetes." *Post Script* (Commerce: East Texas State University) 11, no. 2 (Winter 1992).

Spencer, Herbert. "The Physiology of Laughter." *Macmillan's Magazine* 1 (1860): 395–402.

Staiger, Janet. *Perverse Spectators: The Practices of Film Reception*. New York: New York University Press, 2000.

Steinberg, Cobbett. *Reel Facts: The Movie Book of Records*. New York: Vintage Books, 1978.

Sterritt, David. "Confessions of a John Cassavetes Fan." *Christian Science Monitor* (10 May 1994).

Stevenson, James. "John Cassavetes—Film's Bad Boy." *American Film* 5 (January/February 1980): 48.

Stokes, Melvyn, and Richard Maltby, eds. *Hollywood Spectatorship: Changing Perceptions of Cinema Audiences*. London: British Film Institute, 2001.

Stravinsky, Igor. *Poetics of Music in the Form of Six Lessons*. New York: Vintage, 1956.

Suls, Jerry. "Cognitive Processes in Humor Appreciation." In *Handbook of Humor Research, Vol. 1, Basic Issues*, ed. Paul E. McGhee and Jeffrey H. Goldstein. New York: Springer-Verlag, 1983, 39–58.

Taylor, Richard, ed. *The Poetics of the Cinema*. Oxford: Russian Poetics in Translation Publications, 1982.

Thomas, Barbara. "'Gambler' Tops Thomas' 10 Best." *Atlanta Journal*, 5 February 1975.

Thompson, David, and Ian Christie, eds. *Scorsese on Scorsese*. London: Faber and Faber, 1989.

Thompson, Kristin. *Breaking the Glass Armor: Neoformalist Film Analysis*. Princeton: Princeton University Press, 1988.

———. *Eisenstein's* Ivan the Terrible: *A Neoformalist Analysis*. Princeton: Princeton University Press, 1981.

———. *Storytelling in the New Hollywood*. Cambridge, Mass.: Harvard University Press, 1999.

Thomson, David. "The Decade When Movies Mattered." In *The Last Great American Picture Show: New Hollywood Cinema in the 1970s*, ed. Thomas Elsaesser, Alexander Horwath, and Noel King. Amsterdam: Amsterdam University Press, 2004, 73–82. Originally published in *Movieline* (August 1993): 42–47, 80.

Thurman, Judith. "'Opening Night': The Risks of Acting Your Age." Rev. of *Opening Night*. *Ms.*, no. 9 (November 1980): 29.

Tudor, Andrew. *Monsters and Mad Scientists: A Cultural History of the Horror Movie.* Cambridge, Mass.: Basil Blackwell Ltd., 1989.

Vale, Eugene. *The Technique of Screenplay Writing: A Book about the Dramatic Structure of Motion Pictures.* New York: Crown, 1944.

Viera, Maria. "Cassavetes' Working Methods: Interviews with Al Ruben and Seymour Cassel." *PostScript: Essays in Film and the Humanities* 11, no. 2 (Winter 1992).

Von Gunden, Kenneth. *Postmodern Auteurs: Coppola, Lucas, De Palma, Spielberg and Scorsese.* Jefferson, N.C.: McFarland, 1991.

Wall, James M. "Time, Space and 'The Exorcist.'" Rev. of *The Exorcist. Christian Century* 91 (30 January 1974): 91–92.

Walsh, Moira. Rev. of *The Godfather, Part II. America* (15 February 1975): 116.

Wexman, Virginia Wright, and Gretchen Bisplinghoff. *Robert Altman: A Guide to References and Resources.* Boston: G. K. Hall, 1984.

Wilson, Christopher P. *Jokes, Form, Content, Use and Function.* London: Academic Press, 1979.

Wood, Robin. *Hollywood from Vietnam to Reagan.* New York: Columbia University Press, 1986.

Woodward, Kenneth L. "The Exorcism Frenzy," *Newsweek* 83 (11 February 1974): 60–66.

Woody Allen Standup Comic: 1964–1968. Audio CD. Rhino, 1999.

Yaquinto, Marilyn. *Pump 'Em Full of Lead: A Look at Gangsters on Film,* Twayne's Filmmakers Series. New York: Twayne; London: Prentice Hall, 1998.

Zimmerman, Paul D. "Godfathers and Sons." Rev. of *The Godfather, Part II. Newsweek* (23 December 1974): 78–79.

Zuker, Joel Stewart. *Francis Ford Coppola: A Guide to References and Resources.* Boston, Mass.: G. K. Hall, 1984.

INDEX

CPSIA information can be obtained at www.ICGtesting.com
Printed in the USA
LVOW130607230812

295581LV00002B/61/P